AF720469

EU Fiscal Policy Coordination in Hard Times

EU Fiscal Policy Coordination in Hard Times

Free Riders on the Storm

Charlotte Rommerskirchen

OXFORD
UNIVERSITY PRESS

OXFORD
UNIVERSITY PRESS

Great Clarendon Street, Oxford, OX2 6DP,
United Kingdom

Oxford University Press is a department of the University of Oxford.
It furthers the University's objective of excellence in research, scholarship,
and education by publishing worldwide. Oxford is a registered trade mark of
Oxford University Press in the UK and in certain other countries

© Charlotte Rommerskirchen 2019

The moral rights of the author have been asserted

First Edition published in 2019

Impression: 1

All rights reserved. No part of this publication may be reproduced, stored in
a retrieval system, or transmitted, in any form or by any means, without the
prior permission in writing of Oxford University Press, or as expressly permitted
by law, by licence or under terms agreed with the appropriate reprographics
rights organization. Enquiries concerning reproduction outside the scope of the
above should be sent to the Rights Department, Oxford University Press, at the
address above

You must not circulate this work in any other form
and you must impose this same condition on any acquirer

Published in the United States of America by Oxford University Press
198 Madison Avenue, New York, NY 10016, United States of America

British Library Cataloguing in Publication Data
Data available

Library of Congress Control Number: 2018955012

ISBN 978–0–19–882901–0

Printed and bound in Great Britain by
Clays Ltd, Elcograf S.p.A.

Links to third party websites are provided by Oxford in good faith and
for information only. Oxford disclaims any responsibility for the materials
contained in any third party website referenced in this work.

für Füße
von Vogel

Acknowledgments

Many thanks to all the interviewees who generously gave me their time. This would have been a very different book were it not for their willingness to answer the email of a stranger.

The German Academic Scholarship Foundation has sponsored my undergraduate, graduate, and postgraduate studies. I am very grateful for the numerous benefits and opportunities which this has brought to me. Moreover, this research has been made possible by funding from the University Association for Contemporary European Studies (UACES Travel scholarship), the University of Edinburgh (College Postgraduate Research Scholarship and Sir Bernard Crick Fellowship), the MERCURY Project through the European Union's Framework VII programme, and the European Research Council under the European Union's Seventh Framework Programme ((FP7/2007–13)/ERC grant agreement no. 291733). Many thanks to Frances Burgess and Caroline Laffey for friendly reminders about and speedy help with reimbursement claims and procedural matters. Parts of this book were written while I was a visiting researcher at the University of Notre Dame and the University of Queensland. I would like to thank Notre Dame's Nanovic Institute for European Studies and UQ's School of Political Science and International Studies for their hospitality.

I'm lucky to count Iain Hardie and David Howarth as my mentors and am very grateful for their sharp criticism and support on all fronts of academia throughout the various stages of writing this book. Here I would like to acknowledge David's pain vis-à-vis my deficient use of English grammar—he has suffered in the making of this book which he read before the competent and efficient team at Oxford University Press took over. I am very thankful to my editor at OUP, Dominic Byatt, as well as three anonymous reviewers.

I first presented the idea for this book at the 2014 Warwick Manuscript Development workshop; many thanks to Ben Clift, Len Seabrooke, and Holly Snaith for valuable comments. Cornel Ban, Kristen Hopewell, and Alison Johnston showed me how to write a solid book proposal, and Edinburgh's IPE Research Group hothoused my own. In the process of writing this book, I benefited from comments and advice in various forms from many colleagues including Stephen Bell, Laura Cram, Michele Chang, Mark Hallerberg, Ailsa

Henderson, Dermot Hodson, Erik Jones, Manu Moschella, John Peterson, Lucia Quaglia, Waltraud Schelkle, and Jason Sharman.

The bulk of this book was written in the department of Politics and International Relations at the University of Edinburgh. I am very lucky to have first studied and now to work surrounded by smart and fabulous colleagues. Amongst them I would like to particularly thank Donald MacKenzie who made the transition from PhD to lectureship smooth and sweet sailing.

My family have been a source of resolute support and our 'Edinburgh village' stepped in when needed. Philippe has read a good deal more about fiscal policy coordination than he could possibly ever wish to know and has contributed much more to this book than criticizing its methods. A final 'Dankeschön' to Emilie and Kaspar, my hiccupy fieldwork companions who, once born, contributed to this book by merit of being delightful and well-sleeping babies. This book is dedicated to my wonderful mother Eva.

Contents

List of Figures

List of Tables

List of Abbreviations

BB	budget balance
CDU	Christian Democratic Union (Germany)
DG Ecfin	Directorate General of Economic and Financial Affairs
ECB	European Central Bank
Ecofin	Council of Economic and Finance Ministers
EDP	Excessive Deficit Procedure
EERP	European Economic Recovery Plan
EFSF	European Financial Stability Facility
EIP	Excessive Imbalances Procedure
EMU	Economic and Monetary Union
ESM	European Stability Mechanism
EU	European Union
fQCA	Fuzzy Qualitative Comparative Analysis
FRSI	Fiscal Rule Strength Index
G20	Group of Twenty
GDP	Gross Domestic Product
IMF	International Monetary Fund
IR	international relations
LTROs	long-term refinancing operations
MAP	Mutual Assessment Process
MDH	market discipline hypothesis
MIP	Macroeconomic Imbalances Procedure
MTOs	medium-term objectives
OECD	Organisation of Economic Co-operation and Development
OLS	ordinary least squares
OMT	Outright Monetary Transactions
PB	primary balance
PSB	primary structural balance

QCA	Qualitative Comparative Analysis
SB	structural balance
SGP	Stability and Growth Pact
SPD	Social Democratic Party (Germany)
TEU	Treaty on the Functioning of the European Union
WTO	World Trade Organization

1

Introduction

1.1 The Perfect Storm

It was a perfect storm. When the President of the European Commission announced the European Economic Recovery Plan (EERP) in late 2008, Europe's economies were in deep water. The US subprime mortgage crisis had morphed rapidly into a global financial crisis, with calamities in different corners of the financial universe precipitating and amplifying one another. What followed became known as the Great Recession (2008–10), which in turn paved the way for the European Debt Crisis. A British cabinet minister, speaking off the recorded, summarized the cascade of events: 'the banks are fucked, we're fucked, the country's fucked' (Wintour 2009: 539). The World Bank (2010) estimates that the Great Recession has resulted in an increase in poverty for 64 million people globally. From the start of 2008 to the spring of 2009, the crisis knocked US-$30 trillion off the value of global shares and left a painful legacy of private and public debt, high unemployment, and growing inequalities.

Events caught policy-makers off guard. This was particularly the case in Europe. The financial crisis, so went the prevalent thinking at the time, was confined to the shores of the US—a symptom of greedy US capitalism to which the economies of Europe were immune. In Brussels, Jean-Claude Juncker, later President of the European Commission and then Prime Minister of Luxembourg, proclaimed in September 2008 that '[it] shouldn't be said that Europe is on the brink of recession' (*Financial Times*, September 16, 2008). Three days later, Lehman Brothers initiated the largest bankruptcy proceedings in US history. The very same day, the European Commission's economic division, the Directorate General of Economic and Financial Affairs (DG Ecfin), gathered for its autumn forecast and, as one participating official recalls, 'beamed with optimism' for what lay ahead.[1] When recession struck in the fall of 2008, policy-makers around the globe started to reconsider the fiscal and monetary orthodoxies of economic policy-making that had been widely accepted since the 1980s. The first step was to support ailing financial institutions with substantial bailout programs. On the monetary policy front, the European Central Bank (ECB), the Federal Reserve in the US, and other national central banks have reduced interest rates to unprecedented lows and many central banks have since then engaged in 'unconventional' direct operations in financial markets. Those financial sector and monetary policy responses were implemented remarkably swiftly and broadly in unison.

Not so fiscal policy. As the first signs of economic recession reached Europe, a fierce discussion of appropriate fiscal policy responses to the crisis took place whose echoes peal today. Not only did the crisis catch EU policy-makers by surprise; it also caught them off script. The extraordinary scale of economic fallout presented EU leaders with a new challenge for which they had failed to prepare, namely the coordination of fiscal policies in times of crisis. For the first time since the Maastricht Treaty in 1992 heralded the coordination of macroeconomic policies among EU member states, the 'potent forces' of public finances were collectively directed toward stimulus. In sharp contrast to the past decade of consolidation and constraint, fiscal policy coordination during the Great Recession presents a novelty: a study in fiscal expansion.

This book draws on multiple methods of analysis and asks what comes of EU fiscal policy coordination in times of crisis. In so doing, it follows the tradition of analyzing the politics of 'hard times' (Gourevitch 1986). I seek to dispel three prevalent myths regarding the state of EU economic governance according to which free riding is rampant, austerity reigns, and member states are at the mercy of markets. First, I demonstrate that contrary to clamorous contention, fiscal policy in hard times did not fall into a beggar-thy-neighbor trap. Instead of waiting for other members to pick up the tab to stimulate crisis-stricken economies, or stimulating despite unsustainable levels of debt (both are types of first-order free riding), countries' fiscal policies matched their room for maneuver. Second, although EU efforts to coordinate stimulus policies ultimately failed, these attempts have shaken up the parameters of collective action. The flexible application of existing rules since the start of the Great Recession and the newly created framework for economic governance demonstrate a move away from the narrow surveillance of fiscal headline indicators toward broad macroeconomic surveillance that recognizes the twin nature of free riding, as both 'too much' and 'too little' spending. EU fiscal governance is frequently portrayed as strong and rigid. I argue that it is floppy and weak. This means that EU rules and procedures hardly imposed a harsh doctrine of austerity on its members and drove member states into self-defeating budget consolidation. My findings and arguments thus challenge the body of research chastising the EU's 'austerity delusion' (e.g. Blyth 2013; Schaefer and Streeck 2013). Third, I argue that EU fiscal policy coordination is beset by second-order free riding. While first-order free riding refers to members benefiting from a collective good (in this book, economic growth and stability) without contributing to its production, second-order free riding refers to free riding on the provision of incentives toward collective action. Put differently, second-order free riding is about the challenge of sanctioning non-cooperation. I argue that EU member states failed to enforce collective action within the group. Here this book goes beyond first-order accounts of fiscal policy coordination.

Flexibility is an asset; weakness is not. Weak rules are detrimental to EU stability and growth even in the absence of first-order free riding. In other words, weak rules pose a threat even when they are (broadly) respected. This is, so my argument goes, because weak rules are used as a justification for delegating 'discipline' to financial markets whose interests and behavior are a poor fit for EU collective action. This paradoxical relationship between first- and second-order free riding, where the latter arises despite the former, prompts us to revisit two narratives about the state of EU fiscal policy coordination, one from 'team stupid' and one from 'team feeble'. According to the first, the Stability and Growth Pact (SGP) (which is at the center of EU fiscal policy coordination) is a rigid, counterproductive tool that encourages procyclical fiscal policy and imposes damaging constraints on public finances. According to the second, the SGP is sabotaged by an internal enforcement problem which has promoted excessive government spending. These positions are clearly at odds with each other. If, on the one hand, the SGP is weak, then it cannot, by definition, restrict public finances. If, on the other hand, the SGP is counterproductive, then member states must heed it for it to have this effect. I argue that there is a different link between the SGP's weakness and its harmfulness for EU collective action. 'Team stupid' is right in that there is an asymmetry and 3 percent fetish built into the SGP. But the SGP and related rules have been applied (increasingly) flexibly. These are not imposing a rigid constraint on economic policy choices. 'Team feeble' is rightfully concerned about a lack of in-house enforcement of fiscal rules. This lack, however, is problematic not because it would invite policy-makers to plunge headlong into free riding, but because it empowers bond markets who in turn impose a harsh and erratic constraint on fiscal policies. Unable to enforce discipline at the EU level, fiscal policy coordination openly and deliberately endorses market discipline as fiscal policy sheriff. This, I contest, is a key quandary of EU fiscal policy coordination. If member states are left at the mercy of fickle markets, they are so by their own design. The untenably high costs of this choice have been painfully visible since the European Debt Crisis erupted in late 2009. Containing market discipline is not doing away with gravity. There is nothing natural about the current set-up of collective action; neither is it condemned to be an immutable, permanent feature of economic cooperation.

1.2 A Tale of Two Crises

In scrutinizing fiscal policy coordination during the Great Recession, this book spans both the international financial crisis erupting in 2008 and the European Debt Crisis that took off in late 2009. These hard times are not obvious candidates for successful coordination: 'Under the pressure of rapidly mounting economic distress... unilateral measures, based on national self-interest, promised a higher return and more immediate payoff than cooperative steps with longer-run benefits' (Kahler 2013: 28). A word on the temporal boundaries of this book: setting start and end points for a series of events as complex as an economic and financial crisis, with its various channels and different effects on member states' economies, is bound to present stylized facts. In the following discussion, the Great Recession is situated between the collapse of Lehman Brothers in the fall of 2008 and the agreed expiration date of the EERP in late 2010. This period forms the empirical core of this book. Time will tell when to mark the end point of the (at the time of writing becalmed) European Debt Crisis.

1.2.1 *The Economic and Financial Crisis*

European leaders were slow to grasp the scope of the financial crisis and to gauge the true rate of exposure of their banking sectors (e.g. Almunia 2008a). Their view was that the crisis was created in the USA, blaming it on 'irresponsible Anglo-Saxon Financial Capitalism' (*Financial Times*, May 16, 2010) and believing that it would mainly be confined to its geographical boundaries. In the words of the former German finance minister Peer Steinbrück (2008a), 'there is no reason—and I do say this very intentionally—to doubt the stability of the German financial system. The German system of universal banking has been shown to be more robust and resistant than the American banking system'. It was only in mid-2008 when several financial institutions in the UK (Northern Rock), Belgium/the Netherlands (Fortis), Germany (Hypo Real Estate), Belgium/France/Luxembourg (Dexia), and Ireland (notably Anglo Irish Bank) were rescued by their respective governments that the true scope of the crisis became clear. European financial institutions, inflicted with a severe shortage of capital and substantial asset write-downs, were hardly immune to the global financial turmoil. As policy-makers implemented emergency bailout plans to prevent the banking sector from collapsing, the near simultaneous breakdown in demand in almost all of the EU's major trading partners further aggravated the shock to the real economy and the financial sector, pushing Europe's economies into (deep) recession. Subsequent stimulus programs, in addition to the working of automatic stabilizers, came at a high and immediate fiscal cost. Alongside the abrupt decline in economic activity and revenue losses caused by the recession, financial sector support programs, automatic stabilization, and discretionary fiscal packages contributed to a rise in government deficits and debt. Countries that prior to the Great Recession experienced the build-up of large macroeconomic imbalances were more vulnerable to sudden stop dynamics, and experienced a more pronounced and protracted economic downturn. These imbalances worsened during the Great Recession as credit and housing booms evaporated. The persisting weakness of the banking sector mattered for the perceived credit risk of sovereigns given that the European banking system is one of the largest investors in EU government debt. Thus the financial and economic crisis of 2008–9 contributed directly to events that would lead to the European Debt Crisis.

1.2.2 *The European Debt Crisis*

Just one year after marking a decade of existence, the Eurozone (the bloc of EU members who have adopted the Euro as common currency) descended into the most serious crisis of its short history. In contrast to the economic fallout of the Great Recession that has proliferated globally, the European Debt Crisis is a markedly Eurozone phenomenon. That is to say, it is a homemade European banking crisis that reflects macroeconomic imbalances and, consequently, the exposure of banks in numerous member states to potential debt default (Schelkle 2012b).[2] In similar fashion to the events of 2008, the European Debt Crisis has been met with surprise by European policy-makers. At the end of 2008, the possibility of a full-blown and contagious debt crisis was considerably underestimated (European Commission 2009). Through 2008 and 2009, European sovereign debt raised little concern; the focal point of worry was the stability of the banking sector. Yet the global financial crisis caused a reassessment of asset prices and growth prospects, particularly for countries with growing macroeconomic imbalances. When the Greek Finance Minister announced in October 2009 that the debt ratio for 2009 had been 'miscalculated' by the previous government and was 12.8 percent of GDP (substantially higher than the 3.6 percent initially reported), Greek access to global capital markets began to deteriorate. The unfavorable country-specific shift in market expectations increased the penalty already imposed by markets due to the country's worsening macroeconomic performance. Concerns over Greece's solvency were further stirred when the then ECB president Jean-Claude Trichet announced that the central bank would phase out acceptance of BBB-rated bonds[3] in 2010. This raised the specter that Greek bonds would become ineligible for the ECB's long-term refinancing operations (LTROs). These provide financing to banks in the Eurozone, with the central aim of providing sufficient liquidity. Since domestic banks are usually key purchasers of sovereign debt, this mechanism was considered as a way to circumvent the ban on bond purchases by the ECB. When the ECB temporarily suspended Greek government debt from being used as collateral in LTROs, all three major credit rating agencies, 'the fire accelerants of the crisis',[4] further downgraded Greece's status to that of 'junk status'. The resulting adverse borrowing conditions forced Greece to accept the conditionality of EU financial assistance and to give up large parts of its sovereignty in matters of national economic management. Since May 2010 Eurozone member states and the International Monetary Fund (IMF) have been providing financial support to Greece through three Economic Adjustment Programs.

The European Debt Crisis has not been confined to Greece alone; it has put severe pressure on the bonds of other Economic and Monetary Union (EMU) countries. EU policy-makers were propelled into creating new institutions in order to provide financial assistance to member states. The first wave of such assistance was provided under the European Financial Stability Facility (EFSF). As it became clear that the turmoil in the sovereign debt and financial markets was unlikely to come to an end soon, EU policy-makers agreed to the creation of the European Stability Mechanism (ESM). It was installed in October 2012 as a permanent intergovernmental organization and took over provision of stability support to Eurozone member states, ringfencing some €750bn for countries in need. Since Greece first received assistance, a further four Eurozone member states have asked for financial support as of 2018. In November 2010, Ireland officially requested financial assistance from the EU amounting to a joint financing package of €85bn; this was followed in April 2011 by Portugal, who received a package of €78bn. Spain requested financial assistance in June 2012, worth a total of up to €100bn. At the time of writing, the last country to request financial assistance is Cyprus; it was agreed in April 2013 that the ESM would provide €10bn to the Republic. However, concerns remain that other countries will need financial assistance from the ESM. Ten years after the international crisis erupted, EU member states find themselves with disquietingly fragile macroeconomies and financial sectors. The stakes of the financial assistance programs within the Eurozone were high indeed, from the survival of the common currency, to the fear of contagion in other EMU member states, to the economic hardship in program countries. It is thus perhaps understandable that the first episodes of EU financial assistance, in Hungary, Latvia, and Romania (EU members, but Eurozone outsiders), received scant attention.

1.2.3 *In the Shadow of the European Debt Crisis*

The European Debt Crisis has sparked a rapidly growing literature on the EU's experience, analyzing the crisis' causes, considering appropriate policy responses, and comparing the trajectories of different countries (e.g. Sandbu 2017; Matthijs and Blyth 2015; Brunnermeier et al. 2015; Henning 2017; Schelkle 2017). In light of the enormous challenges and far-reaching consequences of the European Debt Crisis, this burgeoning body of work is centered on possible solutions, identified predominantly in new financial regulation and reforming EU economic governance. The study of fiscal policy coordination during the Great Recession has been eclipsed by the events of 2010/11. What is more, given the renewed concern about fiscal consolidation and the quest to identify appropriate instruments to rein in public deficits, the brief period of stimulus spending (2008–10) seems but a distant memory. This book pays attention to a short-lived period of commonly agreed fiscal expansion. I argue that a comprehensive analysis of the determinants of fiscal policy outcomes and their coordination in exceptional times is of interest to those who wish to better understand the possibilities and conditions for collective action in good times and in bad. Financial crises are costly and thus clearly have fiscal implications. Close ties between sovereigns and banks furthermore mean that financial fragility spells trouble for government bonds. The failure of effective fiscal policy coordination has been used as a justification for abiding by market discipline.

The political legacy of the Great Recession reawakens dormant questions. When is austerity 'too much of a good thing' (Corsetti 2012)? When is fiscal expansion warranted? When are member states free riding on other member states' growth policies? In the 1990s such questions provoked tensions when designing the architecture for a common European currency. The most visible testament to these is the creation and reform of the SGP whose compound name is an attempt to mollify two frequently conflicting policy goals (Dyson and Featherstone 1999; Heipertz and Verdun 2010). During the Great Recession the debate on the merits of active demand management intensified. Since 2008, Germany has repeatedly been accused of engaging in beggar-thy-neighbor policies, 'waiting for other less well-placed countries to do most of the work and reaping the benefits once exports pick up' (*Financial Times*, November 26, 2008). In the wake of the Great Recession, charges of stimulus free riding were replaced by heated debates engaging both policy-makers and academics on the question of austerity policies. The public row surrounding Carmen Reinhart and Kenneth Rogoff's (2010) influential and contested article 'Growth in a Time of Debt', which was repeatedly used as justification by austerity-minded policy-makers like the German Finance Minister Wolfgang Schäuble (2011), is perhaps the most prominent academic example. Criticism was particularly leveled against the speed of fiscal consolidation. On the one hand, Charles Wyplosz (2013) warned that 'adopting contractionary fiscal policies in the teeth of a double-dip recession never made sense'. On the other hand, the ECB Vice-President Victor Constancio, consistent with the central bank's reputation as a fiscal hawk, proclaimed that seeking to stimulate economies by stopping measures aimed at cutting government debt would merely increase countries' borrowing costs rather than triggering growth (*The Economist*, April 24, 2013).

The heightened visibility and consequentiality of fiscal crisis responses make the study of public finances in times of crisis particularly compelling (cf. Schelkle 2012b: 375). The Great Recession presents a new opportunity to examine EU and domestic-level responses to a global economic shock, and by comparing national differences, to draw future lessons for policy coordination. It is the opportunity offered by a 'bad-weather test' (Heipertz and Verdun 2010: 174). The appeal of such a test lies in its revelatory properties; 'prosperity blurs a truth that hard times make clearer' (Gourevitch 1986: 17). A full appreciation of 'how we got there' is especially warranted in the context of the shift of scholarly attention to the European Debt Crisis and the revamped architecture of the EU's economic governance. A deeper understanding of the realities of and processes for fiscal policy coordination during the Great Recession should improve our understanding of the post-2011 reforms that have led to the most comprehensive supranational system of economic and budgetary surveillance to date.

1.3 Methods of the Book

This book uses a mixed-method research design. With respect to the large body of political economy literature on European integration and more specifically fiscal policy coordination, the methodological plurality of this study aims at bridge-building. Here I aspire to plant a study that goes beyond the dominating 'monocultural accounts' (McNamara 2009). Regression analysis will be employed to form a basis for testing the three guiding hypotheses, and notably to assess the determinants of fiscal policy outcomes. The data used in the statistical analyses presented in Chapters 4 to 8 covers the years 2008–14. The empirical material will be appreciated in relation to the qualitative material, particularly the rich interview material with fifty-three key bureaucrats and policy-makers. The combination of nuanced interview material with arguably more blunt econometric techniques seeks to enrich our understanding of fiscal policy coordination in hard times. Interviews were conducted at the European Commission, the European Council, the European Parliament (EP), and Permanent Representations of the Member States to the EU, Eurostat and the IMF. The decision to interview broadly across different institutions is based on the 'fragmentation of responsibilities' (Hodson and Maher 2001: 645) of fiscal policy coordination. Furthermore, I carried out eighteen interviews with fixed-income managers, investors, and market analysts. Interviews took place between 2011 and 2017. Most of the information gathered during the interviews was explicitly 'not for attribution'; that is to say, the information could be used and quoted provided that the individual would be granted anonymity (see Appendix 3). I supplement these interview sources by drawing on extensive primary document analysis as well as the rich secondary literature and contemporary news accounts. By drawing on multiple methods of analysis, I seek to strengthen the book's methodological and empirical rigor.

1.4 Outline of the Book

This study explores the state, dynamics, and legacy of fiscal policy and its coordination among EU member states during the economic and financial crises of 2008–10. Chapter 2 traces the development of and key procedures for EU fiscal policy coordination. Here I introduce the book's main cast of institutional actors, member states, as well as new and old procedures. In so doing it charts fiscal policy coordination from the establishment of the SGP in 1999 to the post-crisis reforms, including the creation of the European Semester. Chapter 3 provides a theoretical treatment of fiscal political coordination in the EU. Fiscal policy coordination is marred by a classic collective action problem; it pays to be egoistical. Member states have an incentive to under- or over-stimulate their economies, despite a common interest in coordinated policies. Building on Mancur Olson's premises on collective action failure (1965), I developed three consecutive research questions which will guide the empirical investigation. These questions scrutinize 1) the EU's group latency, 2) evidence for or against free riding behavior, and 3) incentives to achieve collective action.

In a first step I examine the drivers of fiscal policy outcomes and establish whether EU member states form a latent group for which collective action is inherently challenging. The existence of group latency is said to render the provision of incentives necessary in order to motivate group members to contribute to the production of the collective good in question. Hence, in a second step, I analyze the evidence for and against fiscal free riding during the Great Recession. Rampant free riding would suggest ineffective incentives to curb or boost public spending. In a third step, I investigate the workings of different incentives, identified in fiscal rules and market discipline. This allows me to test whether these incentives mattered for public finances in times of crisis.

Chapter 4 sets out to examine the determinants of fiscal policy outcomes and gets to the issue of latency. EU members form a diverse union. What are the implications of economic and political diversity for public finances and by implication for collective action? Answering this question, I analyze time-series cross-sectional data from the twenty-seven EU member states over a three-year period (2008–10). I focus on a range of fiscal policy measures, from bespoke summaries of stimulus packages to statistically less ambiguous headline indicators of public finance. The empirical analysis asserts that the deficit bias attributed to contemporary public finances was stronger during the Great Recession. Political factors have shaped public finances markedly. I argue that fiscal policy outcomes were not apolitical products of the harsh economic logics of compulsion, but a complex result of intervening political features. Faced with a common shock, member states did not merely respond to the economic imperative of crisis management, but identified different solutions to similar problems. The standing temptation of free riding is thus amplified by political and economic diversity.

Latent groups provide a seedbed for free riders. Chapter 5 thus tests whether fiscal policy coordination was marred by collective action failure. Specifically, both stability and growth free riding are investigated. The central claim of this chapter is that accusations of stability or growth free riding are not borne out by factual evidence. First, I demonstrate that despite their greater ability to free ride, larger and more open economies implemented larger stimulus programs. To better distinguish between growth and stability free riding, I consider fiscal response strategies vis-à-vis a country's fiscal space; that is, a country's room for spending public money without undermining fiscal sustainability. This allows me to ask whether countries stimulated 'too much' in relation to a small fiscal space (stability free riding) or 'too little' in relation to a large fiscal space (growth free riding). In so doing, I construct a new composite indicator based on the EU's Excessive Imbalances Procedure. Results show that, by and large, member states stimulated their economies in line with their fiscal room for maneuver. These findings are contrasted with the political discourse of late 2008 and 2009, when accusations of growth free riding were widespread. Accusations of beggar-thy-neighbor politics were rife; first-order fiscal free riding was not.

Solutions to free riding, be it stability or growth free riding, are thought to be found in the provision of incentives. Chapters 6 and 7 ask which incentives may have kept free riding at bay. Specifically, I analyze two types of incentives: fiscal rules and market discipline. The empirical findings suggest that domestic fiscal rules, such as debt brakes, did not impact on the fiscal policy responses to the Great Recession. Similarly, EU-level fiscal agreements, the SGP, and the newly created EERP did not impact on fiscal policy choices. First, the majority of domestic fiscal rules were equipped with exceptionality clauses. As a result, they did not impose stern constraints on fiscal policy choices in hard times. Second, I argue that in terms of fiscal policy outcomes, the EERP and the SGP were meaningless; member states adopted stimulus programs as they saw fit with little concern for EU-level agreements or

EU-wide aims of stability and growth. It would be a mistake to assume that just because member states predominantly resorted to an increase in public expenditure to combat recession, these policy choices were driven by EU-level incentives. Instead, discretionary stimulus spending as a response to the economic downturn has been a default option for developed and (to a lesser extent) emerging market economies.

Free riding is endemic. But it is not the type of first-order free riding that politicians publicly chastised. Instead, fiscal policy coordination is burdened by a serious internal enforcement problem. The argument presented here is different from the usual decrying of a lack of enforcement in fiscal policy coordination. The lack of enforcement is not a problem because it invites member states to engage in rampant fiscal free riding. Instead I argue that without internal enforcement, fiscal policy coordination has come to rely on market discipline, with dire consequences for its members. In contrast to fiscal rules and intergovernmental agreements, the incentives provided by market discipline are found to impact public finances. This market discipline effect is stronger for Eurozone member states. Here market participants scrutinize fiscal policy choices and outcomes more critically in the absence of unilateral soft and hard debt monetization. The qualified success of market discipline as an Olsonian incentive is due to its external nature. In contrast to the politicized hang-ups of peer pressure and peer discipline, financial markets sanction fiscal policy as a by-product of credit risk pricing, a process that is comparatively sheltered from political capture. Yet, particularly since the eruption of the European Debt Crisis, the high costs of outsourcing the role of fiscal disciplinarian have become blatantly evident. The inability of member states to enforce coordination internally—that is, countries' unabashed second-order free riding—has left vulnerable countries at the mercy of erratic and procyclical market behavior. What is more, market discipline is asymmetric: while stability free riding was punished, there continue to be no effective incentives in place to limit growth free riding. Financial markets are more concerned about stability (credit risk) than about growth, at least in the short to medium term. Neither fiscal rules nor market participants disciplined governments who failed to stimulate the national economy. This leaves policy-makers' excoriated 'deficit and debt bias' to counteract the temptations of growth free riding. The current set-up is bound to be insufficient to rebalance EU economies.

Chapter 8 considers the determinants of fiscal policy outcomes during the consolidation years (2011–14). Echoing Chapter 5, I find that despite heated charges of free riding, member states' fiscal consolidation was by and large in line with domestic fiscal space. Those with limited space consolidated public finances more than those with larger fiscal space. This finding suggests that there was no first-order collective action failure in EU fiscal policy consolidation. Proponents of fiscal rules would credit the strictures of the SGP or newly created debt brakes for bringing about consolidation. Yet there is no convincing evidence (both based on interviews and on the statistical material analyzed in Chapter 8) that these rules mattered for fiscal policy outcomes. Instead the outsourced Olsonian incentive lies in financial market pressure—this holds for the stimulus years and for the consolidation years alike. Financial markets held considerable sway over public finances, and this market discipline is now felt across the EU, as the equal responsiveness of Eurozone and non-Eurozone governments to bond market pressure suggests. Market discipline is not felt equally across the EU. A prominent emerging fault line runs between program (debtor) and those who fear the threat of market panic on the one hand, and credit countries who remain largely insulated from the vagaries of international capital markets on the other.

Looking ahead, the legacy of the crisis years is already shaping the future of fiscal policy coordination. The two main aspects of change concern purview and pliancy. First, fiscal policy has ceased to be defined in narrow 'low-deficit' targets and instead is set to encompass a twin notion of free riding: growth free riding and stability free riding. Second, fiscal policy coordination has become more flexible and as a result more adaptive to the challenges of sound public finances in the twenty-first century. While the institutional architecture for collective action has been strengthened, there is little reason to be optimistic as to the containment of endemic second-order free riding. Member states are continuing to rely on market discipline as erratic enforcers of rules they are unable to bring to bear among each other. The concluding Chapter 9 interrogates key themes of this book vis-à-vis developments beyond EU borders as well as beyond the Great Recession, and proposes three avenues for future research pertaining to the relationship between first- and second-order free riding, the role of policy consensus in fending off free riders, and the black box of market discipline.

This book tackles a deceivingly mundane and dry topic. Yet fiscal policy is the making of decisions about how to collect and spend across people and generations; it is at its core political. In the words of one interviewee from the European Commission's DG Ecfin, 'the budget is one of the ultimate expressions of sovereignty' (interview, April 2015). This portrait echoes a now-famous characterization by Rudolf Goldscheid, the founder of fiscal sociology: 'the budget is the skeleton of the state stripped of all misleading ideologies' (quoted in Schumpeter [1918] 1995: 6; see also Blyth 2013; Levi 1989). With the dawn of the Great Recession, the fiscal skeleton has come to haunt European integration.

Notes

1. Interview, April 2011. To preserve guarantees of confidentiality, I identify interview subjects by date only and institutional affiliations only where permission was granted (Appendix 3).
2. It follows that the very name 'Sovereign Debt Crisis' is misleading and can, at best, only account for half of the crisis. Blyth (2013: 5ff) discusses the political ramifications of giving labels to this 'financial-cum-debt-crisis'.
3. Credit rating agencies, such as Standard & Poor's, Moody's, or Fitch, use an alphabetical system to denote the credit worthiness of debt securities. AAA is accordingly the highest/best rating. Anything lower than a BBB-rating is considered a speculative or junk bond. In addition to the ECB, many government pension funds are required by law to only invest in highly rated bonds. Insurance companies and mutual funds often have similar internal thresholds.
4. German fixed-income manager, interview, March 2014.

2

Fiscal Policy Coordination

A Primer

2.1 Before the Storm

This book examines fiscal policy coordination in times of crises. As such, it is not the place for a history of the Euro (see Dyson and Featherstone 1999) or for an extensive review of fiscal policy coordination during the first decade of the Economic and Monetary Union (EMU). Although the empirical core of this book spans the years of the Great Recession (2008–10), the reader will find that the discussion enters both pre- and post-crisis territory; as in Pharaoh's dreams, 'the fat years and lean years are, of course, interconnected' (Gourevitch 1986: 9). A little historical context and the introduction of key aspects of fiscal policy coordination are desirable in order to make sense of what follows. To this end, this chapter considers the key developments of pre-crisis fiscal policy coordination, before turning to the creation of the European crisis agreement, the European Economic Recovery Plan (EERP), and finally the reform packages post-crisis. It will do so largely chronologically. Despite impressions to the contrary, the procedures for fiscal policy coordination are extensive, although enforced and reinforced with little political and legal power. The byzantine complexity of rules, procedures, mechanisms, and committees aimed at effective fiscal policy coordination has progressively increased during the last decade. Particularly after the Great Recession, member states agreed to the most substantial and meaningful overhaul of fiscal policy coordination and economic governance mechanisms.

2.2 A Faulty Centerpiece

Fiscal policy coordination before the Great Recession evolved around the so-called Stability and Growth Pact (SGP; Heipertz and Verdun 2010). The SGP's origins date back to a proposal by the then German Finance Minister

Theodor Waigel (encouraged by the Bundesbank) in 1995, which insisted on the necessity of a fiscal rule that would prevent countries with poor fiscal discipline records from attempting to 'free ride' on the budgetary 'prudence' of other states. In spite of its double-barrel name, stability free riding takes centerstage. First, the SGP's preventive arm specifies a deficit limit of 3 percent of GDP, which provides an early-warning mechanism that may lead to policy recommendations being made to a member state if deemed necessary. The 3 percent ceiling was very much the heart of the rule—so much so that Waigel's insistence thereof earned him the moniker 'Monsieur Drei-Komma-Null' among his European colleagues. Second, its dissuasive arm governs the Excessive Deficit Procedure (EDP), which is triggered if the deficit should breach the 3 percent threshold. The decisions on the EDP are subject to a highly politicized procedure that notably involves the consent of Ecofin, the Council of Economic and Finance Ministers. Theoretically, noncompliance can lead to a suspension of commitments or payments from the EU's structural and investment fund for all member states, and for Eurozone members it could lead to sanctions in the form of a non-interest-bearing deposit of up to 0.5 percent of GDP, which could turn into a fine if the deficit persists.

The economic and political logic of the SGP was contested well before its creation. Notably, Jacques Delors, the architect behind the new currency union, considered the provisions a 'great disappointment' (Dyson and Featherstone 1999: 741); his vision of the EMU was one where a balance between the economic and monetary pillar should be ensured by comprehensive economic policy coordination. Yet the SGP was strongly biased toward a preoccupation with monetary policy, whilst fiscal policy was to be evaluated by its low-inflation merits. This focus contrasted with Delors' plan favoring fiscal and structural requirements of a viable EMU, which would be able and willing not only to address asymmetric shocks, but also to advance economic growth and employment. Many prominent economists chimed in with this critique of the SGP (e.g. Buiter et al. 1993; Eichengreen and Wyplosz 1998). What is more, many policy-makers seemed equally disenchanted with the SGP—Commission President Romano Prodi's 'stupid' verdict being a notorious example.

2.2.1 *The SGP in Action*

A first stress test for the SGP arose in 2003 when the French and German deficits were (again) above the 3 percent threshold. In line with Treaty provisions, the Council decided to label German and French deficits 'excessive'. The symbolism of receiving a 'blue letter' from Brussels with regards to missed deficit targets is particularly humiliating in the German context. Not only was Germany the self-styled parent of the SGP, but the 'blue letter' is widely associated with the embarrassing warning notes that schools send out every summer to pupils who are about to fail a class. Commentators and oppositional politicians echoed this 'humiliation' aspect (Howarth and Rommerskirchen 2013). The long-suspected toothlessness of the SGP was then confirmed when Ecofin suspended the EDP, the procedure that was designed to lead to fines for non-compliers. Protest was heard, notably from the Netherlands, Austria, Finland, and Sweden. The Dutch finance minister, Gerrit Zalm, even accused the bigger member states of 'bullying' smaller ones, complaining that countries had been intimidated by France and Germany (*Sunday Times*, November 30, 2003). Many observers and scholars interpreted the absence and eventual suspension of sanctions as the death of the SGP (e.g. Begg et al. 2004).

Because of the non-application of the EDP, the Commission pursued legal action against the Council, although with little success: the European Court of Justice ruling scolded the Council, stating that it 'cannot depart from the rules laid down by the treaty' (*Financial Times*, July 13, 2004). However, at the same time, the Court avoided key questions on the nature and concatenation of the SGP's procedure, as well as on the division of power between Council and Commission in the enforcement of national budgetary discipline. The Court ruled that the Council had the right to not adopt the Commission's recommendation, but that it did not have the right to then adopt its own recommendation instead, thus overwriting the Commission's proposal. The decision gave governments leeway in interpreting the EU's controversial set of budget rules, 'leaving [the SGP] vulnerable to political maneuvers' (Sadeh 2006: 11). The decision of the Council of Finance Ministers in November 2003 not to impose sanctions on countries that had breached the deficit limit for two years in succession left the SGP in limbo throughout 2004. By then, most member state governments favored reform.[1]

2.2.2 *Reforming the SGP*

Reform came in 2005 with German and France using their joint political heft to get the revised SGP through heated debates within the Council. An important change concerned the introduction of differentiated 'medium-term objectives' (MTOs). Whereas the old SGP merely stated that member states should maintain medium-term budgetary positions that are 'close to balance or in surplus', under the new SGP each member state would present its own country-specific MTOs. While maintaining a safety margin with respect to the 3 percent deficit limit, the MTOs should take into account the economic characteristics of each state. The reformed SGP also introduces new provisions concerning the adjustment effort that should be made in order to reach the MTOs. This adjustment should be equal to 0.5 percent of GDP per year as a benchmark, with more effort in good times, and possibly less in bad times.

A central revision of the EU's fiscal rules is the extension of exemption criteria. Previously only negative growth and events outside the control of the member states were permissible. Now member states could evoke a host of reasons that will allow for a postponement of the steps toward being reprimanded or even fined under the EDP. The negotiations of these 'expenditure exceptions' were not unlike a bazaar where each state tried to strike bargains and cater to their personal budgetary realities and preferences (for a summary, see Morris et al. 2006). Various factors were to be discounted against the national deficit. This list of items contains a large number of spending provisions ranging from the concrete to the vague (such as investments, education, defense, foreign aid, research and development, structural reforms, European unification, and international solidarity). During the reform negotiations it was clear that member states sought to include spending items that were especially important for the make-up of their respective public finances. Germany, for instance, canvassed for the inclusion of state expenditure toward reunification, while France tried to insert military expenditure (Howarth 2007).

However, the central escape clause within the SGP was left unchanged by the 2005 reform. This clause stipulates two specific conditions that warrant the breach of existing rules: closeness and temporariness. First, the waiver provision stipulates that a deficit of more than 3 percent of GDP should not be considered excessive and hence may warrant an exemption of the rules *if and only if* it stays close to the 3 percent threshold (TEU 126, 2–3). In order to fall under the escape clause, the deficit ratio must *always remain close* to the reference value. Second, any excess over the reference value must be temporary. In order for the excess to be considered temporary, the Commission's budgetary forecast must indicate that the deficit will fall below the reference value following the end of the unusual event or the severe economic downturn. Any deficit above 3 percent that is neither close to the reference value nor temporary should be considered excessive, irrespective of exceptional circumstances. We will encounter these two stipulations, closeness and temporariness, in action in Chapter 6.

The reformed SGP was applied at a time of economic upturn. The center-right Barroso Commission sought to restore compliance with the SGP by recommending corrective action against all members in breach against expectations that it 'would turn a blind eye to excessive budget deficits' (Hodson 2013: 311). To the degree that the economic climate improved, so too did compliance with the SGP. In 2008 the Commission presented an optimistic scenario for public finances in the EU: no Eurozone country was to run a deficit in excess of 3 percent and corrective procedures only remained active for two non-Eurozone members, Hungary and Poland, with the latter expected to soon come to a close. And yet despite broad compliance immediately before the crisis hit, European fiscal policy coordination remained contested. In particular, the newly elected French President, Nicolas Sarkozy, argued that 'institutions, procedures, directives and rules are not ends in themselves', and challenged what he considered to be 'pseudo-dictatorship of the market' inherent in the SGP (*New York Times*, July 5, 2007) before announcing that France would put off balancing the French budget until 2012 (Clift 2008: 205–7). An escalation of the brewing conflict between Germany and France about rule compliance was postponed if not abandoned by the economic and financial crisis.

After the first decade, few would call fiscal policy coordination a success. This raises the question: what does the failure to coordinate fiscal constraints in comparatively rosy times tell us about the prospects for coordination in hard times? An implicit assumption running through the SGP literature is that of the 'deficit and debt bias' of modern democracies, a notion made popular by the public choice school. In a nutshell, policy-makers who wish to maximize their electoral support are said to incur larger budget deficits than would be advisable and ultimately sustainable. The SGP sought to counter-balance this bias with a clear commitment to 'sound' fiscal policies. But in times of crisis the challenge is not to coordinate fiscal constraints, but fiscal stimulus policies. Given governments' deficit spending propensity, is this task likely to be easier than imposing fiscal constraints? If governments resisted a deficit ceiling, would they be more inclined toward group-oriented behavior that expressly encourages expansive fiscal policies? The EERP sought to provide a framework for doing so.

2.3 The European Economic Recovery Plan

The first wave of crisis reactions in 2008 did not address the question of stimulus coordination, but was instead aimed at the financial sector. These efforts were predominantly unilateral (Pauly 2009). Seemingly oblivious to the clear signs that the financial crisis would have severe repercussions for the real economy, the Council's conclusion (Ecofin 2008) on October 7, 2008 stated that the reformed SGP 'is the adequate framework and should be fully applied. It contains flexibility to allow for fiscal policy to play its normal stabilization function . . . relatively large European automatic stabilizers can help cushion the slowdown, while respecting the 3 per cent of GDP deficit threshold'. This assessment was wrong. Problematically, the SGP did 'not allow for discretionary fiscal expansions, unless a country has significantly over-achieved its budgetary objectives' (Larch et al. 2012). At an emergency summit on October 12, member states reached an agreement on national responses to ensure liquidity for financial institutions; yet concrete fiscal policy measures and targets were not addressed. Instead, member states vaguely pledged 'to coordinate measures to address the consequences of the financial crisis on the real economy' (Eurogroup 2008); key terms such as 'stimulus' and 'discretionary spending' were notable only in their absence. The Commission finally proposed a more detailed EU recovery framework on November 26. At the heart of the EERP is the call on member states to implement an immediate budgetary impulse amounting to €200bn (1.5 percent of EU GDP), composed of a budgetary expansion by member states of €170bn (around 1.2 percent of EU GDP) and EU funding in support of immediate actions in the order of €30bn (around 0.3 percent of EU GDP). The EU funding was mainly invested into infrastructure programs and linked to other existing programs such as the European Structural Funds and the European Globalisation Adjustment Fund.

The EERP includes the understatement that fiscal efforts 'may lead some Member States to breach the 3 per cent GDP deficit reference value'. In fact, all member states except Sweden and Estonia were in violation of the 3 percent ceiling at some point between 2008 and 2010. Furthermore, the EERP (2008) relaxes the 'temporary' criterion of the SGP; the speed of corrective action was contingent on the speed of recovery, which meant that the Commission introduced greater leniency with respect to rectifying the excessive deficit situation. The EERP neglected to make explicit or implicit reference to the 'closeness' criterion of the SGP. The qualification of the Commissioner in charge of the economic governance portfolio 'that [close] means a few decimals, not many decimals' (*Financial Times*, November 27, 2008) did not find its way into official agreements or guidelines. What is more, the EERP did not introduce an actual limit on stimulus spending, either in absolute or relative terms. The European Council approved the EERP on December 12, 2008, in doing so advocating a recovery plan that was seemingly at odds with a strict reading of the SGP. This development is noteworthy. After decades of championing low deficits and debt levels, the Commission emerged as an unlikely advocate of stimulus policies throughout the EU, relaxing the application of existing rules under the SGP. The crisis framework laid out in the EERP represented a first attempt not to coordinate fiscal constraints, but rather fiscal expansion. This book presents an in-depth study of the challenges therein.

2.4 After the Crisis

The years after the Great Recession saw a considerable renovation of the EU's entire economic governance edifice. The reform umbrella is called 'the European Semester' which lays out the EU's policy-making calendar. Under this process the Six-Pack (2011), the Two Pack, and the Fiscal Compact (both 2013) seek to broaden and strengthen existing rules. The Semester, by introducing a common calendar for fiscal policy-making and coordination, aims at strengthening the European framework for surveillance of budgetary policies. Whereas the application of the SGP has suffered from admonishing or applauding budgets ex post facto—that is, after member states had (in most cases) already finalized their budgets—the new process introduced a coordination of budgetary and economic policies ex ante. Together these reforms spelt both a continuation and widening of fiscal policy coordination. In many ways the European Semester 'was long in coming' (Carstensen and Schmidt 2015: 9). In particular, the idea of getting to national policy-makers 'in time to make a difference' (interview, February 2017) was on the Commission's wish-list well before the crisis. This meant that the Commission's team working on the reform proposal could 'open drawers full of relevant ideas' (interview, April 2011).

2.4.1 *Something Old*

Reforms are designed like militant forces are said to be trained: to fight the last war, not the next one. As the European Debt Crisis was quickly and wrongly cast as a crisis of fiscal profligacy, cure and vaccine were identified in stronger fiscal rules. On the European level, sanctions for breaches of the SGP's stipulations (which now covered both the 3 percent of GDP for deficits and the 60 percent of GDP for debt levels) were to kick in earlier. Failure to reduce the deficit adequately could result in fines of 0.2 percent of GDP, which could rise to a maximum of 0.5 percent were statistical fraud detected (the latter is a nod to Greek statistics and the failure to sanction fabricated statistics). Penalties can now cover a suspension of EU regional funding, even for non-Euro-area countries. The question over automatic sanctions for noncompliance was once more on the table. The original 1995 Stability Pact foresaw automatic sanctions for deficits above 3 percent of GDP. In 2011 German negotiators were again lobbying for automatic sanctions against fiscally wayward states. True to a long-standing French position on the issue, Nicolas Sarkozy obtained the German Chancellor's concession that sanctions for infringement would not be automatic as part of the so-called Deauville Deal. Specifically, the Commission recommendations to impose sanctions under the EDP may be overridden by the Council only by qualified majority. Overriding the Commission is still possible; doing so requires a larger coalition of member states. Crucially, reverse majority voting is not extended to all decisions taken by the Council. The key decision to place a country under EDP in the first place continues to be governed by the old qualified majority process.

On the domestic level, the intergovernmental Fiscal Compact called on member states to enshrine a German-style debt brake in national law. This reform was indeed a prerequisite for action on the part of the European Central Bank[2] and later financial assistance under the European Stability Mechanism (ESM), a textbook quid pro quo. It is on these grounds that the ratification of the SGP has been followed and welcomed by market participants (interviews, February and August 2015)—because it secures ESM eligibility, not because they cherish the disciplining effect of domestic debt brakes. The German Chancellor Angela Merkel (2011) followed tried and tested rhetoric when proclaiming that this pact represented 'an important step towards Stability Union', with Germany leading the way. The idea of a 'German debt brake' for Europe continues to be popular in Berlin. Yet this narrative ignores the fact that numerous EU countries had already adopted budget balance rules before 2008. What is more, in light of Germany's noncompliance with the SGP and insufficient national rules, Ecofin had previously repeatedly suggested the creation of a 'national stability pact' in Germany and other countries to boost compliance with the Maastricht criteria and to make the attainment of the MTOs within the SGP framework more credible. Already Jacques Delors, one of the Euro's key architects, had put the idea of 'national ownership' forward. With the Fiscal Compact the German government upgraded a predominantly domestic policy issue to the European level. Namely, the German debt brake project was designed to hamper the deficit spending of Länder governments and tied to the federalism reform. This reform, passed by parliament in summer 2009, was one of the most significant fiscal policy reforms achieved in Germany since 1949. The German government played down the fact that this new set of rules was as yet untested (the brake obliges all levels of government to adhere to a structurally balanced budget from 2020 onwards and thus enshrines the problematic concept of the 'black zero'). The solutions identified in the Fiscal Compact offer an old disciplinarian remedy to fiscal policy coordination and are biased toward preventing stability free riding. This one-rule-fits-all approach defies compelling evidence that this type of numerical ceiling is not equally efficient for all types of governments (Hallerberg et al. 2009). Even where the fiscal governance mode corresponds to a country's polity, it is not clear that 'debt brakes' provide a fiscal cure in the light of endemic financial instability and growing macroeconomic imbalances. Spain offers a case in point; in line with its underlying political environment, the country implemented a debt brake which covers 100 percent of general government finances in the early years of the Euro—far more than the 53 percent currently covered by the German debt brake. In Spain, gross central government debt as a percentage of GDP rose from 40 percent in 2008 to 100 percent in 2014. It is useful to look at developments of the fiscal rules index developed by the European

Commission which score the strength of domestic fiscal rules. During the first decade of the Euro, Spain scores higher than Germany in the EU's Fiscal Rules Index. More broadly speaking, advances in fiscal rules have clearly not effectively counteracted developments in debt levels post-2007. Whereas the average EU Fiscal Rules Index improved steadily from −0.66 in 1997 to 0.53 in 2011, debt levels have reached an all-time high (with an EU average of 83.1 percent of GDP in 2011). Chapter 6 will consider the role and power of fiscal rules in times of economic and financial crises, when the demands for stimulus policies or, in many instances more importantly, financial sector rescue packages are pressing.

2.4.2 *Something New*

The real innovation of these reforms, so I argue, is the creation of the so-called Macroeconomic Imbalances Procedure (MIP). This marks a departure away from a single-minded focus on stability free riding toward a more balanced appraisal of stability and growth free riding. Macroeconomic imbalances refer to 'any trend giving rise to macroeconomic developments which are adversely affecting, or have the potential adversely to affect, the proper functioning of the economy of a Member State or of the economic and monetary union, or of the Union as a whole' (EU Regulation No. 1176/2011). Specifically, the MIP established a scoreboard to provide an early-warning signaling device for potentially harmful macroeconomic imbalances in member states. Although this procedure should be interpreted against a global recognition of the threat of imbalances, and indeed the role that imbalances have played in the International Financial Crisis of 2007/8, the challenge of rebalancing has particular salience for the EU. There 'was genuine appetite to have a more holistic view of potential weaknesses across the EU' (interview, March 25, 2015).

Analogous to the SGP, the annual MIP has a preventive arm, where policy recommendations can be issued by the Council to tackle imbalances early on, and a corrective arm where 'excessive' imbalances have been identified and an action plan is requested from the member state concerned. Noncompliance with the Council recommendations can eventually, at least on paper, lead to financial sanctions. In the 'Scoreboard for the Surveillance of Macroeconomic Imbalances' (DG Ecfin 2011), the Commission stresses that the indicators are neither policy targets nor policy instruments. Instead the results of the scoreboard are interpreted from an 'economic perspective', with thresholds for the indicators merely being a starting point to serve as alert levels. The 'scoreboard is the least interesting aspect' (Commission interview, February 2017). According to another Commission official, 'strictly speaking [the scoreboard] is not needed at all. The indicators are there purely to legitimize the Commission's right to dig into issue areas that are sensitive nationally' (interview, February

2017). For Scharpf (2011: 29), the MIP 'replaces the rule-based approach of the Stability and Growth Pact with a highly discretionary regime of supranational economic management'.

As early as 1941, Keynes bemoaned that adjustment under the old Gold Standard was 'compulsory for the debtor and voluntary for the creditor'. The MIP replicates this deflationary asymmetry as the scoreboard for discretionary intervention by the Commission sets current account balance thresholds at 6 percent for surplus countries and 4 percent for deficit countries (see also Moschella 2014). The current account balance records the balance of transactions of a country with the rest of the world. Note that originally no surplus value was foreseen in the procedure, and that this value was only included after the European Parliament successfully used its new co-decision powers and demanded a more balanced approach (interviews, March 2011 and February 2017). The Van Rompuy Task Force[3] report (2010) justifies the asymmetric thresholds by arguing that 'the need for policy action is particularly pressing in Member States showing persistently large current account deficits and large competitiveness losses'. The asymmetric notion of imbalances appears to have a qualitative component too; as one (German) Commission official put it, 'the EU is experiencing imbalances because [other countries] import garbage from China, not because we export high quality machinery to the rest of the world' (interview, May 2011).

While the MIP marks a new development in fiscal policy coordination, the recognition of coordination challenges beyond deficit and debt figures clearly predates its creation. The most direct institutional precursor for the MIP can be found in the form of the Broad Economic Policy Guidelines (BEPGs), a set of overarching economic policy objectives. Whilst superficially similar to the MIP, the BEPGs had a blind spot with respect to imbalances. According to the European Commission, 'macroeconomic imbalances have been continuously monitored within the context of the EU's BEPG' (2012). Yet, on reviewing the annual Council Recommendations on the BEPGs from 1996 to 2008, macroeconomic imbalances were addressed only once. Whereas some parts of the Six-Pack, notably the common fiscal calendar under the European Semester, had been on the Commission's wish-list pre-crisis, the MIP appears to represent a genuine rethink in economic governance for the EU.

2.5 Conclusion

Fiscal policy coordination is in flux. New reform proposals such as those found in the *Four* or *Five Presidents' Reports* (Van Rompuy et al. 2012; Juncker et al. 2015) log an ambitious laundry list culminating in 'fiscal union'. Such a union would foresee a transfer of fiscal decision-making on national budgets to the EU level in exchange for insurance in the form of automatic stabilization provided by a Euro fund. The very notion of 'completing monetary union' is misleading. First, it risks neglecting non-Eurozone member states who are very much involved in economic cooperation. Second, it suggests a finality that is unlikely to match an evolving economic and political landscape. Although there is persistent continuity for some ideas and procedures, the SGP and its fear of stability free riding chief among them, new innovations and reforms have made inroads. Twenty years after Theo Waigel successfully lobbied for the SGP, it has been (mostly intelligently) modified and complemented by a set of new procedures. Respecting a magic deficit threshold is no longer the only game in town for fiscal policy coordination. This means that fiscal policy coordination has become more complex and more nuanced. It is argued that 'simple' fiscal rules 'can better steer financial market reaction of excessive deficits' (see Keleman and Teo 2014). If that is the case, then a more complex system of economic policy coordination is desirable on the grounds of financial markets' patchy track record in policing public finances and the questionable fit between market goals and EU collective action goals. I argue that reforms, where they mitigate market discipline, and thus curb second-order free riding, are to be welcomed. In the following chapters I discuss how the developments during the Great Recession have helped us move away from a narrow surveillance of fiscal headline indicators toward broad macroeconomic surveillance that recognizes the twin nature of freeloading as both 'too much' and 'too little' spending. Chapter 3 will present the theoretical framework of this book, building on Mancur Olson's theory of collective action. Chapters 4 to 7 are then set in the years of the Great Recession, the Stimulus Years. Here I will draw on this chapter's discussion on the shortcomings of national fiscal rules, the SGP, as well as the fiscal roadmap during the Great Recession, namely the EERP. Chapter 8 then takes us into the territory of the Consolidation Years and analyzes fiscal policy outcomes and collective action from 2011–14. Here I will further develop the key arguments of this book, particularly on the relationship between first- and second-order free riding, as well as between stability and growth free riding.

Notes

1. New member states from Central and Eastern Europe were against SGP reforms which they feared would undermine monetary union in advance of their membership (Chang 2006: 113).
2. Specifically, its long-term refinancing operation providing liquidity for banks.

3. In March 2010, member states, with the German Chancellor taking the lead, appointed the Council President Herman van Rompuy as the chief mediator under the Van Rompuy Task Force to work on a proposal to reform the existing economic governance architecture. The Task Force was composed of the finance ministers of the then twenty-seven member states, thus making it a distinctly intergovernmental group. In parallel to the Task Force, the Commission was working on its own proposal.

3

Theorizing Fiscal Policy Coordination

3.1 The Marriage Plot

One interviewee at a Permanent Representation to the EU (February 2017) asserted that 'there is a clear idea: Coordination is better than no coordination'. Why would sovereign states agree to coordinate their national fiscal policies? Answerers to this question have one key aspect in common: *interdependence*. There is no coordination in independence. The interdependencies of EU economies transform domestic fiscal policy outcomes into a transnational public good. The EU Treaty recognizes this specifically by stating that member states' economic and, by implication, fiscal policies are regarded as a 'matter of common concern' (Article 121, TFEU). Domestic fiscal policies can be either to the detriment or to the benefit of EU-wide stability and growth—thus the specter of growth or stability free riding. Commission President José Manuel Barroso was testifying to interdependence when he evoked the veteran 'sinking or swimming together' metaphor. Interdependence was and continues to be experienced outside the EU, of course; the bust of an investment bank in the US can lead to a surge in piracy off the Horn of Africa. Yet European integration has created a web of interdependence between sovereign states unprecedented in width and breadth.

The earliest entry that the *Oxford English Dictionary* offers on the term interdependence stems from a letter by Samuel Coleridge, in which the Lake Poet alludes to his 'unfitness for a state of moral and personal union and lifelong interdependence'. The EU is frequently compared to a marriage. Long before the events discussed in this book, political scientists and economists have drawn on matrimonial metaphors. Andrew Hughes Hallet and Maria Luisa Petit (1990) compared the coordination of fiscal and monetary policies to a 'forced marriage', Niels Thygesen (1993) discusses a 'honeymoon effect' for public finances in the run-up to the Economic and Monetary Union (EMU), Rudiger Dornbusch (1996: 110) considers the Maastricht Treaty a 'prenuptial agreement', Bernhard Winkler (1999: 52) muses that 'candidate countries for EMU play the role of the groom who has to woo a skeptical bride', and Martin Feldstein (2000: 12) stresses that the 'EMU is meant to be a marriage made in heaven with no room for divorce'—before the crisis in Greece brought on the menace of a 'big, fat Greek divorce' (*The Economist*, June 20, 2015) and the 2016 Brexit referendum triggered a flood of break-up notes. The choice of metaphor invariably carries a judgment about the state of the union. A high-ranking official at one of Brussels' Permanent Representations illustrated his reserve toward the strength of the Eurozone by pointing out that for some members the union 'is a money match, not a love match' (interview, February 2017).

This chapter provides a theoretical framework to organize the research agenda of this book and derive hypotheses about the shape and (mis)management of interdependence in times of crises. The starting point is the collective action problem that interdependent member states face when setting their domestic fiscal policies. Discussions on the causal relationship between interdependence and coordination have a standing tradition in both political science and economics. Henry Wallich's textbook definition (1984: 85) makes the link explicitly, defining coordination as 'a significant modification of national policies in recognition of international economic interdependence'. While EU member states are interdependent in a wide range of ways, from environmental hazards to cultural fads, this book focuses on the *economic* interdependence of member states and the *political* interdependence at the heart of the thus arising collective action problem. Trade links are key to understanding the free riding concerns during the Great Recession, but not the only ones. Contagion in European bond markets was not only based on trade relationships, but also made concrete by groupings of countries with (perceived to be) high sovereign risk which gave rise to offensive acronyms.

3.2 Theorizing Collective Action

Since the 1980s, scholars from politics and economics have reinvigorated debates about international cooperation, discussing the constraints and opportunities for macroeconomic policy coordination in the face of interdependence (e.g. Oye 1986; Bryant and Portes 1987). Analyzing fiscal policy coordination in hard times, this book addresses a specific collective action problem. The theoretical foundation of this book can be found in the literature on the logic of collective action, particularly Mancur Olson's seminal work (1965). Granted, various scholars have analyzed free riding behavior and ways to curb free riders prior to Olson. But, as Keith Dougherty (2003: 250) argues, 'these ideas were not prominent. Most of these theories were hidden in a mass of written works that were totally disregarded until Olson gave them relevance again'. Despite Olson's prominence in the political science canon, EU studies have shown comparatively little interest in engaging with his work, beyond a few perfunctory citations. The *Journal of Common Market Studies*, one of the leading journals on the politics and economics of European integration, has in its fifty-year history published a single article that engages with Olson's theory of collective action with respect to EU economic policy cooperation (namely Schelkle 2005).

Olson's original work focuses on the actions of individual people. In it we encounter farmers and unionists, party members and churchgoers. Although his is therefore not a state-centric theory, I argue that its insights are readily scalable from the individual to the arguably most successful organization of all time. Given the prominence of the state, and the centrality of cooperation and conflict in IR, this book on EU member states and their failed attempts to coordinate fiscal policy is not an outsider. Using a state-centric lens of collective action is hardly a novel approach (see for instance Lisa Martin's work on nuclear proliferation (1993)). The question of scalability or the so-called 'level of analysis problem' has preoccupied social sciences, and within them IR, for decades. At its heart, according to David Singer (1961), lies 'a problem of ontology: of whether the properties or behavior at one level of analysis can be reduced to those at another'. This challenge needn't be insurmountable, as the example of Robert Axelrod's (1984) seminal work on cooperation suggests. Here Axelrod discusses the motivations of individuals (be they soldiers or senators) and sovereign states within the same framework. My premise that Olson's theory applies, and pertinently so, to international collective action problems rests on two assumptions. First, Olson focuses on a variety of organizations whose existence can be explained by the provision of public goods and the reduction of externalities (such as security, infrastructure, or labor rights). The EU can be analyzed in similar terms. The 2012 Nobel Peace Prize recognized the EU's most important achievement as 'the successful struggle for peace and reconciliation and for democracy and human rights'. The public goods function of the EU relevant to this book considers the economic realm, namely in supporting stability and growth for its member states. The provision of public goods is the prerequisite for free riding. EU cooperation thus is meant to advance the welfare of its members in a manner comparable to Olson's labor unions, cartels, or corporations. Second, for EU member states, just as for Olson's farmers, it pays to be egoistical. For individuals and states alike, this is a matter of incentives. Individuals holding positions of influence or interest, from the highly visible German Chancellor to behind-the-scenes EU bureaucrats, populate this book. Yet this analysis frequently amalgamates country positions and, particulate in the quantitative section, relies on states as units of analysis. J. David Singer (1961: 78) dubbed the nation state 'our most comfortable resting place'. And yet I would argue that the decision to focus on EU member states in this account of free riding was not motivated by plush scholarship, but by its analytical capacity. To paraphrase David Lake (2010): states decide to free ride. They enlist the help of market forces. They choose whether and at what level to stimulate their economies. States enter economic governance agreements, or not, and choose whether to abide by their provisions.

The starting point for the logic of collective action is the so-called moral hazard problem; a situation where the provision of insurance, by diminishing the incentive to prevent a particular outcome, may make this outcome more, not less, likely. Moral hazard, in other words, encourages risk-taking. These unintended consequences of insurance have been studied in a wide range of fields from health (taking care of your body), to finance (taking care of your money), to agriculture (taking care of your crop). Olson's work rests on the premise that individual rationality is not sufficient for collective rationality. Donald MacKenzie and Yuval Milo (2003: 116) call this 'the possibility of a delightful paradox', namely that 'the very markets in which homo œconomicus appears to thrive cannot be created (if they require the solution of collective action problems, as in Chicago) by homines œconomici'. Olson's insight challenges Adam Smith's invisible hand, where the pursuit of each individual's self-interest in competitive markets is said to further collective wellbeing. Olson notably described how a situation in which the benefits of a public good cannot be successfully limited to those that positively contribute to its generation causes this good to be provided at suboptimal levels, if at all. In this book the public goods in question relate to stability and growth. The bifurcation between stability and growth is a conceptual one. Although it mirrors the debates of policy-makers at that time, the economic relationship between stability and growth is not necessarily adversarial. To give an example, fiscal consolidation can well have a negative impact on EU stability if economic growth reaches critically low levels. Proponents of swift and strong consolidation programs, reversely, have pointed to the notion of 'expansionary fiscal consolidation' where belt-tightening is said to spur economic growth. Section 3.2.1 unpacks these issues further.

3.2.1 *Too Much*

The pre-crisis focus on stability free riding received backing from the community of central bankers. Mervyn King (1995), the former governor of the Bank of England, disclosed that 'central banks are often accused of being obsessed with inflation. This is untrue. If they are obsessed with anything, it is with fiscal policy'. This admitted obsession is not limited to domestic fiscal policy, but also extends to EU-wide fiscal policy coordination. The European Central Bank (ECB) continues to be one of the staunchest supporters of the Stability and Growth Pact (SGP)—a pact that seeks to prevent '*too much*' spending in relation to a country's fiscal room for maneuver. Over the past ten years, the ECB has communicated intensively on fiscal policies in both positive and normative terms, especially in comparison to other central banks (Allard et al. 2013). The reason for central bankers' preoccupation with fiscal policy and its coordination is, again, one of interdependence. Specifically, it lies in the interdependence between monetary and fiscal policy. If central bankers want to fulfill their mandates, fiscal policy needs to be conducted in a low-inflation-friendly fashion—although there is room for disagreement about what this would look like. Note that this 'dance at arm's length' (Bodea and Huemer 2010) is commonplace in other developed and emerging market economies too (Moser-Boehm 2006). During the height of the crisis in 2011, the ECB turned to 'slow dancing' in Italy and Spain: Jean-Claude Trichet (jointly with the respective countries' governors, Mario Draghi and Miguel Ordóñez) signed letters to the Italian and Spanish prime ministers listing the consolidation measures expected in return for the ECB's bond-buying program (cf. Henning 2017: ch. 7). It appears that when Berlusconi's government did not follow through with the reforms, the ECB suspended Italian bond purchases until the installment of a technocratic government under Mario Monti.[1] Trichet did not invent the quid pro quo of central banking. To give one prominent example: cajoling President Clinton to balance the federal budget in 1998, Alan Greenspan all but promised that the Federal Reserve would lower short-term interest rates as a reward for fiscal prudence.

The assumed threat of '*too much*' (stability free riding) within the EU ranges from inflationary dynamics to full-on sovereign debt crisis resulting in bailout calls. Considering the first, fiscal policy coordination has been guided by the doctrine of fiscal discipline for the sake of price stability. As Charles Wyplosz (2006: 225) points out, the economic logic of the SGP 'is rooted in the strong evidence that large inflations are always the consequence of runaway deficits'. Unsustainable levels of debt would lead to demands of higher wage settlements and higher interest rates by purchasers of government debt to be compensated for expected inflation. As a result, governments would try to force monetary financing upon their central banks. Central to the SGP's creation was the claim that high deficits would cause inflation (e.g. EMI 1996). This assertion was reiterated in the reformed SGP (e.g. González-Páramo 2005), in the aftermath of the recession (Stark 2010), and in the context of the European Sovereign Debt Crisis (Bundesbank 2013). Yet there is strong evidence that the link between deficits and inflation, as expressed by Thomas Sargent and Neil Wallace's 'unpleasant monetarist arithmetic', is tentative at best and does not apply to low-inflation advanced economies (Catao and Terrones 2005). Substantial increases in public debt and deficit levels in the wake of the Great Recession have not led to an 'outbreak of inflation'. The opposite is true with central bankers across the EU fending off the specter of deflation.

But the ultimate moral hazard fear concerns not inflationary dynamics, but member states counting on help. Walter Bagehot was already worrying about perverse incentives to rescue banks in nineteenth-century London. A wave of International Monetary Fund (IMF) bailouts in emerging markets and developing countries during the second half of the twentieth century caused concern over biased investors and policy-makers alike. The US system is frequently cited as one example of moral hazard contained with the decision in 1841 of the federal government to decline bailing out eight troubled states that subsequently defaulted. In the US and other 'fend-for-yourself' federalist systems like Russia, Switzerland, Brazil, and Canada, sub-state borrowing thus traditionally attracts interest rate premiums to compensate for the heightened default risk in a no-bailout system. In the context of European integration, warnings that a bailout of one member state would only be a matter of time have been heard since the early 1990s (Bovenberg et al. 1991). E(M)U membership, so the argument goes, provides insurance in the form of bailout solidarity. This insurance in turn insulates members from risk and makes risk-taking more likely, thus exacerbating the likelihood of a bailout being necessary. Chapters 7 and 8 will return to the parlous misconception of this 'moral hazard' argument. Moral hazard features heavily in the so-called No-Bail-Out Clause found in Art. 125 of the TEU. It states that neither the Community nor any member state can be liable for the debt commitments of other member states. This provision not only prohibits the assumption of a member state's debt; it also prohibits EU liability for such commitments. This clause is only one of a number of institutional arrangements for sound fiscal policies at the EU level. It should be seen as complementary to the prohibition of monetary financing (Article 123 of the TEU), the prohibition of privileged access to financial institutions (Article 124 of the TEU), the SGP, and the fiscal provision to avoid excessive government deficits (Article 126 of the TEU), and the no-inflationary bailout obligation of the ECB (that is, the central bank accepting a higher level of inflation). The apparent policy dilemma posed by the high costs of actually sticking to Art. 125, as has been illustrated in the debates on 'Grexit' (Greece leaving the Eurozone), gives further rise to the call for fiscal policy coordination as a means to avoid any excessive debt situation in which a bailout might become preferable.

In the fall of 2008, initial stability free riding concerns warned of risking economic stability at the altar of economic stimulus programs. The fear was that some member states would engage in more discretionary spending than would be advisable with respect to their fiscal space, knowing that other member states would exercise sufficient fiscal constraint for inflation and interest rates (and for the EMU's corresponding central bank policies) not to react. Along similar lines, some member states might prefer to push their fiscal consolidation back to a politically/economically more auspicious date, hoping that other member states will provide sufficiently stabilizing policies for the EU as a whole.

3.2.2 *Too Little*

The name of the SGP already signals the common interest in both stability and growth—never mind that it had very little to say about growth in the first decade of the Euro. And yet few policy-makers would neglect the importance of economic growth for the wellbeing of individual countries and the union as a whole, particularly in light of aging populations and steadily rising welfare bills. The phenomenon of stability free riding had been warned of even before the introduction of the Euro (Inman and Rubinfeld 1992; Portes 1993), analyzed after stage III of the EMU (Chari and Kehoe 2007; Bonatti and Crisitini 2008), and revisited during the current economic and financial crisis (De Grauwe and Moesen 2009). Concerns over growth free riding—that is, 'too little' spending in relation to a country's fiscal room for maneuver—have been less prominent. A charitable reading of neglecting growth in free riding debates prior to the Great Recession would point at the well-established awareness of national policies toward achieving economic growth and thus elevating the need for European-level collection action.

The starting point for growth free riding is the existence of cross-border leakages or spillovers. The more open an economy, the more of its spending leaks into other economies. Member states who limit their spending can thus benefit from the externally generated expansion of demand without having to infer the high costs of budget deficits. Analysis for the time span of 1965 to 2003 suggests that a German fiscal expansion has quite strong effects on its smaller neighbors; an increase in public spending by 1 percent of GDP in Germany leads to a more than 0.4 percent normalized increase in GDP for Austria, Belgium, and the Netherlands after two years—while the corresponding number for Greece is only a 0.06 percent increase in GDP (Beetsma et al. 2006). Given these leakages, Germany is, on the one hand, frequently called 'Europe's engine' as Europe's largest economy, producing a fifth of the EU's GDP. On the other hand, its export-growth model and economic openness make it a prime candidate for (accusations of) growth free riding.

Although allegations of 'beggar-thy-neighbor policies', i.e. too restrictive fiscal stances, are not an entirely new feature of post-crisis debates (e.g. Dullien and Fritsche 2006; Gros and Belkle 2007), the Great Recession has unbalanced the political agenda. This is not only an EU but also a global trend in international macroeconomic policy coordination, as for instance expressed in the 2008–10 G20 policy pledges (Rommerskirchen and Snaith

2017). Prior to 2008, a broad consensus on the merits of prioritizing low inflation and low deficits was secured by the apparent stability of the pre-crisis decades in the developed world. The crisis threw the fallacies of this paradigm into stark relief, illuminating systemic risk in corners of the economy that lay beyond the conventional boundaries of macroeconomic policy regulation and coordination. Faced with the limitations of existing governance strategies in predicting, let alone preventing, the economic fall-out, policy-makers across the globe sought more nuanced and integrated guidelines on macroeconomic management. One of the strongest common denominators amongst the crisis narratives was the identification of global imbalances as a key source of financial and economic instability (e.g. Frieden 2009; Willett and Chiu 2012; Bird 2012). On the fiscal side, the (re)discovery of imbalances meant examining surplus countries, who 'have fostered the crisis through their single-minded determination to pursue export-led growth' (Jones 2009).

In the fall of 2008 concerns over growth free riding started to dominate debates on fiscal crisis responses. Simply put, the stimulus program in one country is likely to also stimulate other economies. In order for this effect to be optimal, member states should coordinate their fiscal stimulus with each other. In the presence of positive spillovers arising from stimulus programs, the absence of coordination will lead member states to refrain from undertaking fiscal efforts to stimulate their economies, as was the case in the 1970s (de Grauwe 2009). A similar logic applies to the cost-benefit analysis when facing fiscal exit strategies. In the context of macroeconomic policy, 'exit strategy' refers to the withdrawal of economic stimulus programs and a return to sound public finances through comprehensive consolidation strategies. Once one member state starts the process of fiscal contraction, this will not only curb economic activity on a domestic level but also create negative spillovers in other states (see In't Veld 2013). Whereas the initial benefit of a return to sound fiscal principles is enjoyed only by the first member state, the costs of consolidation are accrued by other states as well. The likely reaction of other states is to follow the fiscal exit strategy, which will further reduce economic activity. This reduction could offset the positive effects on budget deficits. Non-coordinated exit strategies could therefore potentially hamper the recovery across national borders. This effect has been heatedly discussed in the debate on fiscal multipliers of austerity.

3.2.3 *Asymmetrical Interdependence*

The previous discussion presented growth and stability on EU-wide public goods, on whose production member states would have an incentive to free ride. Since Adam Smith's enumeration of public goods, the list of public goods has been expanded and modified over time. Classic/pure public goods are defined by two characteristics: non-rivalry and non-excludability. First, the consumption of this good by one party does not reduce others' ability to consume it. The second condition refers to the good being in joint supply; one party cannot be supplied without simultaneously supplying others. The notion of asymmetrical interdependence is part and parcel of international policy cooperation. By way of example, consider the 'grand-daddy of all public goods' (Nordhaus 1991), climate change. Some countries are highly vulnerable to global warming, with many low-laying island states on the brink of flooding; others, such as frigid Russia, might even welcome a thaw (Victor 2011).

The public goods of stability and growth have variable interdependence thresholds. Not all member states are, for instance, negatively affected by the sharp increase in interest rates on sovereign borrowing. Indeed, quite the opposite is true; Germany, in a 'flight to quality', benefited from investors pulling out of troubled EMU states. In a similar vein, closed economies are less affected by other member states' decisions to stimulate national economic demand. This does not pose a conceptual problem for this research: the literature on public goods is accommodating to such nuances and heterogeneous exposures (Rao and Kalpagam 1977). These variable thresholds fit within a broader portrait of EU member states' intergovernmental relations where 'asymmetrical interdependence' (Keohane and Nye 1989) dominates.

Growth and stability are public goods that affect all EU members where and to the extent that their economies are interdependent. Although Eurozone membership presents new challenges to European integration, for example with respect to market–state relationships, this issue of free riding concerns all EU states. I argue that the distinction between Euro and non-Eurozone countries, particularly post-Brexit, becomes increasingly brittle. Denmark, for instance, is not a member of the Eurozone, yet pegs its currency to the Euro with the Denmark's Nationalbank effectively shadowing the ECB (unless it is busy defending the parity with the Euro). Fiscal leakages mean that growth free riding is a concern for (particularly open-economy) members, whether or not they have adopted the single currency. Stability free riding can create negative dynamics that affect all EU members. For example, George Osborne (2013), then UK Chancellor of the Exchequer, repeatedly excused missed deficit reduction targets by pointing at the Eurozone crisis. What is more, the specter of bailout, which is the ultimate moral hazard of stability free riding, could affect all EU members. Financial assistance is not limited to the Eurozone. The initial wave of bailouts in 2009 (Latvia, Hungary, and Romania) took place outside the currency union. In the second wave of bailouts, non-Euro countries contributed to the financial assistance of Eurozone countries with the bilateral loans from the United Kingdom, Denmark, and Sweden amounting to €4.8bn. As one interviewee (April 2015) from a non-Euro EU country put it, fiscal policy coordination was an 'EU-wide matter', particularly given the 'need to keep as close as possible'.

Having made the case for the inclusion of *all* twenty-seven EU member states in this study, the case for the exclusion of non-EU states must also be made. Interdependence is not confined to the EU. EU affairs clearly matter for outside countries, even those without strong trade links or geographical proximity. Consider the deep hit that the Mexican peso took in the wake of Brexit. The peso is a proxy currency for less liquid European market currencies and was thus vulnerable to large sell-offs. Furthermore, fiscal policy coordination was not confined to the EU. While national governments forged and fudged their response to the economic crisis, three supranational organizations (the G20, the IMF, and the Organisation for Economic Co-operation and Development (OECD)) attempted to coordinate these policies (Armingeon 2012a). Particularly the attempts, and self-proclaimed success, of macroeconomic coordination within the G20 come to mind. The G20, a comparatively young multilateral forum, is an interesting, yet compared to the EU experience, less rich case. Fiscal policy coordination amongst G20 member states is a rather fledgling area of coordination compared to that in the EU. This distinction must be seen against the backdrop that fiscal independence among dispersed G20 countries is much lower than among EU states. Collective action problems are therefore less pronounced with respect to stability or growth free riding. Consequently, incentives to motivate group-oriented behavior are scarce. The existing architecture in the EU dwarfs international agreements on public finances. Even the EERP, however evasive it may be, is still the most substantial intergovernmental agreement on the coordination of fiscal policy responses during the Great Recession. This is not to suggest that fiscal policy coordination among states outside the EU is not worth studying. Emphatically it is (see Kahler and Lake 2013). But the unique experience of the EU is not readily transposed to other countries, which is why it would stretch this study to include other countries, however strong their economic interdependence with the EU.

3.3 Get Over It

Depending on group composition, Olson (1965: 50) distinguishes between three kinds of groups: privileged, intermediate, and latent. In a privileged group, 'each of its members, or at least some of them, has an incentive to see that the collective good is provided, even if it has to bear the full burden of providing it himself' (ibid.). Accordingly, a collective good may be provided even without any group organization, coordination, or additional incentives.

In an intermediate group, 'no single member gets a share of the benefit sufficient to give him an incentive to provide the good himself, but the group does not have so many members that no one member will notice whether any other member is not helping to provide the collective good' (ibid.). In an intermediate group, a collective good cannot be obtained without some level of group coordination. The third, the latent group, 'has no incentive to act to obtain a collective good because, however valuable the collective good might be to the group as a whole, it does not offer the individual any incentive to bear . . . any of the costs of the necessary collective action' (ibid. 51). The greater the latency of a group, the lower the probabilities of a public good being provided, and the greater the chances of collective action failure. The way out of the social dilemma for latent groups is the provision of incentives that will 'stimulate a rational individual in a latent group to act in a group oriented way' (ibid.). The three main hypotheses of this book are developed systematically from Olson's theory of collective action and consider group latency, free riding/collective action failure, and finally the provision of incentives.

3.3.1 *A Logic of Consequences*

Olson's account starts with the premise that individual rationality (it pays to be egoistical) does not lead to group rationality (successful collective action). This starting point situates Olson within the rational-choice literature. The following account of free riding in times of crisis is marked by a *logic of consequences*, not a *logic of appropriateness* that, for instance, collective action scholar Elinor Ostrom presents in her work (1990). Kathleen McNamara (1998) stresses that the development of a neoliberal economic policy consensus among European leaders was a crucial driving force for the establishment of the EMU. Her account stipulates a strong logic of appropriateness surrounding the so-called sound money paradigm. Yet this consensus did not extend to fiscal policy. It concerned a narrow set of monetary policy practices evolving around the notion of central bank independence and firm inflation targets in the run-up to the EMU. Delegation to the ECB has taken monetary policy out of the domestic policy ring and thus largely insulated it from domestic pressure and contention. Not so fiscal policy, which remains (firmly) in the hands of national policy-makers. Fiscal policy continues to be in search of consensus (Brunnermeier et al. 2016). According to interviewees at the European Parliament (March 2015) and the European Commission (March 2015 and February 2017), there 'cannot be a general consensus', as 'we are too different' and 'politically it's years and years away, so we have the proxy of enhanced fiscal governance [that is, rules] with all its imperfections'. The switchmen on the EU tracks of fiscal policy ideas continue to disagree.

This lack of consensus is 'inimical to the prospects for group action' (Olson 1965: 59). Yet consensus is neither a necessary nor a sufficient condition for collective action. According to Olson's premises (ibid. 59–60), the self-interested rationality to free ride still prevails, even under agreement about the desirability of coordination. For example, few policy-makers would advocate that everybody should ignore the SGP, but many have claimed the right for their country to flout it. The missing link between individual and collective rationality then gives rise to a situation within a political economy that appears irrational. As Allan Drazen (2000a: 410) concludes, 'a goal of political economy is to show how policies which seem suboptimal (hence, irrational in terms of basic welfare economics) can in fact be shown to be the result of the political mechanisms under which the decisions of rational, self-interested agents are agreed'. This book's analysis of collective action (failure) is hence also an attempt to explain the seemingly irrational state of policy (non-)coordination.

3.4 Research Hypotheses

Three main elements of Olson's theory guide this study and inform the three-step testing design. In a first step, Chapter 4 examines whether EU member states can be characterized as a latent group in terms of fiscal policy choices. Specifically, by identifying the determinants of fiscal policy choices, I am able to draw inference on group latency. If group latency is high, Olson warns of free riding behavior. The second hypothesis, tested in Chapter 5, therefore considers evidence in favor of or against stability and growth free riding during the Great Recession. In the final step, the findings of the second hypothesis are interrogated vis-à-vis the presumed need for incentives to motivate group members to contribute to the production of the collective good in question. In so doing, Chapters 6 and 7 examine the working of different separate and selective incentives and whether they matter for public finances in times of crises.

3.4.1 *Latency Hypothesis*

There is no latency litmus test. Instead of wielding a color-coded test stripe, the use of latency is a conceptual device. Latent groups are by definition conflictual groups where the temptation for free riding renders collective action failure epidemic and 'harmony' (Keohane 1984) is elusive. To test for group latency in EU fiscal policy coordination, I will first examine the determinants of fiscal policy outcomes, which in turn either contribute or fail to contribute to the public goods in question (i.e. stability and growth). The first hypothesis tested in this book is that:

H1: FISCAL POLICY COORDINATION IN THE EU TAKES PLACE IN A LATENT GROUP

I will model latency as a function of the economic and political environment of fiscal policy-making. Game theoretic approaches link diversity of group membership with collective action failure (Ostrom 1990). More diverse groups have more diverse interests, which frequently get in the way of cooperative agreements (cf. Snidal 1994: 62–7). This dynamic is particularly apparent with respect to global trade agreements, where 'the heterogeneity of preferences increased to such an extent that it did not increase the scope for issue linkages, but rather scuppered it' (De Bièvre 2014: 223). Waltraud Schelkle (2017) offers a different take on diversity, arguing that heterogeneity can be an asset, not a liability. The very fact that member states were not hit equally by the crisis means that some are, at least in principle, in a better position to keep the European engine churning without provoking the wrath of the bond gods. The contribution to the collective goods of stability and growth then becomes means-tested with a country's fiscal space as the key yardstick for pitching in. In addition to a diverse economic landscape, EU fiscal policy coordination takes place within a diverse political landscape. Fiscal policy is rarely only the result of a reflexive response to an economic impulse. Chapter 4 draws the link between diversity and latency by establishing whether these heterogeneous variables had an impact on fiscal policy outcomes during the Great Recession. Building on the theoretical considerations and empirical findings of the existing literature, I identify the political-economy factors that are likely to impact on a state's fiscal response to the financial and economic crisis, and by proxy likely to influence its contribution to fiscal policy coordination. Given the diverse political landscape of EU member states with differing electoral calendars, partisan outlooks, and executive and legislative makeups, fiscal policy outcomes are likely to be heterogeneous across member states and I expect these outcomes not to merely be a function of the state of the economy.

3.4.2 *Free Riding Hypothesis*

Group latency gives rise to free riding. According to the free rider problem, individuals only partially bear the adverse consequences of reducing their effort concerning fiscal stimulus or consolidation policies. The empirical study of fiscal policy coordination in times of crisis is challenging; in the absence of clear numerical rules for fiscal stimulus policies, measuring the success of fiscal policy coordination is problematic. This challenge is echoed in the skepticism of an interviewee from a member state's Permanent Representation in Brussels, who, when told about the subject of this book, quipped, 'so how are you going to write about something that does not exist?' (interview, May 2011). There is little reason to organize a project on the chimerical promise of measuring the immeasurable. First, as a proxy for group-oriented behavior, I will consider national stimulus programs vis-à-vis the self-imposed EERP value of 1.2 percent of GDP. Second, I will consider fiscal packages in relation to a country's fiscal space. To do so, I will construct a measure of fiscal space based on the indicators used in the newly created Macroeconomic Imbalances Procedure (MIP) to obtain a suitable yardstick for crisis responses. Fiscal policy coordination is found in member states shouldering fiscal expansion in accordance with their fiscal room for maneuver. Fiscal response strategies that fall short or (largely) exceed a country's fiscal space are an indicator of growth or stability free riding, respectively. Finally, I identify two main factors that are likely to contribute positively to the incentive and opportunities for free riding, namely economic exposure and political clout. This allows me to test empirically the lure of free riding.

H2: FISCAL POLICY COORDINATION WAS MARRED BY FREE RIDING
In order to ascertain and explain the phenomenon of fiscal free riding during the Great Recession, two main 'free riding variables' are explored. These relate to the size of a member state and its trade openness, aspects that can elucidate both a country's political ability and its structural capacity to free ride. Both relate to the notion of asymmetric interdependence discussed in section 3.2.3.

3.4.2.1 CLOUT

Studies on compliance rates with the SGP of small and large member states have suggested that size matters when it comes to respecting the E(M)U's fiscal rules. In the words of a senior Commission official, it may seem that 'there is one rule for the big guys and a different standard applied to the small ones' (interview, February 2017). A similar distinction between small and large countries applies to fiscal consolidation. The price of fiscal consolidation tends to be higher in large countries because fiscal multipliers are greater—put simply, the higher the multiplier, the more painful the deficit reduction (Buti and Pench 2004). Since the beginning of the EMU, large countries have grown considerably more slowly than smaller countries, which has hampered their retrenchment efforts (Fatás and Mihov 2003). Looking at compliance with the SGP, Jürgen von Hagen (2006: 33) notes that it is the small states that respect it, which 'matters the least, since a fiscal crisis in a small EMU Member State would hardly threaten the stability of the common currency'. With the benefit of hindsight, this statement surely requires further qualification—Greece is home to 2 percent of the EU population. An alternative argument to the big-versus-small member-states divide highlights the impact of state power at the decision-making stage. The political clout of a member state is closely related to its ability to shape agreements according to its preferences (Thomson et al. 2007). If large member states are able to influence the outcome of negotiations, this will positively impact their ability and willingness to comply with a given agreement. Looking back in history, the alleged degree of preference attainment did not prevent Germany and France from breaching the SGP's 3 percent threshold. This book considers a comparatively short time-frame, where agreeing and enacting coalitions are largely identical in Germany and France. But given the rapidly altered economic and political realities of policy-makers, the preferences held at the negotiation stage in late 2008 are not necessarily the same as throughout the Great Recession. Based on the economic/political clout literature, I suspect that the larger a member state's clout, the more likely it is to free ride. This assumption fits within the Thucydidean tradition of power relations where the strong will do what they will and the weak will do what they must.

3.4.2.2 OPENNESS

Openness is another key factor said to influence a country's propensity to free ride. Small countries tend to be more open. Small countries with small domestic markets have limited opportunities to exploit economies of scale, which leads them to expand their market size through international trade (Alesina and Wacziarg 1998). In fact, large parts of the discussion on the fiscal policy choices of open economies discuss small *and* open countries. Ever since David Cameron's influential study (1978), numerous scholars have found a positive correlation between a country's openness (trade exposure) and government expenditure. Cameron (ibid.) puts forward a 'compensation hypothesis' and explains this by suggesting that small economies are more likely to shelter their economies from the competitive risks of the international economy. However, a second strand of the literature examining the fiscal policy choices of open economies questions the effectiveness of public spending. The Meade model (1951) suggests that at times of collapsing aggregate demand, economies that are more closed (or less open) should opt for larger fiscal stimuli. Trade openness implies lower fiscal multipliers, as a share of the stimuli would 'leak'. During the Great Recession concerns over such 'leakages' were strong amongst EU member states (Cameron 2012). Larger stimulus packages should compensate for such leakages. At the same time, export-oriented open economies are structurally better placed to free ride; it pays more to be egoistical. Thus I expect open economies to be more likely to freeload.

3.4.3 *Incentives Hypothesis*

Group latency creates necessary but not sufficient conditions for the failure of collective action. In other words, free riding behavior is not an inevitable policy outcome for latent groups. To overcome free riding and non-group-oriented behavior in latent groups, Olson (1965: 51) proposes separate and selective incentives to stimulate cooperation and to instill a *logic of consequences*. Notably, incentives should not work indiscriminately like the promise of a collective good, but rather be targeted selectively toward the individual in the group. Negative incentives are defined as punishments that leave an individual on a lower indifference curve than she would have been had she contributed her share of the cost toward the provision of the collective good.[2] Positive incentives, on the other hand, are defined as any reward that leaves an individual on a higher indifference curve and thus makes group-oriented behavior more appealing (Kühn 1963: 365–70). These incentives can then mobilize latent groups into collective action by altering the cost-benefit calculus of individual members. Following Olson's (1965) argument, the hypothesis tested in Chapters 6 and 7 is:

H3: FREE RIDING WAS KEPT AT BAY BY INCENTIVES

I focus on two kinds of incentives which are thought to shape fiscal policy coordination. I first examine the impact of fiscal rules on stimulus policies, distinguishing between domestic and EU rules. Second, I analyze the role of financial market participants, specifically the impact of bond markets, in shaping public finances. While fiscal rules originate from within the collective action group, market discipline is an external incentive. This has important consequences for the market–state relationship underpinning fiscal policy coordination and points to a fundamental problem in the EU's approach to moral hazard.

3.4.3.1 FISCAL RULES

A fiscal rule is '[a] permanent constraint on fiscal policy, typically defined in terms of an indicator of overall fiscal performance' (Kopits and Symansky 1998: 2). Different institutions (fiscal rules) provide the framework within which individuals and groups define their preferences and thereby shape the strategic choices of policy actors (North 1990). The theory of collective action is closely linked to the study of institutions, as these are considered to be the preferred loci of overcoming social dilemmas. Elinor Ostrom (quoted in Peters 2011: 52) stresses that cooperation is most efficient if institutionalized, because institutions are a means to 'prescribe, proscribe, and permit' behavior.

The time-inconsistency of the political business cycle is evoked by the then Portuguese Prime Minister (and later Commission President) Barroso's poetic praise for the SGP helping 'a government to tie itself to the mast and resist the sirens who are trying to lure us to destruction with seductive songs of more state spending and bigger bureaucracies' (quoted in Tanzi 2004: 65). The literature on EU fiscal rules presents mixed evidence for a disciplinary effect. All things considered, a large body of literature finds no significant effect from EU-level fiscal rules (Freitag and Sciarini 2001; LeMay-Boucher and Rommerskirchen 2015). Although the effectiveness of the SGP is almost exclusively studied in the context of the EMU, it is worth stressing that it applies to all EU member states, albeit without the possibility of sanctions for those outside the Eurozone. In contrast, the literature on domestic fiscal rules, such as the Golden Rule[3] or debt ceilings, largely shows that they reduce budget deficits (Alt and Lowry 1994; Alesina and Bayoumi 1996; Debrun et al. 2008). What is more, these studies suggest that balanced budget rules work better when they are stricter (e.g. Bohn and Inman 1996; Lutz and Follette 2012). Mark Hallerberg (2004: 221) thus concludes that 'the source of fiscal discipline is at the domestic level'.

Fiscal rules are meant to rein in the deficit and debt bias of contemporary public finance. Yet in times of crisis, the question becomes how domestic and EU-level expenditure rules impact *anti-cyclical* spending. If strong fiscal rules reduce the deficit bias of policy-makers, do we assume that the same rules exert this moderating influence even in times of crisis, when a) most rules do not apply because of built-in exceptionality clauses and b) the overarching European crisis framework under the EERP explicitly calls for expansionary fiscal policies? At the EU level the question arises whether the coordination of fiscal stimulus is more successful than the coordination of fiscal restraint. If the EERP now empowers member states to pursue expansionary fiscal policies that are in line with their alleged propensity to spend, are governments more likely to listen to it? For domestic fiscal rules, two scenarios are plausible. On the one hand, member states with stronger fiscal rules might have been more attuned to the necessity for fiscal consolidation once the recession stopped and therefore implemented more moderate stimulus programs, which are more easily reversed. On the other hand, it can be assumed that countries with strong fiscal rules were in a better budgetary position to flout their fiscal thresholds to begin with and therefore had more room for maneuver to follow the EU-wide call for fiscal expansion. This logic is summarized in the Commission's endorsement of domestic fiscal rules: 'Enforced national expenditure rules... help to counteract forces leading to pro-cyclical fiscal policy in good times and thus prevent the need to retrench in bad times' (European Commission 2004: 37). Stronger rules would therefore make countries less likely to engage in stimulus free riding.

3.4.3.2 MARKET DISCIPLINE

The literature on market discipline examines if and how financial market participants constrain sovereign borrowers. This alleged ability is described by the market discipline hypothesis (MDH; see Bishop et al. 1989; Lane 1993). Ever since the post-Bretton Woods era, market discipline has been seen as a force for fiscal prudence, with proponents '[applauding] the way international financial markets would discipline government policy and force states to adopt more conservative, "sound" fiscal... programmes' (Helleiner 1996: 324). Market discipline is said to be able to 'deter a borrower from maintaining an unsustainable path of borrowing' (Lane 1993: 83). To this end, the MDH hinges on the responsiveness of both financial markets and national policy-makers. On the one hand, financial markets must react to fiscal policy changes. On the other hand, however, borrowers must respond to market signals. For market discipline to work, policy-makers have to respond to and thus avert ever-growing interest penalties before high debt levels with increasing rollover risk become unsustainable. If not, market punishment risks turning into fiscal bloodletting: aggravating the very illness it is supposed to cure.

To analyze the responsiveness of financial markets, fiscal policy outcomes are modeled as determinants of a government's borrowing costs, measured as bond spreads, credit default swap spreads,[4] interest expenditure (debt servicing costs), or changes in interest rates. The majority of empirical studies point to a significant effect of market punishment for 'excessive' fiscal policy (Bernoth et al. 2004; Dewachter and Toffano 2012). Whilst empirical studies of the first side of the MDH (the market's responsiveness) are abundant (Codogno et al. 2003; Afonso and Strauch 2007; Faini 2006), the second side of the MDH (borrowers' responsiveness) has been comparatively neglected in the literature. This book is interested in the second side of market discipline. Does market punishment offer a strong incentive for 'sound' fiscal policies? Do sovereign borrowers react to interest rate penalties demanded by financial markets? The existing literature suggests that credit market punishment restrains sovereign borrowers (de Haan and Sturm 2000; Heinemann and Winschel 2001). However, this impact is asymmetric: reactions in times of increasing borrowing costs are more pronounced than in times of decreasing interest rates (Molnar 2013; Nickel et al. 2010). Interest rates qualify as 'separate and selective' despite well-documented contagion effects; at their origin they are country-specific. Financial market discipline is likely to provide a particularly strong incentive because it takes the form of both punishment (high interest rates) and reward (low interest rates). It offers both carrot and stick.

3.5 Conclusion

This chapter has set the stage for the following empirical chapters. In the remainder of this book I will test the three hypotheses and explore in more detail the collective action problem at the heart of EU fiscal policy coordination. Therefore, this study uses an Olsonian analysis to understand public finances in hard times. I deliberately steer away from EU-centric theories. Instead I argue that dusting off Olson's contribution to the study of free riding brings two key advantages. First, it offers a parsimonious yet comprehensive lens through which to study collective action. Second, by relying on a theory that has not emerged out of an attempt to engage in EU sui generis theorizing, this book seeks to build bridges between the study of economic cooperation in Europe and beyond. Many of this book's central themes, particularly the debates surrounding austerity and the power of (bond) markets, will be familiar and relevant to readers with no knowledge of or limited interest in EU affairs.

Building on Olson's theory of collective action, I have presented three hypotheses that will guide the following four empirical chapters. These relate to the group latency of EU membership, the evidence for collective action, and finally the provision of incentives to keep free riding at bay. The theme running through this chapter is that the interdependence of EU economies requires cooperative solutions to common problems. In fiscal matters this is particularly true during the Great Recession, when 'people have understood through the crisis that we are all bound together' (Commission official, interview, March 2015). A distinct feature of fiscal policy coordination during the Great Recession is the bifurcation of group-oriented behavior, with growth and stability both being included in the rubrics of collective action. Both forms of first-order free riding are made possible by the strong interdependence of EU economies. Interdependence issues the tickets to free ride.

Notes

1. As Randall Henning (2017: 135) mentions, the suspension of purchases is an educated conjecture because the ECB does not publish a country-specific breakdown of transactions.
2. In microeconomic theory, an indifference curve is a graph showing different bundles of goods, or in this case of fiscal policy actions, between which an actor is indifferent. At each point on the curve, she has no preference for one bundle over another.
3. The golden rule stipulates that over the economic cycle, the government should borrow only to invest—not to fund current expenditure.
4. Credit default swaps are a credit derivative, which allows the buyer to purchase insurance against the risk of default.

4

Policy Needs Politics

4.1 Convergence, Diversity, and Coordination

The motto of the EU, 'United in diversity', is misleading. Although originally a respectful nod to the 'many different cultures, traditions and languages', the eradication of economic diversity has been part and parcel of the common market. The EU seeks to promote economic, social, and territorial cohesion by 'reducing disparities between the levels of development of the various regions' (Art. 174 TEU). Convergence, not diversity, has guided economic policy coordination. This is evident in the Copenhagen criteria, which determine whether a country can join the union in the first place, and later the Maastricht criteria, which examine whether a country is fit to adopt the common currency. The Five-President Report calls for economic structure to 'converge towards the best standards in Europe' (Juncker et al. 2015) and explicitly seeks to minimize diversity. Economic convergence remains the goalpost for cooperation. But the focus on economic diversity, let alone doing away with it, risks sidestepping political diversity. What are the political dynamics behind fiscal policies that run either counter to or in favor of stability and growth? What impact does partisanship have on the stimulus policies adopted? Does political fragmentation matter for fiscal crisis responses? What role do elections play in governments' economic programs?

The underlying assumption of this chapter is that with diverse political landscapes, EU member states face the challenge of collective action under latency. Latency emerges thus not solely out of heterogeneous economies, but is also a result of diverse political geography. This chapter further seeks to answer the question of whether fiscal policy choices during the Great Recession were characterized by a so-called 'deficit bias'. Specifically, I will analyze the spending and borrowing bias emanating from political processes and structures. Informed by the political economy literature on public finances, this investigation is guided by the notion that fiscal outcomes do not emerge in a political vacuum. Instead, they are influenced by a complex battery of factors describing the political environment within which actors bargain for their favored policy outcome. Accordingly, this chapter seeks to elucidate the choices and constraints of the fiscal politics during the Stimulus Years, 2008–10.

By focusing on diversity instead of group size, this chapter moves beyond Olson's original model of latency and joins ranks with the second-generation collective action literature (Poteete and Ostrom 2004: 439–45). The standard assumption among IR scholars is that group size and group diversity are related. With larger numbers, the heterogeneity within the group will typically also increase. This is especially likely in international settings. What we know about fisheries, oil fields, and orange production also applies to IR. This link between diversity and group size applies to multi-, intra-, and supra-national organizations, where less-developed economies have joined a core group of more developed ones (Snidal 1994)—the EU being a case in point.

The focus on diversity emerges from the nature of the two public goods at the center of this book: stability and growth. First, although Olson does not give a numerical threshold, his examples of large groups (the American Medical Association and farm cooperatives) are different types of organization than the EU. Size, according to Olson, matters because it renders free riding visible or invisible, actionable or unactionable. A latent group then 'is distinguished by the fact that if one member does or does not help prove the collective good, no other member will be significantly affected and therefore none has reason to react' (Olson 1965: xx). What Olson had in mind was that in large groups the collective good could be supplied without the contribution of any single member. Yet, securing stability and growth in the EU is malleable and contested. Although the Stability and Growth Pact (SGP) aimed at presenting a winning formula with its 3 percent deficit threshold, group-oriented behavior is more complex and less uniform than paying union member fees or vaccinating one's child to sustain herd immunity. When France and Germany violated the SGP in 2003, they could rightly point to the fact that this did not seem to spell trouble for EU-wide stability and growth—this comes close to the fiscal equivalent of speeding on an empty road in the middle of the night. Where no discernible damage was done, member states were thus acting in a latent group without 'reason to react'. This is contrary to the treatment of Greece seven years later, whose behavior has been sanctioned with reference to the threat its economic devastation posed to *other* member states. The harsh conduct of Greece stands in contrast to France, for example, which got away lightly with repeatedly violating the SGP before, during, and after the Great Recession—'because it's France, duh', in the explanation of the Commission President (*Reuters*, May 31, 2016). On the bond side, as one German bond investor recalled with a tone of resentment in his voice, 'France has not been punished by the markets, despite the fact that they didn't do their homework' (interview, April 2014).

Olson assumes that diversity could increase the likelihood that one member of a subgroup would provide the public good in question—an idea later developed in Charles Kindleberger's observation that hegemony can bring about international economic cooperation (1986). Yet oligopolistic action—that is, the provision of a public good by one group member—is rarely possible. Accordingly, stability and growth do not apply to Olson's *exploitation hypothesis*, according to which better-endowed members should carry a disproportionate burden of collective provision for the small members—a provision that, for instance, rang true for NATO allies at the start of the Cold War when the US nuclear arsenal was thought to protect Western Europe from further Soviet expansion (Olson and Zeckhauser 1966). Instead stability and growth frequently require the participation of all member states, albeit at different levels. Prior to the economic and financial crisis, the overall stability (if measured by sovereign bond spreads) was essentially a 'best-shot' scenario with member states (including, now famously, Greece) paying almost the same interest rates on government borrowing as Germany—although substantial differences in debt servicing costs remained (Rommerskirchen 2015). Yet at no point in time was pure oligopolistic provision of both public goods feasible. Even Germany, the Economic and Monetary Union's (EMU's) 'weak' (Eichengreen 1987) or 'reluctant' (Bulmer and Paterson 2013) hegemon, is not in a position to singlehandedly provide stability and growth—leaving questions of political feasibility aside. Neither can Germany maintain liquidity, solvency and the political conditions for adjustment (cf. Schelkle and Mabbett 2015), nor does it have the economic resources to provide for growth throughout the EU. For all the clamor surrounding Germany's trade surplus, higher internal demand in Germany would be but a flash in the pan for struggling Greece; 'admittedly, it's not going to be a deal breaker' (Commission, interview, February 2017; see also Beetsma et al. 2006). Other core countries, notably the Netherlands and France, stand to benefit from an expansive fiscal policy in Berlin given stronger trade linkages—not to mention its biggest trade partners outside the EU, namely the USA and China (and soon the UK).

This chapter is organized as follows: I start with a presentation of the data and methods of the empirical analysis, after which the research design and empirical methods employed are discussed (section 4.2). The following section presents the empirical findings and discusses various robustness tests (section 4.3). In the discussion, three key findings are considered in greater detail (section 4.4). Here the empirical results are compared to the existing literature and analyzed vis-à-vis additional documents and interviews on the politics surrounding fiscal policy coordination during the Great Recession.

4.2 Let's Get Fiscal

Fiscal policy is inherently concerned with resource allocation and distribution and is thus at the core of state activity. Fiscal policy creates conflicts of interest both with respect to its macroeconomic function (i.e. to ensure fiscal sustainability and stabilization of the economy) and its microeconomic function (i.e. to ensure efficient and effective allocation of public resources). The government provides budgetary support to the economy, which can be broadly captured by the year-on-year change in the general government budget balance as a share of GDP. Given that countries have country-specific levels of deficit and debt levels, it makes sense to take the previous level into account—hence the interest in changes. Government revenues and expenditure make up the overall fiscal balance. Looking at the overall budget balance (BB), one can distinguish between the primary balance (PB), the structural balance (SB), and the primary structural balance (PSB). For the PB expenditure on interest is filtered out. While interest payments are to a large extent dependent on a country's economic outlook and debt sustainability, they can be subject to fluctuations outside the control of national policy-makers (so-called pull factors).

The PSB excludes not only interest expenditures but also spending linked to the operation of automatic stabilizers. Automatic stabilizers are features of the tax and spending system that react automatically to the economic cycle in order to reduce the severity of its fluctuations. These include not only unemployment benefits and progressive taxation, but also sick leave or early retirement provisions. The structural deficit requires two inputs: first, the cyclical position of the economy as measured by the output gap (the distance between actual and potential output), and second, the responsiveness of the BB to the economic cycle, as expressed by budget semi-elasticities. The semi-elasticities measure the reaction of the balance-to-GDP ratio to cyclical conditions and are derived from national tax codes as well as regression analysis. The PSB is generally used for the purpose of budgetary surveillance by both national governments and international institutions, including the European Commission, the Organisation of Economic Co-operation and Development (OECD), the International Monetary Fund (IMF), and the European Central Bank (ECB). Changes in the PSB are considered to be indicative of discretionary policy decisions and not merely a product of output fluctuations. The basic idea in using changes in the PSB is that, once the budget is purged of its cyclical component plus interest expenditure, any remaining difference across time should indicate deliberate policy interventions.

4.2.1 *A Matter of Discretion*

One interviewee in the Commission pointed out that 'discretionary spending is not a statistical term but for Ecofin [the Council of Economic and Finance

Ministers] to decide what is what' (interview, May 2011). Indeed, there is no consensus in the literature on the appropriate methodology for the construction of a cyclically adjusted measure of fiscal policy (Giavazzi and Pagano 1995). Following the Commission's definition (European Commission 2009), a country's discretionary crisis policies are defined as the change in the PSB relative to the preceding period. When the change is positive (negative), the fiscal stance is said to be expansionary (restrictive). The usage of cyclically adjusted BBs as an indicator for discretionary fiscal policies has been favored by numerous studies (e.g. Ballabriga and Martinez-Mongay 2002; Wyplosz 2006). Martin Larch and Matteo Salto (2005) from the European Commission, however, criticize the PSB approach for ignoring the effects of over- or underestimating growth in the planning phase of the budget, coupled with inertia in the implementation phase. The PSB deteriorates (improves) when potential growth is over- (under)estimated. In the context of the 2008 to 2010 period it is well documented that growth assumptions were too positive (European Commission 2008), which means that the size of the discretionary fiscal policy would be overestimated. Put differently, a change in the PSB does not necessarily point to active fiscal stimulus policies such as tax cuts or expenditure increases. Instead the change can simply stem from passive behavior in the event of lower-than-projected underlying growth. The inertia of fiscal policy in the implementation phase is said to aggravate this. Yet the majority of countries reacted swiftly with emergency budgets and revised stimulus plans, fine-tuning their budgets as late as 2010. Consequently, possible 'inertia bias' inherent in the PSB should be less acute during the Great Recession. I accept the critique that the PSB is likely to give a somewhat exaggerated measure of discretionary policy. At the same time, Martin Larch and Alessandro Turrini (2011) concede that 'despite its many downsides... the cyclically-adjusted budget balance remains to date one of the key indicators for the analysis and conduct of fiscal policy making'.

4.2.2 *Fiscal Policy Measures*

Scrutinizing fiscal policy and its coordination, this book will consider four common indicators of fiscal policy:

1) the change in the budget balance (Δ BB)
2) the change in the primary budget balance (Δ PB)
3) the change in the structural balance (Δ SB)
4) the change in the primary structural balance (Δ PSB)

Additionally, I will consult the available figures on stimulus packages. These crucially rely on subjective policy evaluation to determine which fiscal measures qualify as crisis measures and which do not. Adopting a centripetal measurement approach has three advantages. First, it is a welcome robustness check for empirical analyses. To address the quality issues generally signaled in connection with the measurement of fiscal policy outcomes—available data is not based on a unanimously agreed methodology—I used different measures to assess the robustness of results. The four measurements then each account for a distinct, albeit overlapping and highly correlated, aspect of fiscal policy. What is more, when scrutinizing fiscal choices during 'hard times', it seems undesirable to completely purge these 'hard times' from the fiscal outcome variables. I am specifically interested in the role of automatic stabilizers (see section 4.3) and the varieties of fiscal policy choices along a sliding scale of discretion. Different understandings are likely to prevail with regards to what counts as discretionary and what does not. However, since this book considers fiscal policy coordination within the EU, the year-to-year changes in PSB and the PB are therefore useful measurements to investigate member states' fiscal policies in the light of the European Economic Recovery Plan (EERP) and related communications. At the same time, given the substantial role of automatic stabilizers—the automatic stabilization provided was greater, overall, than the discretionary measures (Public Finances in EMU 2010: 22)—it would be short-sighted to ignore their impact, especially when evaluating free riding. It is therefore necessary to include both structurally adjusted and non-cyclical measurements. Are fiscal policy outcomes, which are thought to carry little discretion, driven by different determinants than those based purely on discretional policy choices? Second, this strategy enables comparison with other studies on fiscal outcomes which predominately use the change in BB for fiscal performance or the change in the cyclically adjusted primary deficit for the discretionary element of public finances. Third, data for stimulus packages is available for 2009–10 only; relying exclusively on this measure would therefore reduce the temporal scope of the empirical investigation. What is more, there is evidence that policy-makers were already responding to the economic downturn in 2008. The average budget deficit in the EU worsened in 2008 to 2.3 percent of GDP from 0.8 percent in 2007 (Public Finances in EMU 2009) and we cannot simply assume that this was the result of non-discretionary fiscal policy. Excluding the year 2008 risks presenting an unduly shortened analysis of fiscal response strategies.

4.2.3 *Crisis Policies?*

Fiscal policy outcomes *during* times of crisis are not equivalent to fiscal policy outcomes *because* of crisis. A case in point can be found in Germany, where the change of the commuter tax allowance (*Pendlerpauschale*) and of tax deductibility of social security contributions reduced government revenue by about

0.8 percent of GDP (Zohlnhöfer 2011). The government chose to abstain from offsetting their fiscal effect and did not re-finance the thus-created expenditures. This led German and European authorities to count these expenditures under the discretionary fiscal stimulus package. Another example can be found with respect to education spending in Malta. The increase in expenditure related to education (amounting to 0.34 of GDP) was presented as stimulus spending, whereas it arguably had little to do with the economic and financial crisis, but was 'already planned and sold as part of the electoral campaign in the previous year' (interview, April 2011). These are not the only examples of governments branding their 'normal' fiscal policies as crisis responses (see Watt and Nikolova 2009: 12; Armingeon 2012a: 9). Fiscal policy is noisy. When the Beatles' live album from the legendary Hollywood Bowl concerts was remixed, a new app was able to filter out the most famous screams in pop history. There is no functional equivalent for public finances. In identifying the discretionary elements of fiscal policy, one is left with less refined filters. Concerning the intentionality of crisis policies, then, a degree of uncertainty will remain unresolved. Indeed, as depicted in Table 4.1, the data on these stimulus packages varies considerably depending on the source.

Table 4.1. Fiscal stimulus figures in comparison

	COM[a]	OECD[b]		ECB[c]	IMF[d]	Watt[e]
Country	total	total	total	total	total	total
BE	2.2	1.6	1.4	0.8		0.9
CZ	3.5	3	2.8			
DK	2.2	2.5	3.3			2.2
DE	4.1	3	3.2	2.3	3.6 (3.9)	2.64
IE	1.7	4.4	8.3	1		
EL	0.6		0.8	0		
ES	3.2	3.5	3.9	2.9		4.6
FR	3	0.6	0.7	1.1	1.5 (2.3)	1
IT	1.6	0	0	0	0.3 (0)	0.2
CY	5.1			0.1		
LU	5.6	3.6	3.9	2.6		1.75*
HU	2.6	4.4	7.7			
MT	1.8			3.2		
NL	1.9	1.5	2.5	1.9		1
AT	3.3	1.1	1.2	3.6		2.4
PL	4.8	1	1.2			
PT	1.7	0.8	0.8	1		1.2*
SI	3.3			1.1		
SK	0.9	1.1	1.3	0.1		
FI	4.3	3.1	3.2	3.4		1.5
SE	4.4	2.8	3.3			2.4
UK	2.4	1.4	1.9		1.5 (1.6)	1.5

Note: a) *Public Finance in EMU* (European Commission 2011), discretionary stimulus in % of GDP, b) Composition of fiscal packages total over 2008–10 period as % of GDP in 2008, first estimation published September 3, second estimation published September 7, c) fiscal stimulus package, % of GDP, ECB (2010) d) discretionary measures, in percent of GDP, relative to 2007 baseline (revision made in the Fiscal Monitor November 2010, e) Watt (2009), * 2009 only.

It is important to add that by analyzing fiscal policy coordination during the Great Recession, this study does not venture into the thorny field of assessing the exact size of the impact fiscal measures had on aggregate demand; I focus on the input side (the changes in government finances) and not on the output side (its effect on macroeconomic developments). The extent to which fiscal policy is effective in supporting growth recovery, both in the short and long term, is subject to much debate. Whilst arguably relevant for the production of the public goods in question, a study of the output side would be beyond the remit of this investigation. A focus on the input side is not only empirically more feasible, but also the relevant approach for the study of fiscal policy coordination. The EERP (similarly to the rules of the SGP) makes suggestions about the size of stimulus spending and not about the size of the impact of this expenditure. In so doing, fiscal policies will be considered at face value.

4.3 Data and Methods

This section discusses the empirical research design for this chapter, starting with the dependent and independent variables and ending with the discussion of the appropriate estimation techniques. The model specification is as follows:

$$\begin{aligned}\Delta \text{ fiscal outcome } = {} & \alpha + \beta_1 \text{ L.GDP}_{i,t} + \beta_2 \text{L.debt}_{i,t} + \beta_3 \text{L.AS}_{i,t} + \\ & \beta_4 \text{ Bailout}_{i,t} + \beta_5 \text{ Election}_{i,t} + \beta_6 \text{ Government}_{i,t} + \\ & \beta_7 \text{ Opposition}_{i,t} + \beta_8 \text{ Left}_{i,t} + \beta_9 \text{ Dummies} + \epsilon_{i,t}\end{aligned}$$

The following paragraphs describe the variables used to test the assumptions concerning the determinants of fiscal policy choices. Summary statistics for these variables can be found in Table 4.2. A definition of these variables, including sources, together with other key variables used in this book is listed in Appendix 2.

Fiscal policy: The strategy for capturing a country's fiscal responses to the crisis will be to test four variables separately; the change in budget balance (Δ BB), the change in the primary balance (Δ PB), the change in the structural balance (Δ SB), and the change in the structural primary balance (Δ PSB).

Economic conditions: First, I include the lagged GDP growth rate (*GDP*).[1] Economic growth is likely to impact on fiscal choices. Low (or even negative) rates of economic growth tend to increase budget deficits by reducing revenue and increasing expenditure (notably in the context of unemployment benefits). What is more, the political pressure to bring about economic growth via fiscal stimulus programs increases as economic conditions deteriorate. Second,

Table 4.2. Selected summary statistics

Variable	Mean	Std. Dev.	Min.	Max.
Δ PSB	−0.94	2.88	−15.07	7.21
Δ SB	−1	2.89	−16.21	6.43
Δ PB	−1.97	3.23	−15.79	5.55
Δ BB	0.1	5.48	−7.4	15.7
L. Δ GDP	0.18	5.44	−17.7	10.5
L.Debt	48.97	28.87	3.7	129.7
Bailout	−0.36	2.27	−20.16	0.43
L.AS	−1.16	2.01	−8.15	2.2
Government	0.61	0.26	0.22	1
Opposition	0.51	0.19	0.22	1
Left	0.3	0.46	0	1
Election	0.25	0.43	0	1

Note: Based on cross-sectional data available for all twenty-seven EU countries over the 2008–10 period. Δ is the first difference operator. N = 81.

the lagged debt to GDP ratio (*debt*) represents a country's past fiscal legacy as well as its constraints for future spending in light of fiscal sustainability. Third, the lagged size of automatic stabilizers (*AS*) controls for both the budgetary impact of welfare state provisions and budget elasticities, and for the fact that discretionary fiscal policies are influenced by the size of existing crisis provisions in the form of automatic stabilization. Its measurement follows the European Commission and takes the change in the output gap multiplied by the expenditure-to-GDP ratio (used as a proxy of the semi-elasticities of the BB) (data source: Ameco and European Commission 2010a).

Financial crisis: The variable *Bailout* records the consequences of the bank and other market support operations by public authorities. Including this variable controls for the fact that stimulus measures and financial bailouts are likely to be interrelated policy choices. Controlling for the impact of the financial crisis should reduce the exogenous noise of the bailout blowing up expenditure levels. Furthermore, the variables pertaining to the general economic climate also account for the impact of the financial crisis. On a related note, the cyclically adjusted measure takes into account the magnitude of the crisis and is closely linked to the financial fallout; financial crises lower potential output (Furceri and Mourougane 2009). Specifically, the variable *Bailout* measures the direct costs of these interventions in percent of GDP as recorded by Eurostat (2012). A negative value records costs, whereas a positive value indicates revenue stemming from the financial sector interventions. Cornelia Woll (2014: 13) presents this anecdote on data quality: the German finance minister Wolfgang Schäuble announced in the fall of 2011 that the bailout costs were actually €55bn (!) less than previously announced. An accounting misinterpretation by the agency in charge of unwinding Hypo Real Estate had overstated the liabilities of the bank. Data used in this book's estimations is revised, accounting for the uncertainty about (recording) bailout costs in the mediate aftermath of government assistance. However, this is no absolute guarantee for error-free data—a caveat that applies to all data used in this book.

Elections: The variable *Election* is a dummy variable, equal to 1 if there was a legislative election at the national level in a given year (Keefer 2010). This variable captures the political business cycle, which is based on the premise that policy-makers are opportunistic and voters myopic. Assuming that the expected support for a party will rise with the short-term welfare it delivers, deficits are higher in election years when incumbent governments try to buy electoral support (Nordhaus 1975). A myriad of studies have been developed since the 1970s (for an overview see Drazen 2000b), forming a body of literature that, although theoretically rich and empirically sophisticated, is far from harmonious in presenting evidence concerning the impact of elections on public finances. There is evidence of expansionary fiscal policies in EU member countries before elections, despite the introduction of the SGP (Buti and Van den Noord 2003; Hallerberg et al. 2009: ch. 4; Mink and de Haan 2006). Other studies have, however, cast doubt on the presence and/or strength of a political business cycle (Franzese 2002; LeMay-Boucher and Rommerskirchen 2015). A subgroup of the literature has explored the relationship between fiscal consolidation and elections, again turning up mixed evidence (Gupta et al. 2005; Mierau et al. 2007; Lavigne 2011).

Political fragmentation: To measure the strength of the executive, I include the variable *Government*, which indicates the probability that two deputies picked at random from among the government parties will be of different parties. This variable has a potential range from 1 (government is composed of a single party) to close to 0. This variable is from Philip Keefer's dataset (2010). Analogous to the variable above, I include a corresponding measure for the strength of the legislative opposition, *Opposition*, which indicates the probability that two deputies picked at random from among the opposition parties will be of different parties. This variable, which is also found in Keefer (2010), has a potential range from 1 (the opposition is composed of a single party) to close to 0 (every opposition seat in the legislature is held by a different party). Budget deficits are said to be more likely in countries with fragmented executive or legislative polities. The former, in particular, has received much attention in the literature. Fiscal policy under coalition or fragmented governments[2] is said to suffer from a so-called 'common pool problem' (Weingast et al. 1981). This problem arises because for a typical spending program, the costs are spread over a larger group with benefits being concentrated in a smaller group. The resulting 'overgrazing' of the common pasture (Hardin 1982) then leads to a deficit and debt bias.[3] Fragmentation in the legislature is likewise thought to increase deficits. In fragmented legislative systems, so the argument goes, each party has an incentive to secure as much spending as possible to its political constituents (Mukherjee 2003). To summarize, I expect both government and opposition fragmentation to have a positive impact on the size of the fiscal stimulus.

Government ideology: To account for the executive party's/parties' orientation with respect to economic policy, I include a variable for 'right' and 'left' governments. *Right* takes the value of 1 for parties that are defined as conservative Christian democratic, or right-wing; *Left* takes the value of 1 for parties that are defined as communist, socialist, social democratic, or left-wing. Centre is omitted. The data comes from Philip Keefer (2010). The analysis of the impact of political parties and their ideological inclinations has been the target of considerable scrutiny since the early 1970s. Proponents of the left–right hypothesis regarding public deficits posit a causal relation between political variables and policy outputs (Hibbs 1977: 485). A myriad of studies since then have examined the impact of (different) ideological stances within the executive (Mink and de Haan 2006) and legislative branches (Heller 1997). Various studies have found evidence for increased budget deficits under left-wing parties (De Haan and Sturm 2000; Imbeau et al. 2001), whilst others find no relationship between the party/parties in power and government spending (Pampel and Williamson 1988). Similarly, ideological positionings of government are said to matter for the implementation of fiscal consolidation (Mulas-Granados 2003). Reviewing the literature, William Clark (2009: 49) concludes that the evidence for the 'Hibbsian relationship between fiscal policy and the ideological orientation of the government is mixed at best'. Following the conventional assumption that a left-wing deficit bias is in part due to a propensity to implement Keynesian demand policy, this bias, if it exists at all in the contemporary EU, should be amplified in times of economic crisis when the perceived need (and therefore justification) for fiscal intervention is stronger. This would suggest a positive relationship between the size of stimulus policies and left-wing governments.

In addition, this model includes year and country dummies (see section 4.3.1).

4.3.1 *Econometric Issues*

The bulk of econometric evidence presented in in this book is based on eighty-one observations. This is comparatively few and results should be read with this in mind. The sample size is justified by the fact that it represents a 'complete population' in the sense that all EU countries and the years of the Great Recession during which the EERP applied (2008–10) are included.

Empirically I augmented the numbers of observations with numerous interactions of each variable of interest with a pre- and per-crisis dummy. Doing so for the 1994 to 2010 period, I reject the hypothesis of parameter poolability (i.e. the poolability of the data). Evidence for this claim can be provided in the form of a Chow test for structural change across time. Similar studies on fiscal policy during the economic and financial crisis are likewise left with relatively few observations (Armingeon 2012a; Cameron 2012). Because of the small sample of countries and the limited number of years included, the use of panel data estimation techniques with fixed or random effects may not be appropriate. What is more, the existence of several dummy variables that do not change over time means that the use of fixed effects is not feasible. This is why I prefer to use the pooled ordinary least squares (OLS) estimation technique.

A pooled cross-section (where observations for all countries and for all periods are pooled in one cross-section sample) is analyzed much like a standard cross-section, except that it accounts for variation across time. 'Pooling' offers at least two advantages compared to either a pure cross-section or a pure time-series analysis. First, as the number of observations increases, so do the degrees of freedom. This makes it possible to estimate more fully specified models and to reduce the potential problem of omitted variable bias. Second, pooling makes it possible to control for exogenous shocks common to all countries (by controlling for time effects). The pooling procedure was made popular by Nathaniel Beck and Jonathan Katz (1995), also called the 'de facto Beck-Katz standard' (Plümper et al. 2005: 327) because of its influence on subsequent research. It includes a lagged dependent variable and time and unit dummies (in this study 'year and country' dummies). The analysis of pooled data is econometrically more problematic than a pure cross-section analysis because observations from the same countries are not independent. I use panel-corrected standard errors to address this potential violation of the standard OLS assumptions. The OLS estimator proposed by Beck and Katz (1995) is known to be biased if errors are autocorrelated. To eliminate serial correlation of errors, the authors recommend adding the lagged dependent variable to the right-hand side of the equation. In the public finance literature the inclusion of a lagged dependent variable is a common feature, as authors often point to the path dependency of fiscal policy choices (Davis et al. 1966). In fiscal policy studies the lagged dependent variable is frequently found to be significant and included for theoretical as well as methodological reasons (Hallerberg et al. 2009). Yet when analyzing discretionary fiscal policies, there is reason to doubt the narrative of fiscal path dependency. Aaron Wildavsky's notion of 'budget incrementalism' (1964) has come under attack in research exposing the limited evidence of this account (for a review see Berry 1990). This book is interested in explaining the variations of discretionary fiscal responses, which should reflect the felt needs and political pressures of the contemporaneous year, as opposed to the previous years. 'Sticky' expenditure and revenue are filtered out in both the SB and PSB measures. From a theoretical point of view, the inclusion of a lagged dependent variable therefore *only* makes sense for the cyclical indicators.

Given that our sample only covers three years, it is technically difficult to detect any serial correlation with confidence. I nevertheless test for it (Wooldridge 2002; Drukker 2003) and results indicate that autocorrelation is only an issue in one of the models (BB). This makes sense since this measurement carries less 'discretion' than the cyclically adjusted and PB indicators, thus making it more persistent over time. Including a lagged dependent variable as suggested by Beck and Katz (1995) does not alter the results, nor does it improve the model's fit markedly, as indicated by the R.[2] This is an interesting finding in itself, suggesting that fiscal policy responses during the Great Recession were *not driven* by path dependency. Pooled data from multiple countries observed over a number of years can cause problems when analysts attempt to apply the standard linear regression model. Having discussed the broader methodological issues, the next section, 4.3.1.1, will consider the possible endogeneity of elections.

4.3.1.1 THE ENDOGENEITY OF ELECTIONS

Governments have been known to manipulate the timing of elections, calling elections early in the light of a climate favorable for the incumbent or delaying elections if approval ratings are low. This may give rise to endogeneity. Endogeneity refers to the presence of an endogenous explanatory variable that is correlated with the error term either because of an omitted variable, measurement error, or simultaneity. A further source of endogeneity might stem from unobserved factors. The timing of both elections and fiscal policies could be influenced by a variety of (unobserved) variables, such as social unrest, which are not included in our regression. Looking at the election landscape of the Great Recession, it seems that in a number of instances early elections and public finances were interlinked. For example, in September 2009, the then Greek Prime Minister Costas Karamanlis called for snap elections after discontent with his government's handling of the unfolding economic crisis. In the same year the Hungarian Prime Minister Ferenc Gyurcsány surprisingly announced his resignation tied to the deteriorating economic situation. After protests in Riga over the worsening economic situation degenerated into snowball-hurling riots and an attempt to storm parliament, the Latvian prime minister Ivars Godmanis resigned but defended his austerity plans which were deemed necessary in the light of a €7.5bn bank bailout. Nine governments (Latvia, Slovenia, Slovakia, Greece, Italy, Portugal, Romania, Ireland, and the Netherlands) collapsed between elections between 2008 and 2012 alone. There is reason to assume that the endogeneity of elections should be a wider concern—not only for the 2008–10 period (Heckelman and Berument 1998). This means that the timing of elections is determined by fiscal policy choices and not the other way around. This complex relationship makes it difficult to establish any direction of causality with certainty.

To deal with this endogeneity problem, similar to Joachim Wehner (2010), I therefore enter a new dummy variable, which captures the number of years left in the electoral term of the current government as an instrument for actual elections. This instrument suggests itself; in all countries the electoral term is constitutionally determined (in the sense that there are term limits) and therefore difficult to manipulate. Thus, the assumption that the number of years left in the current term is exogenous to fiscal policy choices is reasonable. At the same time, this instrument is correlated with the actual incidence of elections. This instrument is individually significant in the first stage; however, this does not in itself guarantee a successful identification in the second-stage estimation. Testing for weak instruments, I use the Kleibergen-Paap rk F-statistic, a correspondingly robust version of the Cragg-Donald statistics. The statistics obtained should be compared to 10, the conventional rule of thumb (Baum et al. 2007). The Kleibergen-Paap rk LM-statistic for overall identification allows us to strongly reject the null hypothesis that the equation is under-identified. Consequently, weak instruments may not be considered a problem for all estimations. In short, the results suggest the model used is reliable. I then proceed to test for endogeneity in the variable estimated with instrumental variables; the results of this test show that the null cannot be rejected at a 10 percent level: endogeneity of the *Election* variable is not a problem in this analysis (see Table A4.1 in Appendix 4). I therefore display the results without instrumenting.

4.4 The Drivers of Fiscal Policy Hard Times

Table 4.3 presents the results of the main model. The findings suggest that the economic climate is a key determinant of fiscal policy outcomes. The importance of economic variables is markedly different for the cyclically adjusted models (Δ SB and Δ PSB), where they (together with the year and country dummies) account for only 0.42/0.43 percent of all variation, in contrast to 0.80/0.85 percent in the two non-adjusted models (Δ PB and Δ BB). Political controls then explain 0.35/0.36 percent of the variation in fiscal policy outcomes compared with 0.11 and 0.7 percent in the non-adjusted models. The interpretation is straightforward: *the more discretion policy-makers have in their fiscal policy choices, the more important the political landscape in which these choices take place.*

Table 4.3. Determinants of fiscal policy changes in the EU, 2008–10

	Δ PSB	Δ SB	Δ PB	Δ BB
L. Δ GDP	−1.225***	−1.188***	−0.737***	−1.147***
	(0.248)	(0.243)	(0.185)	(0.238)
L.Debt	0.193***	0.175***	0.173***	0.398***
	(0.052)	(0.050)	(0.037)	(0.050)
Bailout	1.077***	1.077***	0.937***	0.050
	(0.068)	(0.063)	(0.064)	(0.114)
L.AS	3.178***	3.026***	1.620***	3.054***
	(0.603)	(0.584)	(0.473)	(0.634)
Government	−9.537	−12.836	−19.094***	−27.721***
	(8.898)	(8.771)	(5.632)	(10.140)
Opposition	5.071	7.131	13.993***	16.671*
	(7.319)	(7.051)	(5.083)	(9.339)
Left	3.377***	3.332***	2.929***	5.324***
	(1.266)	(1.242)	(0.679)	(0.907)
Election	−1.368***	−1.258***	−0.795**	−0.915**
	(0.364)	(0.349)	(0.310)	(0.421)
Constant	−14.101***	−12.190**	−13.294***	−30.699***
	(5.385)	(5.179)	(3.788)	(5.033)
N	81	81	81	81
R2	0.770	0.790	0.914	0.925

Note: Standard errors are corrected for groupwise heteroskedasticity and contemporaneous correlations across countries of the error terms are corrected with panel-corrected standard errors. * Significant at the 5% level; ** at the 1% level; *** at the 0.1% level. Standard errors listed beside coefficients. Time and unit dummies not shown to preserve space.

The variable *GDP* captures the economic need for government intervention. All coefficients on this variable are negative and economically meaningful, suggesting that policy-makers reacted to a severe economic downturn with less and *not more* stimulus spending, possibly due to limited room for fiscal expansion (simple correlation estimates confirm this relationship both for the lagged and the contemporary GDP measurement). Its coefficient is largest for the measurements with the most discretion attributed (*PSB* and *SB*), which may be because policy-makers here had larger freedom to curb spending. The variable *Debt* has the expected positive sign,[4] a result that points to the strong and disciplining effect of high public debt burdens—a finding to which we will return in Chapter 7. The coefficient for automatic stabilizers shows a positive impact of automatic stabilization on fiscal stimulus policies (automatic stabilization shows up as a negative value, thus the positive coefficient).[5] The variable here records costs and high automatic stabilizers thus enter into the model as negative values. EU states with large automatic stabilizers were also more ready to use discretionary stimulus on top. This link is not merely due to the fiscal costs of automatic stabilization. Instead of implementing a substitution strategy, governments with larger automatic stabilization were also engaging in more discretionary spending to combat the crisis. Automatic stabilizers are an indicator for the generosity of the welfare state. As such, they highlight both the ability of a government to shoulder stabilization as well as expectations with regards to efforts to mitigate the consequences of the economic fallout. This finding is contrary to the recommendation of the European Commission (2009), which advocate that the size of the automatic stabilizers should be a key factor in explaining differences in fiscal stimulus across countries: countries with extensive automatic stabilizers, so the argument goes, should rely less on discretionary fiscal policy spending. The costs of the financial sector interventions (*Bailout*) lead to an increase in fiscal measures to mitigate the crisis. The positive coefficient needs to be read bearing in mind that a negative value of the variable records costs, whereas a positive value indicates revenue stemming from the financial sector interventions.

Turning to the political landscape variables, the coefficients of *Government* and *Opposition* indicate that while opposition fragmentation increases stimulus policies, the fragmentation of the government improves the fiscal position. Note that these two variables are only statistically significant in the structural (not cyclically adjusted) models. A left-leaning government is associated with an improvement in the budgetary position. I also included a corresponding variable measuring right-leaning governments. Here the coefficient was negative and statistically significant in all models. Since the interpretation of the findings remains unchanged and the models' fit did not improve, I parsimoniously excluded this variable in the light of the small number of observations. Furthermore, I find evidence for the existence of a political business cycle (*Election*). The electoral cycle further played out once governments were looking at fiscal consolidation. According to Ignazio Visco (2011), Member of the Governing Board of the Banca d'Italia, 'we are having so many problems because we have an election every other week. This is democracy but it delays reforms'. The following sections 4.4.1 to 4.4.4 unpack these findings.

4.4.1 *Main Street and Wall Street*

Higher costs for bank bailouts are associated with higher stimulus spending. This finding suggests that the severity of the financial crisis, or at least the severity of its consequences for public finances, impacted positively on fiscal response strategies. It appears that fiscal stimuli and financial bailouts are not independent policy choices. According to one interviewee, 'for us [the national government] saving the banks was one thing, but then when it came to getting the stimulus plans right, we wanted to show the people on the streets that we cared about them too. If we have money for the banks, we have money for the people' (May 2011). The results presented here indicate that the financial sector bailouts and stimulus efforts were on par; every

1 percentage point of bank bailout costs led to an equivalent deterioration of public finances for three out of the four fiscal policy measures. The corresponding coefficient in the model with the change in the BB as the dependent variable is not statistically significant. The coefficients of the variable *Bailout* in the other three models are statistically equivalent at around 1 percentage point. Ireland is an outlier in the sample with costs in 2009 representing 20 percent of GDP after Eurostat ruled that the operations of the newly founded National Asset Management Agency, a bad bank, had to be classified within the vernal government sector. Excluding Ireland from the sample, the coefficient for *Bailout* in all models increases (ranging from 2.14 to 1.52). The magnitude here suggests that the fiscal impact of financial sector rescue programs goes beyond the costs incurred. The costs of these operations lead not merely to a deterioration of public finances, but also to discretionary stimulus measures. Bank bailouts and stimulus plans are not rivals as the tensions around financial sector rescue packages (Hellwig and Coffey 2011) would suggest, and as the chant of the Occupy Wall Street movement in the US contests: 'Banks Got Bailed Out—We Got Sold Out'.

Jonas Pontusson and Damian Raess (2012: 24, 27) downplay the link between support given to financial institutions and public finances: 'Suffice it to note, at this point, that most of the support for the financial sector... does not show up in national accounts as current spending and consequently is not part of the estimates of fiscal stimuli... In this sense, fiscal stimuli and financial bailouts can be treated as independent policy choices'. The bulk of financial sector interventions do not show up in the deficit headline figures used in this book to evaluate fiscal crisis policies. They are recorded as liabilities (which are recorded as government debt) and contingent liabilities (which are *not* recorded in the debt level).[6] And yet, the evidence presented here suggests that Pontusson and Raess' (2012) claim of 'independent policy choices' should be taken with a grain of salt. Bank bailouts do very little to stimulate demand and are distinct from fiscal stimulus packages. That does not mean that they are independent policy choices. Government interventions aimed at the financial sector and at the real economy are not independent policy choices.

4.4.2 *Government Fragmentation*

Government fragmentation matters for fiscal policy outcomes. The results of the cross-sectional analysis suggest a diminishing effect of government fragmentation; the less fragmented the executive—that is to say, the more homogenous it is—the more stimulus policies were implemented. It is worth noting that this effect is not conditional on the strength of government. I interacted the fragmentation index with a dummy for minority or majority government and the margin of majority, and the corresponding coefficients remained insignificant in all of the specifications. Furthermore, the inclusion of quadratic and cubic transformations of this variable, as well as the corresponding measurement of opposition fragmentation, was rejected.[7]

Several factors explain this outcome. First, the literature on the deficit and debt bias of contemporaneous public finances emerges from the implicit assumption that this bias is 'a bad thing'. Bjorn Volkerink and Jakob de Haan (2001: 221), for example, introduce their study with the observation that 'most industrialized countries entered the 1980s with their public finances in disarray'. High deficits are considered a negative result of a fragmented, disheveled government. Yet is it possible that in times of crisis, the old equation of political power dispersion and high deficits no longer holds? Arguably, yes. One-party, majoritarian[8] governments implemented larger stimulus programs, all other things being equal, than coalition governments. The main reason for this lies in the fact that the perceived mandate for procyclical spending has reached levels that are unprecedented in recent history. Even the allegedly adverse German electorate received the fiscal package favorably. According to a 2009 survey, only 15 percent of German respondents thought that the second stimulus program was 'too high', whereas 38 percent thought it was 'just right' and 34 percent thought it was 'too small' (survey based on 1,202 respondents over the age of eighteen, *die Welt*, February 12, 2009). Previous analyses predominantly studied counter- and procyclical fiscal behavior jointly. This chapter examines the expansion of counter-cyclical fiscal policies which, although with the benefit of hindsight may not always be beneficial, is at least easily justifiable. In the words of former Commission President Barroso (2009): 'Exceptional times call for exceptional measures'. A strong executive, defined as a single-party government, is likely to be in a better position to react more swiftly and forcefully. This claim is echoed in veto player theory (Tsebelis 2002), which predicts fewer changes in the budget in countries where the government consists of several parties and the ideological distance between parties is large. Crises, so the common narrative goes, are extraordinary events that break away from the practices of normal times (Kahler and Lake 2013: 10–12). Pressures for increased spending may become stronger in economically good times; as resources are more abundant and the benefits from lobbying increase, fiscal policy is likely to become procyclical (Tornell and Lane 1999). Yet in the light of strong domestic calls for stimulus policies as well as explicit EU-level prodding, the bad economic climate increased the perceived need and justifiable scope for government intervention. Looking at crisis budgeting across the OECD, Allen Schick (2009: 11) concludes that in times of crisis, 'when stimulus is the order of the day, the main issues in dispute are how big the increases should be and who should get them'. With the general modus of public finances 'switched to stimulus spending', the benefits for lobbying consequently increased instead of decreasing (Tornell and Lane 1999).

4.4.3 *Opposition Politics*

A fragmented opposition increases deficit spending for two of the four measures (the PB and BB).[9] The more fragmented the opposition (and thus the lower the value of the index used), the higher the deficit spending. The impacts of government fragmentation and opposition fragmentation are thus opposite. This confirms the 'common pool argument' (Hardin 1982) of many fishers depleting the oceans. Note, however, that the coefficient for government fragmentation is always larger than that for opposition fragmentation.[10] Consequently, the fragmentation effects of the executive outweigh any fragmentation effects of the opposition. Existing studies suggest that in times of crisis, we may witness a pure executive mode of policy-making and a 'rally round the flag' effect which makes it difficult for the opposition to criticize or even oppose government policies, similar to what has been described during foreign policy crises (Oneal and Bryan 1995). Describing the mechanisms of crisis budgeting, Schick (2009: 10) considers the tendencies of the budgeting process to become more 'top-down and centralized'. This 'expedites the process, invests political capital and urgency in mobilizing support, and marginalizes those who stand in the way'. Accordingly, decisions are largely taken in small groups involving the executive, which results in a loss of power of typical veto players located in the legislative.

There is evidence that the Great Recession has seen an increase in executive policy-making and a marginalization of the legislative (see Lodge and Wegrich 2012). As one national parliamentarian put it in an interview, 'there was a general feeling that we were treated as "rubber stamp parliament"' (June 2011). In Spain, the government marginalized legislative decision-making, issuing crisis measures as executive orders, which prevent any amendments by parliamentarians (Fleischer and Parrado 2010). Parliament could then only approve or disapprove of these 'royal decree laws' without any real powers to shape and amend. Similar crisis decrees were passed in Romania and Hungary. In the case of the latter, the newly elected government in April 2010 proposed an extensive package of controversial measures, submitting over eighty regulations to parliament without following customary or mandatory consultation procedures (Parrado 2012).

Parliamentarians whose parties were in government were also unlikely to influence fiscal policy outcomes. In most EU countries, notwithstanding the formal powers of the legislature to modify budget bills, the vote on the budget is considered a vote of confidence in the government, according to the OECD

Budgeting Database. In Finland, for example, the government declared the vote on the stimulus package an issue of confidence: i.e. the government would have resigned if it lost, which led to an 'unusually high number of absentees' (interview, June 2012); out of ninety-five votes, thirty-eight parliamentarians abstained (Saramo 2012). Similarly in Belgium, out of 129 votes, forty-nine parliamentarians abstained when the stimulus was approved (Loi de relance économique 2009).

4.4.4 *Spending Left and Right*

The results in Table 4.3 show that left-leaning governments implemented smaller stimulus packages than their right-leaning and centrist counterparts.[11] Christine Lipsmeyer (2011) argues that the Great Recession has seen a departure from 'business as usual' where governments pursue their policy goals in line with their stated ideological outlook. The severe economic downturn constrained politicians in their ability to enact their favored welfare policies; even fiscally conservative governments may turn to extensive stimulus policies to 'buffer people from hardship' (ibid. 977). Along similar lines, the emergency mood of public finances may override particularistic, partisan interests (Schick 2009: 10). There is evidence that in times of economic crisis the party affiliation of policy-makers does not matter for the state of public finances because 'the impact of partisanship is contingent on high levels of economic growth' (Castles 1998: 32). Pointing to a diminishing partisan impact on social expenditure during downturns, 'during economic busts all governments spend more on welfare regardless of ideology' (ibid.). This description of 'default stimulus' in times of economic crisis fits the situation of fiscal policy-making in most EU member states. Turning to liberal Keynesianism as the 'model response to economic crisis' (Pontusson and Raess 2012) was a move that transcended party lines.

This is not to suggest that stimulus spending was readily embraced across the EU: 'fiscal policy coordination is no consensus game' (interview, March 2015). This is perhaps best illustrated with the example of Germany, although other countries, notably Finland and Austria, were initially cautious as well (interviews at Commission and Permanent Representations, April 2011 and February 2015). It bears remembering that for all the focus on Germany, EU politics is usually taking place in malleable country coalitions. As a senior Dutch parliamentarian explained to Mark Hallerberg (2016) in summer 2013, 'our policy at the EU level is to make sure that the Germans remain German'. Dating back to an attempt at demand management in the 1970s, which is frequently portrayed as failed, the German position on stimulus spending was initially negative. This stance is rooted in the conviction of 'basically all leading German academic economists' who stressed that 'fiscal policy

CANNOT work for principal theoretical considerations' (Dullien 2008a). German government officials echoed these views during the negotiations on the EERP. One participant described a heated discussion amongst EU and national officials: 'we were witnessing the worst economic crisis in the history of the EU, and all we heard from the German side was that stimulus doesn't work because of non-Keynesian effects'[12] (interview, April 2011). On December 22, 2008, the then Finance Minister Peer Steinbrück stressed in an opinion piece in the *Wall Street Journal* that 'large-scale stimulus programmes—and tax cuts as well—would not have any effects in real time' (Steinbrück 2008b). Only a few weeks before he had denounced the UK's cut in VAT as 'crass Keynesian[ism]' (*Newsweek*, December 11, 2008). The timing of this is remarkable for two reasons. First, at the EU level member states had already agreed to coordinate substantial stimulus programs. Second, the German recovery package had already been approved domestically. Once concrete stimulus measures were already well on their way, the economy minister called the German crisis response 'a tailored economic growth package, not a classic stimulus program' (*New York Times*, October 5, 2008). On first consideration this linguistic hair-splitting seems to be more a matter of political cosmetics than of economic substance. But in the light of coordination problems, it is important to remember that whether fiscal crisis policies are in line with a policy agreement (such as the EERP) is not all that matters; whether other EU member states perceived them to be so matters too. This is especially so in the context of overcoming a collective action problem, where the incentives for defection rise with the perceived likelihood of other countries complying. By not only arguing generally against stimulus measures, but also denying the nature of the domestic crisis response, the German government was *de facto* undermining the coordination of national stimulus programs.

4.4.4.1 GOING TO CHINA

One would expect that given equal popular support, there would be no partisan effect on fiscal policy choices in times of crisis, in line with previous studies (Castles 1998; Lipsmeyer 2011). Right-leaning parties emerged as 'unlikely actors' championing the motto of 'excessive' spending. Counterintuitively, these parties are in a comparatively better place to advocate this expansionary crisis policy not *despite* but *because* of the fact that it contradicts their perceived pre-crisis paradigms on fiscal policy-making. The reason for this apparent incongruity is that the public does not suspect conservative parties of advocating stimulus spending 'solely' because of the attributed 'ideological tendencies'; the policy is perceived as being an objectively motivated one. Buttressed by an image of fiscal conservatism, right-leaning governments are subject to fewer pressures to justify an increase in spending. Whereas stimulus implemented by the left may be seen as exploiting a crisis for their own ideological agenda, the same program may be considered an economically necessary move if undertaken by a government considered fiscally conservative. The stereotype of a 'fiscal hawk' may then help these parties to secure an agreement on exceptional fiscal policies. This phenomenon of unlikely champions of policies that appear to contradict their policy preferences has been called the 'Nixon-in-China syndrome' (Cukierman and Tommasi 1998): right-wing policies are more likely to be implemented by left-wing parties (and vice versa). This effect has been confirmed empirically by studies on fiscal consolidation (Zohlnhöfer 2007). When the socialist German Finance Minister Olaf Scholz pledged allegiance to the debt brake, his approach was described by a senior Christian Democratic Union (CDU) member as 'show[ing] voters: Look, I am able to handle money although I'm a leftie' (*Reuters*, May 30, 2018).

The embrace of stimulus policies by conservative governments is likely to have political repercussions for Europe's partisan landscape beyond the Great Recession. Toni Judt (2010) appeared puzzled by the fact that 'in a series of European elections following the financial meltdown, social democratic parties consistently did badly; notwithstanding the collapse of the market, they proved conspicuously unable to rise to the occasion'. Indeed, in Austria, the Czech Republic, Finland, Germany, the Netherlands, Sweden, and the United Kingdom, center-left parties made considerable electoral losses (Lindvall 2012). What is more, in Germany, the Netherlands, Slovakia, and the United Kingdom, center-left parties either lost power or were forced to leave governing coalitions (ibid.). The fact that left-leaning governments were not more likely than their right-leaning counterparts to engage in more stimulus spending may help to explain why parties left of the political spectrum were not able to benefit (at least for the moment) from the Great Recession. An analysis of thirty-one parliamentary elections in twenty-six OECD countries from 2007 through early 2011 reveals some evidence of a boost in incumbent governments' electoral support associated with spending on economic stimulus programs (Bartels 2014).

4.5 Conclusion

This chapter has investigated the determinants of fiscal response strategies to the economic and financial crisis, analyzing time-series cross-sectional data from the twenty-seven EU member states during the Stimulus Years (2008–10)—the empirical evidence is based on a relatively small number of observations. Post-war economic history provides evidence that fiscal authorities in industrialized countries may be prone to a deficit bias, which shows up in large and persistent deficits and growing public debts. One result to highlight is that political economy factors are found to have shaped public finances during the Great Recession. This finding confirms Peter Gourevitch's (1986) dictum that 'policy needs politics'.

The determinants of EU fiscal policy during the Great Recession can be summarized as follows:

1. Fiscal policy responses were not contingent on the fiscal policies of pre-crisis years.
2. Larger automatic stabilizers went hand in hand with larger fiscal stimulus policies.
3. Larger bank bailouts went hand in hand with more stimulus spending.
4. The more severe the economic crisis, the less expansive the fiscal policy.
5. The more homogenous the government and the more heterogeneous the opposition, the more expansive the fiscal crisis policies.
6. Election years led to an increase in stimulus spending.
7. Right-leaning governments implemented larger stimulus policies.

The empirical results of this chapter suggest that the heterogeneous crisis responses should be seen not only as a result of different economic profiles (the severity of the recession shock), but also as a consequence of different political landscapes, marked by diverging electoral calendars, government formations, and ideological positions. This heterogeneity has considerable implications for the latency of EU member states and in turn the coordination of fiscal policy choices. Member states without election years falling in the 2008–10 period, for example, were more likely to implement smaller stimulus programs than those where policy-makers faced the electorate. Conversely, right-leaning governments were more likely to have designed larger stimulus plans than their left-leaning counterparts. The differences in the political and economic climate throughout the EU, which are shown to determine the fiscal responses to the Great Recession, mean that the production function for fiscal policy coordination is heterogeneous across member states. Collective action theory would therefore see the likelihood of free riding increasing in groups with 'stressful heterogeneities' (Varughese and Ostrom 2001: 762).

Notes

1. Lagged variables are used to circumvent the endogeneity problem of contemporaneous macroeconomic variables, which raises doubt as to the validity of the estimates and may create biases. Initially I attempted to instrument GDP growth as well as the debt levels with their lagged variables and US GDP and debt levels. As Hallerberg et al.

(2009: 341) note, it is 'notoriously difficult to instrument changes'. Relevant tests indicate the strength of the instruments is fairly weak. At the same time a Durbin-Wu-Hausman test confirmed the endogeneity of both variables (see Table A4.1 in Appendix 4). Similar to Armingeon (2012a), I therefore use the lagged variables.

2. Government fragmentation usually distinguishes between the minority/majority governments and the number of parties in the coalition.
3. More specifically, Hardin (1982) described 'the law of 1/n', according to which the larger the number of grazers (the n) on the budgetary commons, the smaller the fraction of costs that each grazer internalizes. The severity of the common-pool problem increases: the smaller the fraction of the total cost that each grazer has to take on, the smaller become the perceived costs compared with the actual costs.
4. I also added the squared term of the *Debt* variable to control for non-linear effects, but its coefficient was not significant in any of the specifications, nor did it change any of the other coefficients. A RESET test confirmed the exclusion of both the quadratic and cubic term.
5. Following the Commission (2010), I use an expenditure-based measurement of automatic stabilization. Dolls et al. (2010) and Girouard and André (2005) also include revenue-based indicators (such as corporate, personal income, and indirect taxes). To check the robustness of my proxy I also ran the same specification with a revenue-based variable. Analogous to the original measure, it takes the change in the output gap multiplied by the revenue-to-GDP ratio (used as a proxy of the semi-elasticities of the budget balance). Inferences were not affected.
6. Liabilities ranged from 0 to 29 percent of GDP (average value 1.69) and contingent liabilities ranged from 0 to 24 percent of GDP (average value 2.3). Both types of interventions were statistically not significant when included in the main model.
7. Squared and cubic coefficients were not significant in any of the model specifications. A RESET term further confirmed the linear modeling choice.
8. In the sample at hand, all one-party governments also held the majority of seats.
9. Minority governments must bargain with the opposition to pass legislation. Therefore, to test whether the role of the opposition is conditional on the minority/majority status of government, I interacted the fragmentation index with a minority dummy. Both variables were positive and insignificant in all specifications.
10. Both coefficients are statistically different from one another. Coefficient signs remain the same if one of the two variables is excluded.
11. Including the variable 'right' in the model specification with only centrist governments in the base group yields a significant and negative coefficient. The R2, however, does not improve and all other results are virtually identical.
12. The economic assumption behind the opposition to fiscal stimulus is that forward-looking consumers save the proceeds from a debt-financed fiscal stimulus in anticipation of the future tax increases. This behavior then cancels out the impact of the stimulus and creates a so-called non-Keynesian effect.

5

Beggar-Thy-Neighbors

5.1 A Patriotic Stimulus

National policy-makers eyed each other's stimulus efforts suspiciously, wary of free riding EU members and beggar-thy-neighbor crisis responses. According to Michael Glos, then German Minister of Economics, one 'can only hope that the measures taken by other countries... will help [the German] export economy' (*Financial Times*, November 30, 2008).

Statements like this suggest that the specter of free riding was haunting EU collective action. Consider further the example of the French government's support of the car manufacturer Renault under the condition that it repatriated production from Slovenia in early 2009. Unimpressed with criticism, President Sarkozy announced that if the French government gave 'financial aid to the automotive industry we [the government] do not want them to set up a factory in the Czech Republic again' (Rippert 2009). He furthermore urged the carmaker to support French industries involved in supplying parts and services to French automobile manufacturers (*Financial Times*, February 4, 2009). Along similar lines, the German government's rescue package for Opel, a German car manufacturer, raised concerns about possibly discriminatory protection of jobs in German plants. The then acting EU Council president, Czech Prime Minister Mirek Topolanek, warned of a 'protectionist race' in Europe, whilst the then Swedish Prime Minister, Fredrik Reinfeldt, said that he was 'very worried at the growing tide of protectionist economic measures in Europe' (*euractiv*, February 10, 2009). Accusations of free riding spilled over to the G20 level where US delegation repeatedly called for more stimulus spending from EU countries. In a similar vein, Olivier Blanchard, then the International Monetary Fund's (IMF's) chief economist, warned that 'if the circumstances require it, states must be ready to do more—3% or more if necessary' (BBC, December 23, 2008), thus going beyond the originally recommended European Economic Recovery Plan's (EERP's) 1.5 percent of GDP stimulus. At the global level the Bush administration's 'Buy America Act' or

Wen Jiabao's 'Buy Chinese Edict' appeals to the 'patriotic consumer' were at odds with proclamations in support of multilateral crisis cooperation.

The EERP (2008) stipulates that stimulus policies had to be targeted toward the source of economic difficulties with measures that supported businesses, labor markets, investment activities, and households' purchasing power. For national policy-makers the spending target clearly had one over-arching dimension that is, naturally, not mentioned in the EERP; their electorate. The political discourse on discretionary spending does not attempt to conceal potential conflicts of the domestic stimulus targets with the principles of the internal market and more elusive notions of European solidarity, which are evoked in the EERP. During the parliamentary debate on the 2009 stimulus package in Austria, for instance, the parliamentarian Gerald Klug (2008) warned that 'in order that we do not repeat mistakes of the past, the stimulus package should exclusively focus on measures that work domestically'. Similar concerns could be heard from the erstwhile Christian Democratic Union (CDU) shooting star Karl-Theodor zu Guttenberg who demanded that 'our stimulus package should secure jobs in Germany and not jobs in the Far East' (*Reuters*, January 26, 2009). Nationalism and parochialism are built-in features of public spending regardless of the underlying economic conditions (see, for instance, Morris (1997) on welfare protectionism). The use of public finances to further domestic aims should be seen against the standing temptation of 'economic patriotism' (Clift and Woll 2012)—whose allure both predates and outlived the Stimulus Years. The aim of fiscal policy is to promote the welfare of those contributing to it, and in the absence of a 'European demos' or a 'EU taxman', this erects easily identifiable goalposts for public spending. In the context of a crisis, with the state in charge of 'a major injection of purchasing power into the economy' (EERP 2008)—or as one interviewee put it, the 'renaissance of industrial policy' (interview, May 2011)—the discriminatory potential of public spending increases.

Chapter 4 has shown that fiscal crisis responses were not merely driven by a country's economic situation, but shaped by a host of political factors. This, I argue, suggests 'political explanations of economic policy choices' (Gourevitch 2013: 253). As a result, the coordination of fiscal response strategies may be hampered by a high degree of group latency. Latent groups face difficulties in managing collective action, which subsequently gives rise to concerns about free riding. Again, in the context of fiscal policy coordination, free riding behavior can be divided into stability free riding and growth free riding—stimulating 'too much' or 'too little'. This leads to the question of whether there is empirical evidence for free riding beyond the headlines of single initiatives or the undiplomatic fumbles of politicians.

According to the European Central Bank (ECB), measurement of stimulus spending in eleven EU member states did not meet the EERP call to implement fiscal packages of 1.2 percent of GDP. Table 5.1 lists 'non-compliers' with the EERP. According to my own comparison of the data available, I suggest that the figure should realistically read nine member states—still a third of the total. This high figure is remarkable, given that member states agreed on the 1.2 percent only *after* the vast majority of countries had already designed their national stimulus plans. To put this high figure of 'non-compliers' into context, this chapter will analyze the evidence for and against free riding behavior. Section 5.2 will analyze two of the main characteristics of free riding states as presented in the literature: trade openness and economic/political power. Given the small sample size, I will do so by relying on fuzzy Qualitative Comparative Analysis (fQCA). Section 5.3 of this chapter considers fiscal response strategies in relation to a country's fiscal space. To do so, I construct an original composite indicator, based on the EU's Macroeconomic Imbalances Procedure (MIP). Results show that, by and large, member states stimulated their economies in line with their fiscal room for maneuver, as laid out in the EERP. These findings are contrasted with the political discourse of the Great Recession, where accusations of (particularly German) growth free riding were widespread.

5.2 Analyzing Free Riding

This section analyzes free riding by methods similar to those employed in Chapters 1–4; that is, by relying on regression analysis techniques. To test for free riding behavior, I add two 'free riding variables' (trade openness and economic power) to the main model of Chapters 1–4. To measure the trade

Table 5.1. Non-compliance with the EERP's 1.2% of GDP stimulus threshold

COM (2011)	ECB (2010)	OECD (2009)
Greece	**Greece**	**Greece**
Romania	**Slovakia**	**France**
Slovakia	Slovenia	**Italy**
Lithuania	**Portugal**	**Portugal**
	Cyprus	**Ireland**
	Italy	
	France	
	Ireland	
	Belgium	

Note: ECB estimations only include Eurozone member states (as of 2010). OECD estimations are not available for Bulgaria, Estonia, Cyprus, Latvia, Lithuania, Malta, Romania, and Slovenia. Non-compliers in bold.

Source: European Commission (2011) *Public Finances in EMU*, ECB (2010) *Euro Area Fiscal Policies and the Crisis*, OECD (2009) *World Economic Outlook*.

position, I take the average trade position (value of imports + value of exports) as a percentage of GDP for 2008–10. I also tested the size of the population as an indicator of economic/political power, and obtained similar results. These variables capture both a country's political ability and its structural capacity to free ride. If I were to find that, for example, open-economy countries implemented fewer discretionary fiscal policies, this would be evidence for the charge that those countries have a greater incentive (i.e. capability) to engage in fiscal free riding—benefiting from the export possibilities generated by neighboring economies. Consider the example of Germany. In a now-defunct online presence (Germany Trade & Invest), the Economic Ministry maintains a list of stimulus packages in over sixty countries to help the German 'Mittelstand' to seize opportunities to enter new markets and thus emerge with new strength out of the economic crisis (Schelkle 2012a). Specifically, the website offers detailed descriptions of stimulus programs including the relevant sector and—helpfully—contact information. In 2010, French criticism of the strong German trade surplus made headlines amidst clear indicators of a strong German recovery. Jean-Paul Fitoussi, then adviser to Sarkozy, complained that 'the German economic strategy built on growth of exports is uncooperative' (*Financial Times*, February 16, 2010). Yet in contrast to the anecdotal evidence presented above, I find that none of the 'free rider' variables has a significant impact on a country's fiscal policies during the Great Recession. Table 5.2 presents these results. This evidence suggests that although export-oriented open economies are structurally better placed to free ride, economic openness was not a determining factor of fiscal policy outcomes. Similarly, although EU member states with more economic and political clout are likely to be in a better place to get away with beggar-thy-neighbor policies, they are not more likely to free ride.

To further test for free riding behavior, I consider compliance with the EERP. Crucially, the EERP sets an absolute, cumulative reference value for the fiscal programs and not an annual value. Because of this, the number of observations available is limited to twenty-seven (the number of EU member states at that time). With so few observations, it is not feasible to use appropriate techniques such as a probit model. A solution for small-N research designs that is increasingly applied throughout the social sciences is the Qualitative Comparative Analysis (QCA) approach (Schneider and Wagemann 2010; Emmenegger 2011). Ragin (1987) developed QCA initially in order to formalize comparative case study research with small- and moderate-N datasets. This approach is not only advantageous in the light of small numbers of observations, but also given the causal complexity which calls for the necessary modeling of interaction effects and the related loss of degrees of freedom (Ragin 2000).

Table 5.2. 'Free rider profile' and fiscal policy outcomes, 2008–10

	Δ PSB	Δ SB	Δ PB	Δ BB
Power	**−0.000**	**−0.001**	**0.001**	**0.003***
	(0.001)	**(0.001)**	**(0.001)**	**(0.001)**
Trade	**0.702**	**1.182**	**1.030**	**1.105**
	(4.236)	**(4.030)**	**(3.453)**	**(5.839)**
L.Δ GDP	−1.121***	−1.082***	−0.753***	−1.214***
	(0.198)	(0.190)	(0.190)	(0.260)
L.Debt	0.187***	0.179***	0.153**	0.341***
	(0.049)	(0.047)	(0.047)	(0.062)
Bailout	1.052***	1.078***	0.917***	−0.032
	(0.068)	(0.065)	(0.079)	(0.117)
L.AS	2.815***	2.711***	1.636***	3.121***
	(0.487)	(0.465)	(0.476)	(0.660)
Opposition	12.720	15.311*	11.901*	10.020
	(7.035)	(6.595)	(5.531)	(10.185)
Government	−16.908*	−20.902**	−16.290**	−19.319
	(8.091)	(7.515)	(6.203)	(10.939)
Left	4.091***	4.051***	2.951***	5.359***
	(1.029)	(0.977)	(0.729)	(1.045)
Election	−1.342***	−1.236***	−0.792**	−0.895*
	(0.316)	(0.302)	(0.307)	(0.411)
	(0.000)	(0.000)	(0.000)	(0.000)
Constant	−15.082	−8.332	−25.219*	−65.044***
	(14.298)	(11.930)	(12.005)	(15.430)
R2	0.897	0.912	0.914	0.929
N	81	81	81	81

Note: Standard errors are corrected for groupwise heteroskedasticity and contemporaneous correlation across countries of the error terms are corrected with panel-corrected standard errors. * Significant at the 5% level; ** at the 1% level; *** at the 0.1% level. Standard errors listed beside coefficients. Time and unit dummies not shown to preserve space.

5.2.1 *Fuzzy Free Riding*

QCA is distinct from other case-oriented methods because of its use of Boolean algebra and set-theoretical insights to operationalize comparison and detect causal complexity.[1] While it only allows binary variables, its fuzzy-set variant (fQCA) makes it possible to examine continuous and interval-scale variables. The use of fQCA calibrates the causal conditions into sets, which allow for partial membership in a set. Specifically, the membership of each case in a set of conditions may vary between full membership (value 1) and non-membership (value 0) in a set. The value 0.5 describes the crossover point indicating the border between cases that could be 'in' or 'out' of a set, where 0 is a full 'out' and 1 a full 'in'. Given that many of the variables of interest are more complex than binary coding would account for, the fQCA approach is an obvious choice. Using a fQCA-based research process, which is able to detect empirical patterns in the data at hand, I seek to scrutinize fiscal free riding.

I pursue two related methods to measure compliance with the EERP. The first yields a simple dummy, which takes the value of 1 if the total stimulus package (2009–10) is estimated as 1.2 percent of GDP or larger, as the threshold of the EERP states, and 0 otherwise. The second accounts for the relative compliance with the EERP and measures the total size of the stimulus package (calculated by the European Commission 2010a). The outcome variables used in the presentation of the main results are based on the Commission's estimations. Results for a crisp (binary) outcome variable are virtually the same. As a robustness check, I also ran the QCA using the ECB's stimulus measurement. All results hold.[2]

The two conditions thought to influence member states' growth free riding and subsequently compliance with the EERP are trade openness and political/economic clout. Measures are the same as in section 5.2. In addition, I control for economic distress. The third measurement indicates economic distress as a binary outcome, which is a way (albeit crude) of indicating a severe crisis. Economic distress, so the underlying argument goes, puts a substantial constraint on public finances and is likely to limit the scope for stimulus spending—this is appropriate in line with stability free riding as 'too much' spending. The first group of countries qualified to be under economic distress are under IMF program conditionality (Hungary, Romania, Latvia), and the second group belongs to the now infamously and crudely dubbed 'PIIGS' (Portugal, Ireland, Italy, Greece, and Spain)—a grouping that would gain a negative momentum and a life of its own, mirroring the positive experience of countries under the BRICS (Brazil, Russia, India, China, and South Africa) label. These countries experienced the Great Recession substantially differently from the other member states. Although the difficulties faced by these countries are not identical, they are compatible in that they clearly experienced *severe* economic distress. Granted, the economic and financial fallout had devastating consequences across the EU. Yet if the Great Recession was a car crash, these economic distress countries would be in intensive care, whereas the other confederates were 'merely' visiting A&E. Note that the countries in the group of non-compliers identified in Table 5.1, with the notable exception of France and Belgium, do all also belong in the group of 'distress countries'. Greece, according to the Commission, had a modest stimulus of 0.6 percent of GDP, and no stimulus spending at all according to the ECB (see Table 4.1). George Papandreou, the Greek Prime Minister elected in 2009, had promised a stimulus program of EUR 2.5 billion (incidentally the price tag for militarily equipment brought by Greece from France amidst the country's debt crisis), yet once in office this plan was never put into practice (*Financial Times*, October 6, 2009).

Table A5.1 in Appendix 4 displays the fuzzy-set scores for the outcome and the three conditions, as well as the best fit for each country case.[3] Results are presented using letters as abbreviations for the conditions and the outcome. C represents compliance with the EERP/the size of the total stimulus package,

T trade openness, P political power, and D economic distress. Upper-case letters indicate the presence of a condition, while lower-case letters indicate the absence of a condition—for example, T indicates a high level of trade openness and t indicates a low level of trade openness.[4]

5.2.2 *Compliance with the EERP*

To test for growth free riding, I perform a test of each configuration's y-consistency versus its n-consistency and a test between each set's y-consistency and the consistency of all other configurations. I look for the configurations with y-consistencies that are significantly greater than 0.7 (a conventional threshold; see Schneider and Wagemann 2010), as well as significantly greater than their n-consistencies. TPd is the most highly consistent configuration for compliance with the EERP (coverage = 0.502, consistency = 0.940). Figure 5.1 presents the result graphically. Note that for a condition or a combination of conditions to be sufficient, all cases should be located around or above the bisecting line/diagonal (Ragin 2000: 236). While the consistency of the sufficient condition (TPd) is very high, the coverage is less strong.[5] This is visualized in Figure 5.1 by the proximity of country cases to the diagonal vs. the Y-axis. The closer a country case is to the diagonal, the higher the degree

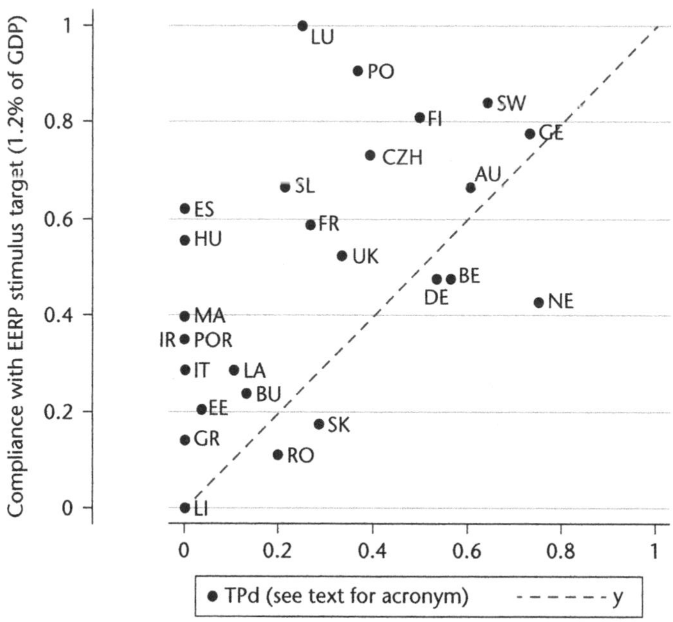

Figure 5.1 Sufficient conditions for meeting the EERP target

of coverage. Overall, the graphical representation of the fQCA analysis does *not* support the finding that member states with open economics and more economic/political power experienced less economic distress or implemented larger stimulus packages (i.e. had better compliance scores). This is in contrast to the implicit or explicit portrait of big, powerful countries as being prone to free riding.

Further visualizing this relationship, the scatter plot in Figure 5.2 plots illustrates the positive correlation between the 3-year backward moving average current account balance (one of the headline indicator used in the Macroeconomic Imbalances Procedure) and the total stimulus package based on estimations of the European Commission (rho = .56). In addition, I transformed the variables in question into ranks to see whether the same findings also hold for Spearman's rank correlation coefficients; the results are virtually identical.

In sum, there is little evidence for free riding behavior. These findings fill a gap in the literature and run counter to accusations of the time. Few studies have empirically analyzed the problem of growth free riding during the Great Recession. Mathias Dolls and colleagues (2010) report a negative correlation (−0.4) between the average annual discretionary fiscal measure and their indicator for openness. Yet these findings are only comparable to a limited extent. First, the authors use the average ratio of exports to GDP for the 2000–4 period, whereas I construct a measure for the time span of the financial and economic crisis that is congruent with the period of the implemented

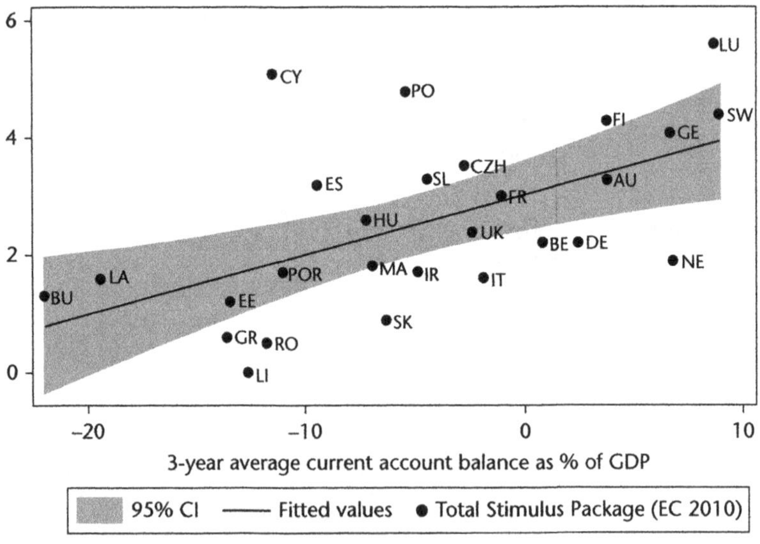

Figure 5.2 Relationship between total stimulus package and account balance

stimulus packages. Second, the motivation for the selection of countries is not clear; Dolls et al. (2010) analyze eighteen EU countries, plus the USA. The inclusion of the USA and the exclusion of nine EU countries are likely to impact upon results. Third, the source for the estimation of the size of stimulus packages differs. It is not entirely clear what their source is. In the text the authors state that they use the estimations of an IMF staff note, yet, from my reading, said note lists only the stimulus packages of the G20 countries. Joshua Aizenman and Yothin Jinjarak (2010) present another analysis of the relationship between openness and fiscal response strategies with regression analyses looking at the variation in the fiscal stimuli during 2009–10 in 112 countries (including twenty-five EU member states). Specifically, they find higher trade openness (measured by the 2000–6 average trade to GDP ratio) to be associated with a lower fiscal stimulus. But the authors do not run separate regressions for country groups (i.e. the EU), and given the inclusion of eighty-seven other countries, the results are not comparable.

5.3 Fiscal Space

Barroso quipped that all EU members are sitting in one (leaky) boat—they make for a rather motley crew. The EERP (2008: 7) states this explicitly: 'To maximise its impact, the budgetary stimulus should take account of the starting positions of each Member State. It is clear that not all Member States are in the same position.' The stimulus package, so the argument goes, should be consistent with a country's fiscal space so as not to threaten the sustainability of public finances, which could have negative spillovers for other member states as well. In order to better distinguish between stability and growth free riding, this section investigates whether member states' fiscal responses matched their room for fiscal maneuver.

Fiscal space refers to 'the capacity of a government to provide financial resources for a desired purpose, subject to the constraint that the fiscal position is sustainable, both over the medium and long-term' (Heller 2005). Or put differently, a country's room for public spending without running into credit risk. Heller's definition gained influence among IMF officials and was originally predominantly applied to developing countries. In the EU, the term 'fiscal space' came to gradually replace the previously preferred 'room for maneuver' in 2009 (interview, March 2011). The discussion within the G20 and the strong presence of the IMF during the Great Recession made the term 'fiscal space' respectable and stripped its association with developing and emerging market economies. Whilst the EERP mentions the 'fiscal room for maneuver', a year later DG Ecfin's Public Finances in the EMU (European Commission 2009a: 192) called on 'countries with limited fiscal space . . . to engage in particularly cautious fiscal policies'. The logic of fiscal space had implications not only for the extent of economic stimulus spending but also for its timing. Focusing on fiscal exit strategies, Marco Buti (2009), Director-General for Economic and Financial Affairs at the European Commission since December 2008, considered that 'while accelerated fiscal consolidation is the immediate priority for the countries with no or little fiscal space, others with better fiscal space can maintain less restrictive stances in the short term, for the sake of growth and jobs in Europe'. The concept of fiscal space has also gained importance in relation to that of the Eurozone's aggregate fiscal stance. In short, countries with fiscal space are urged to use this space to contribute to an expansive aggregate fiscal stance for the Eurozone as a whole. I will return to this point in Chapter 9 of this book.

There are no readily available comprehensive indicators that can be used to measure the availability of fiscal space (Heller 2005; Ostry et al. 2010: 4). Indeed, this is one of the political advantages of the concept; it is 'a judgment call' (Clift 2018: 108). In EU circles the vagueness of the term did raise concerns. The ECB continues to be skeptical of the term and feared that in the absence of clear targets and thresholds, countries would interpret the meaning according to their own preferences.[6] The term 'room for maneuver' is *prima facie* no less vague. But during the first decade of the EMU, member states reached a common reading of the semiotics of this term, namely fiscal policies in line with the SGP. In discussions on public finances it became clear that member states had 'quite different' understandings of their own fiscal space (interview, March 2011). As one interviewee from the Commission put it, 'for Finns, fiscal space is there if you can meet all your fiscal obligations for the next 50 years, for some Southern countries, fiscal space is there if you need to spend more' (April 2011). Elinor Ostrom (1990: 18) described this challenge as a situation where 'the herders can overestimate or underestimate the carrying capacity of the meadow'.

Amidst the European Debt Crisis, a series of new regulations to enhance economic governance in the EU were agreed at the EU level. One of them, as part of the so-called Six-Pack, established a surveillance procedure to prevent and correct macroeconomic imbalances; the MIP. Specifically, the new regulations established a scoreboard to provide an early-warning signaling device of potentially harmful macroeconomic imbalances in member states. I use the indicators scrutinized in this imbalance surveillance to construct a better indicator for a country's fiscal space. Further information can be found in Appendix 1. Specifically, I introduce new sub-scores based on the MIP's scoreboard and use a different weighting strategy with factor analysis. The 'Scoreboard for the Surveillance of Macroeconomic Imbalances' (DG Ecfin 2012) contains ten indicators. What stands out is that with these indicators economic policy coordination not only moves away from a narrow focus on the deficit threshold, but also pays close attention to the state of the private economy. Imbalances are presented as a problem for public policy, but are mapped out as stemming from both the public and private realm of the economy. The MIP in so doing is able to challenge the German narrative of the Eurozone crisis; what Mark Blyth (2013) has called, arguably with a touch of hyperbole, 'the greatest "bait and switch" in modern history' as a crisis of public instead of private debt.

1) Three-year backward-moving average of the current account balance as a percentage of GDP, with a threshold of +6 percent of GDP and −4 percent of GDP;
2) Net international investment position as a percentage of GDP, with a threshold of −35 percent of GDP;
3) Five years' percentage change of export market shares measured in values, with a threshold of −6 percent;
4) Three years' percentage change in nominal unit labor cost, with thresholds of +9 percent for Eurozone countries and +12 percent for non-Eurozone countries;
5) Three years' percentage change of the real effective exchange rates based on Harmonized Index of Consumer Price (HICP) and Consumer Price Index (CPI) deflators, relative to thirty-five other industrial countries, with thresholds of −/+5 percent for Eurozone countries and −/+11 percent for non-Eurozone countries;
6) Private sector debt in percent of GDP with a threshold of 160 percent;
7) Private sector credit flow in percent of GDP with a threshold of 15 percent;
8) Year-on-year changes in house prices relative to a Eurostat consumption deflator, with a threshold of 6 percent;
9) General government sector debt in percent of GDP with a threshold of 60 percent;
10) Three-year backward-moving average of unemployment rate, with a threshold of 10 percent.

The scoreboard not only identifies potentially 'harmful macroeconomic imbalances' but also yields a useful indicator for the identification of fiscal sustainability, which is a country's fiscal space. The alphabet soup of fiscal policy coordination got thicker. Next to the MIP with its in-depth review under the Excessive Imbalances Procedure (EIP), the SGP with its in-depth review under the Excessive Deficit Procedure (EDP) continues to apply. In an accompanying document (European Commission 2011b) the Commission emphasizes that 'the sustainability of public finances will not be assessed in the context of the EIP given that this issue is already covered by the SGP'.

The Commission did not want to be seen as replacing or weakening the existing EDP: 'there may well be a loss of clarity; first we had only one clear indicator and now all of a sudden there are ten. What if the verdicts of the EIP are not in line with the EDP, which recommendations should member states follow?' (interview, April 2011). The *artificial* differentiation between macroeconomic imbalances and fiscal sustainability, I argue, is impractical. In its justification of the choice of indicators, accompanied by a comprehensive review of the literature, the link between each indicator and fiscal sustainability, default, and crisis incidences is meticulously presented. Despite this reluctance, the EIP may be seen as a direct consequence of the main lesson of the European Debt Crisis: 'Fiscal profligacy is neither the sole nor the main origin of Europe's fiscal crisis' (Buti and Carnot 2012: 903). Critiquing the sub-scores of the EIP, Marco Buti and Nicolas Carnot (2012: 903) state that indicators of 'fiscal vulnerability' which take into account variables for financial and competitiveness developments give a better picture of the risk of fiscal crises than purely fiscal indicators. A broader measurement of fiscal space/fiscal sustainability is needed to capture relevant macroeconomic fundamentals. To obtain a 'more complete', theoretically grounded, measure of fiscal sustainability, I use factor analysis and follow recommendation to 'combine as many meaningful single indicators as possible into one composite indicator' (Knedlik and Von Schweinitz 2012). Appendix 1 discusses the construction of the fiscal space indicator; weights are presented in Table A5.1 of Appendix 4.

By and large, the newly constructed indicator (see Figure 5.3) is in line with what one would expect; Germany, Luxembourg, the Netherlands, and Austria have the highest scores, whereas Portugal, Spain, Greece (which has the lowest score in 2009 and 2010), Hungary, Ireland, and Bulgaria have the lowest scores. Furthermore, the EIP fiscal space indicator correlates negatively with a country's risk premium paid on government bonds.[7] Fiscal space is linked to higher interest rates. By this I do not suggest that market participants are superior judges of fiscal sustainability; whether markets adequately price government bonds remains an open and contested question. Despite a broad fit of the indicator, the scores are not perfect predictors for the multicausal outcome of fiscal distress. Notably, the comparatively high scores for Romania and Latvia come as a surprise. The Latvian government applied in late 2008 to the EU, IMF, and regional neighbors for financial assistance amidst a rapidly deteriorating economic situation and short-term liquidity pressure linked to the ailing financial sector. Likewise, Romania needed financial assistance. Although the overall fiscal situation of both countries was dire, they still scored highly on some of the indicators such as private debt, house prices, and government debt. What is more, five out of ten of the fiscal space sub-scores take annual averages (three to five years), and the brisk

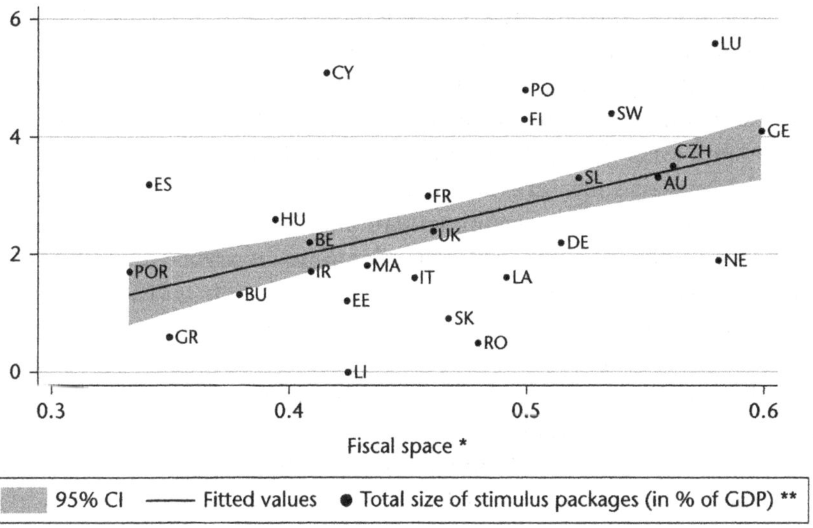

* average fiscal space (2007–10), see text; ** based on Commission estimates (EC 2010)

Figure 5.3 Relationship between fiscal space and stimulus package

economic downturn that led to liquidity problems is therefore less strongly registered than it would be with annual indicators. Note also that Romania and Latvia score well in the Commission's fiscal space indicator (EC 2009a) as well as that of Aizenman and Jinjarak (2010; see Appendix 1 for a more detailed discussion).

5.3.1 *Fiscal Space and Stimulus Spending*

Fiscal space is linked to fiscal policy outcomes. Figure 5.3 summarizes the correlation results. There is a strong positive link between the size of the average fiscal space (2007–10) and the size of the stimulus package as estimated by the Commission (N = 27, rho = 0.48).[8] This finding links up with David Cameron's study (2012), according to which governments with a surplus in the years prior to the crisis generally made more substantial stimulus efforts. Countries with larger fiscal space, such as Germany and Luxembourg, implemented substantial stimulus packages. Countries with less fiscal space, such as Greece and Ireland, engaged in virtually no stimulus policies even before program conditionality limited governments' room to move. Ireland was the first EU country to implement what was later labeled 'austerity politics' in the fall of 2008. Foretokening the experience of crisis-stricken economies amidst the European Debt Crisis, local elites sought to signal Ireland's credible commitment, hoping to stabilize private investment (Ban 2016: 185).

Member states implemented stimulus policies with their fiscal space in mind. Indeed, the recommendation of the Commission makes a case for limited stimulus spending, provided a member state has limited fiscal space. Stimulus spending becomes means-tested. In its 'Report on Slovakia', the Commission (SEC 2009, 1276 final: 8) found the Slovak government's restrained anti-crisis measures adequate given 'the limited fiscal space due to external imbalances'. In its recommendation on the existence of an excessive deficit (SEC 2009, 1271 final: 9), the Commission argued that the Italian stimulus package is 'not expected to appreciably weigh on the government balance, as [it is] planned to have an overall neutral budget impact...The package is an adequate response to the economic downturn in view of the very high debt ratio'. Along similar lines, in the assessment of the Belgian Stability Programme, the Commission points out 'that as a result of the openness of the economy, foreign packages should also contribute considerably to the recovery of the Belgian economy' (ECFIN/52791/09-EN). No public publication related to the Excessive Deficit Procedure, be it authored by the Commission or the Council, encourages any of the nine EERP non-compliers to shoulder more substantial stimulus measures. This, however, is less evidence for successful coordination of fiscal crisis responses under the EERP than for the accommodating EDP application in times of crises.

5.4 Free Riding: Facts and Fiction

The evidence presented in this chapter does not support accusations of free riding. In addition to the quantitative evidence, all interviewees were asked about the occurrence of fiscal beggar-thy-neighbor policies; none named growth free riding of weaker members as a serious concern.[9] In other words, countries with limited fiscal space, which effectively abstained from discretionary spending, were not accused of freeloading. However, three interviewees (interviews, April and June 2011) pointed to Spain as an example where a country had shot beyond its fiscal space in stimulating demand. The MIP fiscal space score corroborates this impression. According to this indicator, Spain had one of the EU member states' worst fiscal space scores but one of the largest stimulus policies. During 2008 and 2009, the Spanish debt burdens increased by 3 percent of GDP due to direct bailouts of the financial sector, and the government amassed a significant stock of liabilities linked to financial market support operations worth around €20bn (EC Public Finances 2010). Ye, both the Spanish government and the European Commission initially claimed that Spain had fiscal room for maneuver to engage in discretionary stimulus spending. During the first decade of the Euro, the Spanish economy had been one of the fastest-growing and most successful economies in Europe. Presenting his government's stimulus policies in parliament, the then Prime Minister José Luis Rodríguez Zapatero contested that the Spanish government was in a strong position to stimulate the economy due to its relatively small debt burden and 'the fiscal prudence of the Socialist government over the past four years' (*Financial Times*, November 28, 2008). This optimism was echoed in the Commission's (EC 2009b) evaluation of Spain's fiscal stimulus package which, although at first glance seemed excessive in the light of its output gap, was considered fine due to 'Spain's comparatively favorable fiscal space'. Tony Barbor (*Financial Times*, November 4, 2008) put Spain in a category with Germany and argued that '[countries] such as Germany and Spain, which practiced fiscal discipline in the years when economic growth was robust, have more room for maneuver than others, such as France and Greece, which did not'. Sebastian Dullien (2008b) was one of the few cautious voices warning that 'a stimulus package in Spain risks just to cover up the country's economic problems without solving them'. In his opinion this amounted to a 'stimulus in the wrong country'—the right one being Germany.

5.4.1 *Playing Up and Playing Down*

Fueled by public disagreements between Sarkozy and Merkel, the free riding debate of 2008–9 focused on Germany. Disagreement between German and French perspectives on fiscal policy-making is not unusual. The joint effort to first resist the application of the SGP in 2003 and then to bring about its reform (critiques would say 'watering down') marks the exception. The frictions surrounding the politics of fiscal stimulus represent yet another iteration of long-standing differences. What stands out here is the discrepancy between allegations and realities of free riding in the French and German fiscal crisis responses. Whereas the Sarkozy-led French government was seen as a motor for fiscal policy coordination both at the EU and the international level, the German government faced criticism for doing too little to stimulate domestic growth and obstructing economic cooperation. Indeed, criticism was voiced both at the EU and the international level. The US government sought to discuss imbalances first and foremost to put pressure on China to appreciate the renminbi faster: 'Originally the issue of imbalances was a way for the US to bash China within the G20, yet for political reasons the Obama administration did not want to single out China and therefore Germany got in the line of fire as well' (interview, April 2011). In these negotiations, Germany became China's most important although by no means sole ally. The other BRICS countries have continually stood in solidarity with China. For instance, when US Treasury Secretary Timothy Geithner attempted to enlist Brazil, he was rebuffed by the then Finance Minister, Guido Mantega, who insisted the

United States was the source of imbalances (Chodor 2017). Korea, itself no stranger to currency intervention, also came out to defend the Chinese government. The Korean Finance Minister, Yoon Jeung-hyun, made clear that 'we may discuss for example the general approach toward foreign exchange rates . . . or the impact foreign exchange could have on the global economy . . . I do not believe that it is appropriate to have a discussion regarding the foreign exchange rate or level of a specific country' (*Reuters*, September 23, 2010).

Whereas Sarkozy was praised for his efforts, Merkel was dubbed 'Madame Non' in the international press not only because her government was hesitant in its domestic crisis response, but also because she was reluctant to call for all member states to implement substantial stimulus programs. In addition, she vetoed the plan for a more coordinated stimulus in the form of a general reduction of VAT, which the Commission had supported (Schelkle 2012a). The remark of the then German Finance Minister, Peer Steinbrück (2008a), who called the UK's cut in VAT 'crass Keynesian', should be seen as a reaction to his government's position against similar EU-wide tax cuts. A *Financial Times* article (November 26, 2008) called for EU officials to name and shame countries not pulling their weight, such as Germany and the Netherlands, 'waiting for other less well-placed countries to do most of the work and reaping the benefits once exports pick up'.

In addition to the difference in political stance, the German and French economies were differently affected by the crisis. Export dependency and the current account position is one of the main factors in determining the contraction of the economy. In particular Germany, the Netherlands, and Austria, where export demand had been strong, were more exposed to the contraction in world trade. The sharp decline in German exports had a devastating effect, notably on investment in plant and machinery, which fell by 21.8 percent in the first six months of 2009 alone (Zohlnhöfer 2011). The *Economist* (May 7, 2009) claimed that with the export-led model sputtering more than most in times of recession, 'the title of export champion may have lost its glitter'. Along similar lines, in a speech in front of the G20, Sarkozy (2009) prided himself that the 'French economy is holding up better than those of its major partners'. Although this portrait of an ailing German economy and a resistant French economy was short-lived, it shaped the free riding parlance during the Great Recession.

Against this backdrop, the realities of stimulus spending hardly live up to the free riding accusations. Germany had one of the largest stimulus packages both in absolute and relative terms. The Germany government, in line with the ordo-liberalisms, has embraced state intervention. Consider Angela Merkel's take on state intervention (2009): '[The state] is not only able to, it has to act'.[10] Germany announced a first set of stimulus measures prior to the EERP agreement. When asked how far EU pressures and agreements shaped

Germany's crisis response, interviewees across the board were skeptical as to whether they mattered at all: 'do you really think German politicians needed someone to tell them that they should help their automotive industry?' (interview, March 2011). Dan Drezner (2014: 165), in his flattering account of international collective action, claims that 'Germany eventually bowed to pressure from economists and G20 peers'. Based on my interview material as well as the process tracing (timing and domestic discourse) of the German stimulus plan, I challenge this narrative. My assessment echoes Miles Kahler's analysis (2013: 44) of the large stimulus programs implemented by the US and Chinese governments, which 'owed little to international pressure or collaboration' (see also Helleiner 2014: 32). Still in contrast to the US or Chinese programs, the initial announcements of the German stimulus programs were timid (by December 2008 France had announced a €39bn plan, whereas the German package pledged only €12bn; Spilimbergo et al. 2009). German policy-makers in charge of stimulus diplomacy are largely responsible for this misconception of a passive government because of their hidebound public embrace of stimulus spending and inconsistent communications. As one Commission official put it, 'the problem was not with the stimulus, but with its non-communication' (interview, March 2011).

If accusations of free riding were not justified given the size of the stimulus packages, they were certainly provoked by a government that in public refused to acknowledge the need for discretionary fiscal spending. Most of this reluctance stems from domestic paradigms of macroeconomic policies. There is, however, also a European dimension to the repeated disavowals of stimulus spending. The German government initially opposed the EERP, as it would encourage 'states to spend money that they do not have' (interview, April 2011). Still, concerning its own stimulus efforts, Commission officials 'heard a lot about helping Volkswagen, but never about applying the Pact' (interview, April 2015). The public reneging on the EERP was aimed at other countries. German policy-makers were aware of the country's favorable fiscal space for stimulus policies, yet did doubt that other countries were in a similarly good situation. The communication strategy directed at fellow EU members was thus one of 'do as I say, not as I do' (interview, April 2015).

Comparing the French and German crisis responses to the Great Recession suggests that while the German stimulus was substantial (albeit poorly communicated), the French stimulus was timid (see Table 5.1). French stimulus spending amounted to merely 0.6–3 percent of GDP, depending on the source (see Table 4.1). Notwithstanding pro-stimulus proclamations and initiatives, 'in practice, the French government relied heavily on the in-built stabilizers of their tax-transfer system with largely symbolic extra spending' (Schelkle 2012a: 131). Mark Vail (2014: 10) claims that the modest French stimulus 'was particularly surprising given France's relatively dire economic situation', indicated by a comparison between French and German unemployment rates (9.5 percent and 7.8 percent of GDP, respectively, in 2009). Yet the difference for 2008 is less stark (unemployment rates of 7.8 percent in France and 7.5 percent in Germany). More importantly, the causality of unemployment rates and stimulus spending is not unidirectional as Vail implicitly assumes. The German stimulus was not high despite low unemployment rates, but unemployment was kept at bay because of generous stimulus spending. The German Kurzarbeit (short-term work) program is estimated to have subsidized more than 1.5 million employees, about 4 percent of the workforce, 'which helped keep unemployment relatively low' (Zohlnhöfer 2011). The case of Germany furthermore shows that a huge and growing current account surplus can go hand in hand with one of the largest stimulus programs. The 'sizeable subsidy to encourage labor hoarding by firms and generous support for the car industry' (Hassel 2014) put German firms in a better position to seek market share abroad.

If one accepts the notion of fiscal space-dependent stimulus, then the French response was in line with its fiscal room for maneuver. Despite being less vulnerable to the decline in export markets, the French economy faces considerable structural challenges, which may threaten the long-term sustainability of public finances. In Figure 5.3 France sits in the middle of the sample. The French government is not the only one to have played up the extent of intervention. In November 2008, the Italian prime minister announced an €80bn stimulus package (*Financial Times*, November 30, 2008). This (presumably aspirational) figure was widely circulated not only in public speeches but also in official documents such as the country's annual Stability and Convergence Report. Yet official estimates show the Italian stimulus to be virtually non-existent (estimated at 0 by the ECB and the Organisation of Economic Co-operation and Development (OECD), and at 0.3 percent of GDP by the IMF). The Council's 2009 country recommendation notes that 'given the already very high debt ratio, any large budgetary deterioration could elicit a reaction from the financial markets, causing a further widening of the already significant spreads between Italian and German bonds. This would result in higher interest rates for the entire economy, outweighing the benefits from the fiscal stimulus'. In light of Italy's limited fiscal space, the absence of a *de facto* stimulus package was welcomed. As one Commission interviewee admitted: 'We were quite relieved that Berlusconi's big announcements amounted to nothing more than hot air' (April 2011).

5.5 Conclusion

Accusations of stimulus free riding are not borne out by factual evidence. What is more, countries with limited fiscal space, as set out in the EERP, by and large abstained from large stimulus programs. This is an important finding since it suggests that member states did shoulder more or less stimulus burden depending on their economic means—thereby eschewing uniform contributions across member states. Despite considerable group latency, free riding behavior amongst EU member states was kept at bay. The absence of widespread beggar-thy-neighbor policies in the EU during the Great Recession mirrors the broader international climate. There is evidence that emerging markets were not protectionist either, arguably because their increasing integration into world trading systems meant that protectionist strategies were not considered beneficial (Haggard 2013). Former US trade representative Susan Schwab (2011) concludes that 'although countries took protectionist measures in the wake of the crisis, the international community avoided a quick deterioration into a spiral of beggar-thy-neighbor actions to block imports'. Despite repeated diagnosis of the 'end of globalization' (e.g. Rugman 2001), world trade and the structures that underpin it are not in retreat. Aggregate regional and global data from the conservative US think tank Heritage Foundation records a continual 4 percent increase in its Index of Trade Freedom between 2008 and 2016.

Accusations of growth free riding *and not* stability free riding dominated. The German government in particular came under fire for alleged beggar-thy-neighbor policies. Yet, despite opportunistic episodes such as the above-mentioned Germany Trade & Invest initiative and the parochial hopes of Michael Glos, there is little evidence for a government-led free riding strategy. If German policy-makers had any systematic free riding intentions, it would be counterproductive to vocally denounce the effectiveness of fiscal stimulus and to dissuade other EU states from implementing programs. Benefiting from other member states' stimulus programs, and actively seeking to do so, is something that net-exporting countries are structurally better positioned to do than net-importing countries. Yet this does not amount to free riding. This chapter has shown that given the substantial German stimulus, the government certainly contributed its share to the production of the collective good—but whether this qualifies as the 'lion's share' (Steinbrück 2010) is a matter for debate.

Notes

1. Boolean algebra can formalize the maximum number of systematic comparisons that can be made in terms of the presence or absence of attributes of interest, across the cases under analysis. Rather than estimate the net effects of single variables, QCA employs Boolean logic to examine the relationship between an outcome and all binary combinations of multiple predictors. Its underlying understanding of

causation is that of multiple conjunctional causation which relies on a configurational approach to causation. It identifies the different conjunctions of *conditions* or 'causal paths', leading to a certain *outcome*. In so doing, it allows for the identification of multiple conjunctional causation and the distinction between sufficient or necessary as causally relevant (Schneider and Wagemann 2010). More specifically, QCA differentiates between causal conditions being necessary but not sufficient, sufficient but not necessary, or necessary and sufficient. The co-existence of various combinations of causal paths that lead to an outcome has been referred to as equifinality of outcomes (Ragin 2000).

2. Chapters 1–4 have argued that the preferred measurement for discretionary fiscal policy is the cyclically adjusted budget balance. This chapter, although still corroborating findings with reference to this indicator, focuses on the stimulus data as presented by the European Commission. This is reasonable since I am interested in the total size of the stimulus package. Furthermore, collective action theory stipulates that information about other group members' intentions is crucial in the provision of a public good. The communication of stimulus programs on a policymaker and public (newspaper etc.) level was dominated by the stimulus figures identical, or at least readily comparable, to those published by the European Commission, other international organizations, and think tanks (such as the IMF and the OECD). Focusing on the realities and accusations of free riding, it is advantageous to work with the same data that member states used in their EU level meetings (interview, May 2011).
3. The transformation of the variables into a fuzzy-value scale was undertaken by creating rank orders of the variable and then standardizing this ranking to range from 0 to 1. For a comprehensive, largely nontechnical discussion of the acquisition of membership values in fuzzy-set analyses, see Verkuilen (2005). The equation for this standardization is (rankedvar—min(rankedvar))/(max(rankedvar) – min(rankedvar)). An exception are the dummy variables for compliance and the existence of economic distress; they are treated as crisp sets.
4. Results are evaluated using both graphical representations as well as descriptive measures such as consistency and scores. Consistency assesses the degree to which a subset relation has been approximated, while coverage assesses the empirical relevance of a consistent subset (Ragin 2006: 291). It is important to note that coverage is only interpreted for consistent results. Coverage for inconsistent results is not a meaningful indicator (Schneider and Wagemann 2010: 209). Consistency and coverage are calculated using the 'fuzzy' command in stata (Longest and Vaisey 2007), an add-on command that is capable of creating, testing, and performing logical reductions on both fuzzy and dichotomous (crisp) set-theoretic data.
5. Consistency trumps coverage. What is more, it is very rare for graphical representations of fQCA analysis to display a 'perfect fit' (with all observations being close to the diagonal); see Ragin (2000).
6. Based on a systematic review of archival material from the ECB, it appears that the ECB did not use the term fiscal space at all prior to 2008. After that the term is used sparingly, mostly in reference to existing literature employing the term and mostly

with quotation marks (even when no source of quotation is given). The ECB's preferred term remains fiscal sustainability.

7. Measured as the interest rates paid on government bonds with ten-year maturity, for the 2008–11 period (N = 107, rho = –0.35, significant at the 0.01 level).
8. Significant at the 0.5 percent level; results for the ECB stimulus estimations are virtually identical.
9. This finding might be biased because of the timing of interviews. Over half the interviews took place in the spring of 2011 when fiscal consolidation and concerns over the spreading debt crisis dominated the calendar of the people interviewed. The focus was therefore likely on stability free riding and not growth free riding. Yet the interview material is remarkably consistent across the interview years (2011–17). To corroborate the absence of growth free riding accusations in interviews, I systematically reviewed newspapers and official EU and domestic government documents of that period and also found no accusations of free riding leveled against countries with limited fiscal space.
10. Almost 10,000 miles south-east of Berlin, the Australian President Kevin Rudd framed his government's stimulus plan as '[saving] capitalism from itself'—during the Great Recession, the appetite for state intervention went global.

6

Discretion Rather Than Rules

6.1 Rules and Rulers

In pre-modern times public finances were largely left to the decisions of autocratic rulers, often spending vast amounts of resources on personal pleasures and pompous palaces. Rulers were not bound by rules. Fiscal policy-making in modern times seeks to break away from the discretionary mode of the past. Fiscal rules have become a ubiquitous check on government in the vast majority of developed, emerging markets and increasing developed economies. They are meant to limit fiscal discretion. In so doing, they put a 'permanent constraint on fiscal policy, typically defined in terms of an indicator of overall fiscal performance' (Kopits and Symansky 1998: 2). Without them, so the underlying argument goes, myopic governments would succumb to the sirens of voter-pleasing and unsustainable deficit spending. Fiscal rules thus bind government to the mast of fiscal responsibility. For Olson, rules are part of a political system's law and order; they are 'requisites of all organized economic activity' (1965: 89). Rules would make collective action possible where self-interested rationality would otherwise lead to free riding.

The deficit and debt biases of public finances, so I argued in Chapter 4, are more pronounced in times of crisis. This has implications for group-oriented policy actions in the context of stimulus spending. With diversity (in terms of political landscape and economic profile), group latency of the EU as a whole increases. Yet, as Chapter 5 demonstrated, despite a high degree of latency, stability and growth free riding was kept at bay. Instead of engaging in beggar-thy-neighbor policies, member states stimulated their economies by and large in line with their fiscal space. If the system worked, how so, and at what costs? Mancur Olson's work (1965: 51) identifies the solution to successful collective actions for latent groups in the provision of separate and selective incentives. As George Varughese and Elinor Ostrom (2001: 762) put it, heterogeneities 'do not have a determinant impact on the likelihood or success of collective action' since groups can overcome 'stressful heterogeneities by crafting innovative institutional arrangements well matched to their local circumstances'. Was the EU's institutional body equipped with such 'innovative' arrangements to curb free riding?

This chapter will scrutinize the impact of fiscal rules on fiscal outcomes, distinguishing between domestic fiscal rules and fiscal policy agreements found in the European Economic Recovery Plan (EERP)[1] as well as the Stability and Growth Pact (SGP) at the European level. These three types of rules related to member states' fiscal crisis responses in that they sought to offer 'prescriptions about what behaviors... are required, prohibited, or permitted' (Ostrom 1986: 5). Most domestic fiscal rules are designed to restrict policy-makers in order to achieve fiscal sustainability. Their main aim is therefore to mitigate the deficit and debt bias of contemporary public finances. The three types of rules analyzed in this chapter both complement and challenge one another. Notably, the EERP explicitly encourages stimulus spending and may even be seen as a counterweight to the existing budgetary framework under the SGP and at the domestic level. Domestic fiscal rules and the SGP both rely solely on the threat of punishment as incentive, without rewards for compliance. The EERP is not even equipped with the (empty) threat of punishment—it is a non-legally binding entente over the conduct of fiscal policy in times of crisis. Yet non-compliance with its letter and spirit may trigger scorn from fellow member states, in that it is akin to the 'reputational costs' associated with breaching the SGP.

This chapter proceeds as follows: First, in section 6.2, the role of domestic budget rules in steering fiscal stimulus programs is tested. Given numerous crisis-driven reforms, the endogeneity of fiscal rules and their implications for statistical estimations are considered in detail. Section 6.3 discusses the roles of the EERP and SGP. I show that both types of rules have made no impact on fiscal policy outcomes. In the light of this finding, I explore both the Commission and member states' roles in the creation of the EERP and the survival of the SGP.

6.2 Rules in Crisis

What happens to rules in times of crisis, when 'exceptional times' are thought to warrant 'exceptional measures', as the statement of the then Commission President Barroso suggests? James Poterba considers the study of fiscal policy choices in times of crisis to be particularly interesting. According to him, fiscal crises provide 'a unique opportunity for studying how fiscal institutions and political factors affect fiscal decision-making' (1995: 1). He reasons that if fiscal rules constrain the flexibility of political actors, then states with and without these rules should respond differently to fiscal crises. Did fiscal rules matter for

Table 6.1. Selected summary statistics

Variable	Observations	Mean	Std. Dev.	Min.	Max.
Rule	81	0.455	0.967	−1.12	2.46

Note: Based on cross-sectional data available for all twenty-seven EU countries over the 2008–10 period.

fiscal policy during the Great Recession, and if so, how? Ex ante, there is reason to believe that fiscal policy coordination can be more successful in times of crisis. First, the call for group-oriented behavior found within the EERP, which is to stimulate within country-specific fiscal space, is likely to be more popular than the restraint advocated by the SGP. Second, the exceptionality provisions of existing fiscal rules should be accommodating of crisis policies and facilitate the coordination of fiscal expansion. What is more, domestic fiscal rules are unlikely to pose a strong constraint on public finances in hard times. As this chapter will discuss, fiscal rules have more functions than curtailing deficit and debt levels. There are more ways for rules 'to matter'. In the case of the EERP, this role points to the Commission's crisis management and its attempt to salvage the SGP. Along similar lines, the debt brakes of the Fiscal Compact are in the short term primarily addressed at bond markets and EU electorates wary of providing financial assistance to confederates.

Analyzing the role of domestic fiscal rules, I employ the fiscal rules index developed by the European Commission (for summary statistics, see Table 6.1). Commission services have compiled a dataset on domestic fiscal rules in force, based on questionnaires sent to EU member states. These surveys request information on the description and definition of the fiscal rule, its coverage, its statutory base, monitoring and enforcement mechanisms, as well as experience applying the rule. Based on the Fiscal Rule Strength Index (FRSI) for each rule, the Commission constructed a time-varying fiscal rule index for each member state by summing up all FRSIs in force in the respective member state weighted by the coverage of general government finances of the respective rule.

6.2.1 *The Endogeneity of Fiscal Rules*

Empirically modeling the impact of fiscal rules on public finances throws up the challenge of endogeneity. The endogeneity of budget institutions is well established in the literature. Fiscal outcomes and budget institutions may both respond to other unobserved variables such as a country's alleged 'Stability Culture' (Howarth and Rommerskirchen 2013, 2017) or voters' preferences in addition to the political environment. If voters have a preference for conservative fiscal policy, they would be in favor of both low deficit and debt levels as well as tight fiscal rules (Poterba 1996). The omitted variable of voters' preferences may then play a role in explaining fiscal discipline. However, it is exceedingly difficult to accurately measure voters' tastes for fiscal outcomes. The use of government party affiliation may be considered a satisfactory, albeit crude, proxy (Holtz-Eakin et al. 1988; Poterba 1995). Including the left–right placement of the executive in the estimation model (variable LEFT) therefore provides a useful control variable. Furthermore, various studies have considered that budgetary institutions can be treated as exogenous variables uncorrelated with social preferences (e.g. von Hagen and Harden 1995).

A second potential source of endogeneity stems from the likelihood that fiscal policy outcomes impact on fiscal institutions and not the other way around, raising concerns about simultaneity. Political institutions are artifacts, not natural phenomena. Therefore, so goes the argument, they can be modified and reconstructed. In several European countries, budget rules emerge as a result of previous fiscal outcomes. Furthermore, although the causal link runs primarily from political economy factors to fiscal policy, it may be the case that fiscal policy choices also influence political and institutional variables (Lavigne 2011). The same logic can be applied to the causality of discretionary fiscal policy and the change of fiscal rules. Mark Hallerberg et al. (2009) emphasize that budgetary institutions are relatively costly to change and are stable over at least the short to medium term, as fiscal performance cannot quickly feed back into altering institutions (see also Debrun et al. 2008). Nevertheless, in their analysis on fiscal governance in EU countries from 1985 to 2004, the authors (2009: ch. 5) also show that countries with histories of fiscal crises have adopted more robust fiscal institutions. Through fiscal crises, the electorate is said to learn the potentially disastrous consequences of having weak fiscal institutions in place. Fiscal crises are, however, neither necessary nor sufficient for institutional reform. Fiscal problems in Italy in the late 1970s and 1980s did not lead to meaningful reform because of limited competition amongst parties (Hallerberg 2004). The fiscal crisis in Sweden in the 1990s did not automatically cause institutional reform, but instead contributed to a general climate for reform (Molander 2000).

The notion of institutional inertia is unconvincing in light of reforms of fiscal rules in the aftermath of the financial crisis. There are many instances during and after the Great Recession where fiscal policy outcomes and institutional reform were clearly interdependent. Consider the introduction of a debt brake in Germany. The resulting cyclically adjusted debt brake envisages a 0.35 percent of GDP limit for federal government borrowing in normal times from 2016 onwards, with a transition period starting in 2011, and the (regional) Länder budgets are to be structurally balanced as of 2020.

To tame his rebellious Social Democrat (SPD) coalition partner, Volker Kauder, when Chairman of the Christian Democratic Union (CDU) parliamentary group, followed the tested logic of package deals and threatened to vote against the second stimulus package if the debt brake was not introduced (*FAZ*, February 1, 2009). Conversely, members of parliament (particularly SPD parliamentarians) who were in favor of a second stimulus package made their approval of the debt brake conditional on the passage of new discretionary measures (interview, March 2011). More debt and more rules, so the German case shows, went paradoxically hand in hand. Consider further the fiscal rule changes enshrined in the 2011 reforms, which were driven by the escalating Eurozone debt crisis. The Austrian government, to cite just one example among many, endorsed a national debt brake, with Josef Pröll, then Austria's finance minister, arguing that 'considering the high indebtedness in Europe, [the Austrian government is] in favor of a *Schuldenbremse*' (*Die Welt*, May 4, 2010). Not only did negotiations on debt brakes and similar measures feature heavily in the political discourse of European crisis leaders, but there is also evidence that the majority of member states have, at least on paper, improved their budgetary institutions. According to information provided in the 2009–10 Stability and Convergence Program, twenty-one EU member states have implemented and/or plan to implement changes in their respective systems of fiscal governance (Ayuso-i-Casals 2010). The European Commission's FRSI indicates a jump from an average of 0.29 in 2009 to 1.7 in 2014. The phenomenon of fiscal governance reform is not restricted to EU member states, as a survey of the adoption of new fiscal rules in response to the economic and financial crisis shows (Schaechter et al. 2012). Whereas in 1990, only five countries (Germany, Indonesia, Japan, Luxembourg, and the United States) had fiscal rules in place that covered at least the central government level, the number of countries with national and/or supranational fiscal rules surged to seventy-six by the end of March 2012 (ibid.; see also Schick 2009: 12).

How then to address the issue of endogeneity? A standard strategy is to instrument the variable, for example with previous levels of its score (Hallerberg 2004). I instrument fiscal rules with lagged values and test for weak instruments; the Kleibergen-Paap rk F-statistic indicated that weak instruments need not be considered a problem for all estimations. The Kleibergen-Paap rk LM-statistic for overall identification allows for strong rejection of the null hypothesis that the equation is under-identified. In brief, the results suggest the model used is reliable. I then proceed to test for endogeneity in the instrumented variable, with results suggesting that *statistically* endogeneity is not a problem in this analysis (see Table A4.1 in Appendix 4). I therefore rely on the original, non-instrumented measure of fiscal rules.

6.2.2 *The Home Story*

The model used to examine the impact of fiscal rules during the Great Recession is as follows:

$$\begin{aligned}\Delta\,\text{fiscal outcome} = {} & \alpha + \beta_1 \text{L.GDP}_{\,i,t} + \beta_2 \text{L.debt}_{\,i,t} + \beta_3 \text{L.AS}_{\,i,t} + \beta_4 \text{Election}_{i,t} \\ & + \beta_5 \text{Government}_{\,i,t} + \beta_6 \text{Opposition}_{\,i,t} + \beta_7 \text{Left}_{\,i,t} \\ & + \beta_8 \text{RULE}_{i,t} + \beta_9 \text{Dummies}_{i,t} + \epsilon_{i,t}\end{aligned}$$

The estimation techniques are identical to those in Chapters 1–5 (time-series estimation with standard errors corrected for groupwise heteroskedasticity and contemporaneous correlation across countries of the error terms corrected with panel-corrected standard errors). The significance and size of the other variables' coefficients are largely in line with the results presented in Chapters 4 and 5. The inclusion of the additional control does not alter the results. Turning to the question of whether fiscal rules mattered in times of crisis, the answer is no. The coefficient for the fiscal rules index (*Rule*) is not significant in any of the model specifications, as shown in Table 6.2. How then can we explain the insignificance of domestic fiscal rules in times of crisis?

Table 6.2. The impact of fiscal rules, 2008–10

	Δ PSB	Δ SB	Δ BB	Δ PB
Rule	**−0.245**	**−0.235**	**−0.140**	**0.009**
	(0.222)	**(0.215)**	**(0.244)**	**(0.306)**
L. Δ GDP	−1.085***	−1.072***	−0.719***	−1.161***
	(0.180)	(0.179)	(0.184)	(0.249)
L. Debt	0.183***	0.168***	0.169***	0.396***
	(0.038)	(0.037)	(0.038)	(0.048)
Bailout	1.036***	1.046***	0.932***	0.047
	(0.061)	(0.057)	(0.066)	(0.109)
L.AS	2.808***	2.727***	1.625***	3.327***
	(0.442)	(0.432)	(0.455)	(0.643)
Government	−17.833**	−19.355***	−19.177***	−31.450***
	(7.562)	(7.503)	(5.825)	(10.080)
Opposition	14.127**	14.340**	14.390***	20.912**
	(6.746)	(6.612)	(5.437)	(9.288)
Left	3.980***	3.842***	2.841***	5.623***
	(0.967)	(0.957)	(0.735)	(0.972)
Election	−1.208***	−1.135***	−0.728**	−0.657*
	(0.309)	(0.304)	(0.304)	(0.390)
Constant	−14.171***	−12.387***	−13.167***	−31.056***
	(3.967)	(3.887)	(3.882)	(4.919)
N	81	81	81	81
R2	0.907	0.913	0.916	0.930

Note: Standard errors are corrected for groupwise heteroskedasticity and contemporaneous correlation across countries of the error terms are corrected with panel-corrected standard errors. * Significant at the 5% level; ** at the 1% level; *** at the 0.1% level. Standard errors listed below coefficients. Time and unit dummies not shown to preserve space.

One explanation for the insignificant coefficient of the fiscal rules index takes into account the exceptionality provisions/escape clauses of existing fiscal rules. 'While the budgetary institutions and political climate in a state may be determined by the same factors that influence the long-run choice of spending level', says James Poterba (1996: 2), 'these factors may have less impact on the way states respond to fiscal stress'. Instead of facilitating coordination, rules become meaningless. The role of escape clauses in macroeconomic policy is to enable policy-makers to reap the advantages of following a rule on average, while still retaining some flexibility in defining policies in response to exceptional circumstances (Drazen 2000a: 127). The trade-off between flexibility and commitment poses the challenge of identifying the optimal level of commitment in a stochastic world. Fiscal rules are inherently arbitrary and non-contingent. Indeed, the 3 percent deficit threshold of the SGP has frequently been under attack for being 'plucked out of the air' (Arestis et al. 2001: 123). According to Martin Larch and his colleagues from the European Commission (2010a: 23), not only the credibility but also the sustainability of a rule-based system hinge on the existence of escape clauses that permit policy-makers to react to especially severe circumstances when compliance with rules is no longer a feasible option. As Jon Elster (2000: 163) highlights, 'tight constitutional self-binding may be incompatible with the flexibility of action required in crises'—a rule-based system should account for various eventualities that are outside the forecast for normal economic and/or political conditions. Otherwise, any political agreement will be forced to catch up with realities and its credibility and sustainability will be undermined by revisions. With the Macroeconomic Imbalances Procedure (MIP), Commission officials have explicitly not tried 'to write the complete contract' (interview, February 2017).

Even high scores on the fiscal rules index may be relatively meaningless, as rules do not fully apply in times of severe recession. By way of example, the German debt brake, a self-proclaimed stern rule to be emulated across Europe (Merkel 2010), allows for exceptions in the event of natural catastrophes and emergencies that are beyond the government's control. It is worth noting that the debt brake, although styled as a rule to save Europe's fiscal malaise by German officials, is in its origins an inwards-looking, domestic project designed to tie deficit-prone Bundesländer to the mast of fiscal sustainability (Howarth and Rommerskirchen 2013). Likewise, the Swedish debt brake is flexible; it allows room for counter-cyclical policy since the government can, if needed, run a structural deficit during a downturn provided it is offset by a correspondingly greater surplus during the next expansion (Fischer 2005). However, the absence of exceptionality clauses does not necessarily mean that policy-makers are bound to the (too) restrictive fiscal rules of sunnier days. In the UK, for example, existing rules—a golden rule and a debt ceiling—were not equipped with an exceptionality clause similar to the German or Swedish one. As a result, existing British fiscal rules under the Code for Fiscal Stability have been put on hold during the economic crisis. Alistair Darling, then Chancellor of the Exchequer, defended this decision, saying that 'to apply these rules rigidly in today's changed conditions would be perverse' (*The Economist*, October 30, 2008). In its November 2008 Pre-Budget Report the UK government announced a temporary departure from its rules until 2015/16 and the implementation of a new temporary operating rule which requires the government 'to improve the cyclically-adjusted current budget each year, once the economy emerges from the downturn, so it reaches balance and debt is falling as a proportion of GDP once the global shocks have worked their way through the economy in full' (HM Treasury 2008: 4). The suspension of existing rules is reflected in the *largest drop* in the fiscal rules index since records began in 1990 for all twenty-seven EU member states (from a score of 2.06 in 2008 to −1.02 in 2009). In a similar vein, the Finnish and Slovak governments announced suspensions of budget rules during the crisis. This is a broader trend—in many Organisation of Economic Co-operation and Development (OECD) countries 'fiscal rules have been vitiated, at least temporarily, by the global economic crisis' (Schick 2009: 3). The exceptionality provisions of fiscal rules are considered in the Commission's questionnaires, which have 'exclusions from the coverage of the rule' as one criterion. Yet the random weighting of the rule does not change if escape is sought; that is to say, when the exceptionality clause applies. Crisis budgeting is 'inherently improvisational' (2009: 9). This means that '[r]ules and procedures are devised to accommodate the needs of the moment, and frequent adjustments are made along the way. Ad hockery is necessary because established procedures get in the way of dealing with the crisis, and new players are brought into the process' (ibid.). It may well be that the FRSI employed in the empirical analysis does not accurately reflect either the 'ad hockery' of crisis budgeting or the variation of existing escape clauses.

6.2.3 *EU-Level Rules*

The EERP, discussed in Chapter 2, represents a considerable shift for fiscal policy coordination in the EU. Particularly, this crisis agreement breaks away from former commitments to fiscal constraints and encourages stimulus spending across EU member states to combat the worst financial crisis since the 1920s. I empirically test the impact of this agreement alongside the SGP by augmenting the sample size and including six OECD countries in the main model. The control group consists of Switzerland, Norway, Japan, Canada, Iceland, and the United States.[2] This inclusion makes it possible to ask whether countries that signed up to the EERP and are, at least on paper, still subject to the SGP adopted identifiably distinctive response strategies to the financial and economic crisis. Are EU countries any different? Specifically, the variable *EU* takes the value 1 for all EU countries in the 2008–10 period and 0 for the six non-EU OECD countries. Controlling for the economic climate and political landscape, one would expect that EU member states would adopt larger stimulus programs than their non-EU counterparts, being spurred on by the creation of the EERP and the flexible implementation of the SGP. Two related caveats apply. The first is that the *EU* variable is a crude, binary measure of any incentives stemming from this elliptical commitment. It could just as well measure EU membership per se or the underlying attitudes to government intervention, which may be different from Japan or the United States. Put simply, the variable is likely to capture much more than the EERP and the crisis-mode of the SGP. However, in the absence of more sophisticated measurements, this empirical strategy is well established in the existing literature on the determinants of fiscal outcomes. Most studies on the effect of Economic and Monetary Union (EMU) membership rely on similar dummies to capture the impact of various EU agreements (e.g. Freitag and Sciarini 2001; Busemeyer 2004).

A further caveat concerns the direction of causality; did the EERP impact public finances or did public finances determine the content of the EERP? Did the explicit flexibility of the SGP cause fiscal outcomes, or did the fiscal positions of member states lead to a system of greater flexibility? The majority of member states announced their own national stimulus programs *prior* to the launch of the EERP. Spain was the first country to implement stimulus policies in line with election promises in spring 2008 and announced new stimulus measures on October 26. Germany announced its first stimulus package (*Konjunkturpaket* 1) three days later. The Chancellor of the Exchequer set out the UK's anti-recession plan on November 14 and the Italian government unveiled an €80bn fiscal package on November 18. Instead of forging an EU-wide coordinated economic stimulus, governments did not wait for the 'green light from Brussels' (interview, April 2011) to simultaneously announce *independently designed* national fiscal policies in winter 2008–9. This raised concerns from former Eurogroup chair Jean-Claude Juncker, who called for better European economic coordination, worrying that 'Member State after Member State is arranging its own plans and programmes' (*Euractiv*, February 10, 2009). Perhaps the relationship between the EERP and fiscal outcomes should best be modeled as bi-directional? In light of the large potential coverage of the EERP, multi-causality should not be much of a problem. After all, the dummy also provides a measurement of EU membership per se, which has (at least so far) not been changed by the scope and design of stimulus programs.

6.2.3.1 EMPIRICAL RESULTS

The inclusion of the six non-EU OECD member states results in a slight change in model specification. Because of data availability and different accounting standards from governmental agencies, the costs of the financial sector bailout as well as the size of automatic stabilization are no longer included. The model used is as follows:

$$\begin{aligned}\Delta \text{ fiscal outcome } &= \alpha + \beta_1 \text{L.GDP}_{\text{i,t}} + \beta_2 \text{L.debt}_{\text{i,t}} + \beta_3 \text{EU}_{\text{i,t}} \\ &+ \beta_4 \text{Election}_{\text{i,t}} + \beta_5 \text{Government}_{\text{i,t}} + \beta_6 \text{Opposition}_{\text{i,t}} \\ &+ \beta_7 \text{Left}_{\text{i,t}} + \beta_8 \text{Dummies}_{\text{i,t}} + \epsilon_{\text{i,t}}\end{aligned}$$

Table 6.3 presents results for the change in the structural balance (Δ SB) and budget balance (Δ BB) only, to conserve space. Including these six countries does alter the findings on the determinants of fiscal policy outcomes during the Great Recession. One change to highlight here, as it is the only consistent one across models, is that elections no longer seem to drive public finances in this broader sample. The variable *EU* is not significant in any of the model specifications. To nuance the investigation, I also included a dummy for Eurozone membership first in the EU sample and second in the sample of EU and non-EU countries. This is thought to capture the fact that the pressures for fiscal policy coordination are potentially greater for Eurozone member states

Table 6.3. The impact of EU and Eurozone membership on fiscal policy outcomes

	Δ SB	Δ BB	Δ SB	Δ BB
EU			**−5.086**	**−2.945**
			(4.638)	**(1.822)**
Eurozone	**−2.036**	**−1.494**		
	(1.766)	**(1.257)**		
L. Δ GDP	−0.174***	−0.178**	−0.178***	−0.181**
	(0.059)	(0.082)	(0.061)	(0.080)
L.Debt	0.018	0.044***	0.026	0.047***
	(0.026)	(0.010)	(0.023)	(0.011)
Government	−12.852	−23.469***	−22.705	−27.840***
	(10.537)	(5.801)	(14.000)	(7.418)
Opposition	6.884	14.500***	12.985	17.172***
	(8.025)	(4.663)	(9.252)	(5.292)
Left	2.475	4.409***	2.916	4.538***
	(2.830)	(1.191)	(2.460)	(1.202)
Election	−0.738	−0.835	−0.634	−0.779
	(0.639)	(0.557)	(0.616)	(0.549)
Constant	1.044	−0.767	3.838	0.596
	(3.096)	(1.366)	(5.784)	(1.938)
N	93	93	93	93
R2	0.495	0.813	0.502	0.814

Note: Standard errors are corrected for groupwise heteroskedasticity and contemporaneous correlation across countries of the error terms are corrected with panel-corrected standard errors. * Significant at the 5% level; ** at the 1% level; *** at the 0.1% level. Standard errors listed below coefficients. Time and unit dummies not shown to preserve space.

than for Eurozone outsiders. Interdependence is higher between Eurozone countries because of the common currency. Again, the variable is not significant in any of the specifications. These findings suggest that the EU's fiscal agreements, whether under the EERP or the SGP, did not influence fiscal outcomes during the Great Recession. Instead, stimulus spending as a response to the economic downturn seems to have been a default option for developed and emerging market economies (te Velde 2011).

In embracing expansive fiscal policies, the EU was hardly exceptional. China sought to escape the Great Recession with a 4 trillion renminbi stimulus package launched in late 2008; that is, US-$586 billion or 12.5 percent of GDP. The International Monetary Fund (IMF), previously skeptical about the usefulness of fiscal policy in times of crisis, came to endorse 'a wider array of fiscal tools for a broader spectrum of countries' (Ban 2015: 168). At the global level, during the G20 inaugural Washington summit, country leaders pledged to 'use fiscal measures to stimulate domestic demand to rapid effect' (*Financial Times*, April 1, 2008). The majority of G20 countries declared their intention to introduce a fiscal stimulus plan prior to the Washington summit; the commitment for coordination is hence only one ex post facto. What G20 leaders sold as an unprecedented entente on macroeconomic crisis management was little more than the concomitance of recession responses. Similarly, just because EU member states predominantly resorted to an increase in public expenditure to combat recession does not mean these policy choices were driven by EU-level incentives. This echoes the challenges of the claim that the Maastricht treaty brought about a period of fiscal consolidation by member states eager to comply with the entry criteria for monetary union. There is evidence that government spending adjustment in the 1990s should be 'characterized as an OECD phenomenon rather than as a phenomenon specific to countries participating in the Maastricht Treaty or the Stability and Growth Pact' (Hercowitz and Strawczynski 2005: 82). Fiscal policy in the EU, despite unique efforts to coordinate outcomes, is not unique after all—in good times or bad. It is highly unlikely that the EU somehow 'made' states engage in or refrain from stimulus spending (cf. Hallerberg 2004: 8).

Martin Heipertz and Amy Verdun (2010: 189) characterize the overall approach to fiscal policy coordination during the Great Recession as 'one of pronounced national action and limited European coordination, the communication of which bordered on the meaningless'. Evaluating the impact of the EERP, virtually all Commission officials interviewed described it as an acknowledgment of member states' unilateral crisis policies; a 'salmagundi of national plans' (April 2011) amounting to 'what member states were comfortable doing anyway' (May 2011), which 'merely stated the existing state of play' (March 2011) and 'rubber-stamped the policy initiatives that member states had already in their pipelines' (April 2011)—in Robert Keohane's terminology

(1992: 176), this hardly represented an 'inconvenient commitment'. As a senior Irish civil servant suggests, pre-crisis, EU constraints were only invoked 'when actually the contents of policy are what we [the Irish government] would do anyway' (quoted in Hay et al. 2008: 189).

6.3 Appealing Exception

The creation of the EERP, in parallel to the survival of the SGP, then poses a puzzle. First, why was the SGP applied given the weak compliance rates and resistance toward the usage of Excessive Deficit Procedures (EDPs) in the past? Second, why did the Commission endorse fiscal stimulus programs, which were in violation of a strict reading of existing rules? 'The opening of the Excessive Deficit Procedure became less of a regulatory process than a weak substitute for binding fiscal policy coordination' (Schelkle 2012b: 377). Various interviewees supported this argument; 'for the Commission it was important to give at least a semblance of normality and to go through the motions, no matter whether they would have an impact on public finances or not' (May 2011). The opening of the EDP, triggered by non-compliance with the SGP's 3 percent deficit threshold, is not a sign of the SGP's 'resilience' (Hodson 2010: 232) but, I contest, its inconsequentiality. During the Great Recession deficits were neither small nor temporary, but substantial, and there to stay for the foreseeable future. As a result twenty-four EDPs were opened. In setting and extending the deadline for correcting these excessive deficits, member states gave themselves considerable room for maneuver in the face of 'special circumstances' and 'unexpected adverse economic events' (Article 126(7)). Since the initial (re)opening of the procedure, the already delayed deadlines for correcting an excessive deficit have been further set and frequently revised. For example, the initial deadline for the correction of the excessive deficit in Spain was revised from 2012 to 2014 to 2016 to 2018.

Amidst the overall 'extremely generous' (interview, May 2011) application of the EDP, the case of Greece stands out. After establishing an excessive deficit in April 2009, the Council decided, as of November 2012, to move to the next stage of the EDP procedure, four times giving notice under Article 121(4) and reinforcing fiscal surveillance under Article 126(9). This represents the first time the two provisions have been applied together. Greece was the only country where the 'exceptionality argument' was not accepted; 'the situation in Greece was a crisis on its own and had very little to do with the economic downturn' (interview, April 2011). Therefore 'the Greek public finances have worsened much beyond what could have been expected to result from the downturn and the financial-sector support measures' (European Commission 2010b). The application of the dissuasive arm of the SGP points to the intergovernmental nature of the 'appeal to exception', which relies on the evaluation of the justificatory circumstances taking place in the Council. Given the spreading debt crisis and the mounting evidence of fraudulent statistics, the general reasoning within the Council was 'to come as hard down on the Greek government as possible, without making matters worse' (interview, August 2011)—but make matters worse it did. One element in understanding the botched policy responses to the crisis in Greece is the pervasive feeling of deceit. A grievance I often heard during interviews was a version of 'they [the Greek government] lied to us'. In the national press this feeling has been translated into indignation and outrage, as exemplified by the infamous cover of Germany's *Focus Magazine* from 2010—of the Venus de Milo statue with her middle finger raised. But for policy-makers (at least, this is my interpretation from over fifty interviews in Brussels), the feeling was one of hurtful betrayal more than anger. Former US treasury secretary Timothy Geithner (2015), in his reflections on the financial crisis, recalls the 2010 G-7 finance meeting in a freezing, tiny Canadian outpost just south of the Arctic Circle where his Europeans counterparts 'spent most of the meal complaining about Greek profligacy and mendacity. There were strident calls for austerity and Old Testament justice'. The treatment of Greece is reminiscent of Argentina's experience with the international community, notably as represented by the IMF, in the middle of its sovereign debt crisis in 2001. Argentina became the 'spoiled child of the Washington Consensus' (Birdsall 2002), with market participants and regulators looking the other way at signs of brewing economic troubles. Similarly, the imbalances that fed the Greek crisis, an 'accident waiting to happen' (interview, February 2017), were only made possible by the neglect of investors and policy-maker groups (above all member states in the configuration of the European Council) eager to hold on to the notion of an Hellenic *Wirtschaftswunder* that would support the success story of the Euro.

Prior to 2011, all decisions related to the SGP's preventive and dissuasive arms were subject to unanimous voting. With all but three (Sweden, Estonia, and Luxembourg) EU member states in excessive deficits during the Great Recession, a scenario where sanctions would bite was deemed 'absurd' (interview, May 2011): 'dogs do not eat dog' (interview, May 2011). What is more, the cost of sanctions increased. Not only are sanctions more counter-productive for a country facing a major economic downturn, but the possibility of retaliation also increases these costs for a punishing country likely to breach the SGP. Punishment is an elastic good (Anderson and Putterman 2006). The quantity of punishment demanded is lower with a higher price. In short, the law of demand holds. Following this argument, one would expect the likelihood of sanctions under the EDP to decrease with an increase in cost. Furthermore, empirical research also suggests that the deliberative nature of fiscal policy coordination may precipitate a general environment of non-compliance. The probability of Eurozone member states being sanctioned under the EDP is inversely related to the number of countries that breach the SGP (de Haan et al. 2003). This could trigger herd effects: 'it is hard to imagine that Member States on the verge of breaching the deficit criterion sometime in the not so distant future will take a tough stance with regard to those countries that already have an excessive deficit' (2003: 20).

Member states seemingly respected existing provisions while granting each other full flexibility in breaching the SGP. This is not to suggest that member states did not benefit from the toothless opening of the EDPs as well. The EU-level and domestic tensions surrounding the de facto suspension of the EDP in 2003 have shown that it may be politically more harmful to suspend the rules than it is to open the procedure with generous correction targets. Despite well-documented breaches, appealing for and contesting SGP exceptionality is taken seriously (e.g. Meyer 2004; Puetter 2004: 864). Generally speaking, member states clearly have an interest in signaling credible commitment and ensuring the commitment of other members. The opening of the EDP therefore served as an affirmation of existing rules and policy-makers' commitment to return to 'fiscal prudence' once the storm was weathered. Instead of signaling the irrelevance of the SGP, appealing for exception and stretching the existing escape clause were thought to express a principled commitment to the EU's fiscal rules.

By opting for an application of the SGP whilst specifically allowing for excessive deficit spending encouraged by the EERP, the Commission improved its relationship with member states (interviews, April and May 2011). Larch et al. (2012: 21) assume that if 'the Commission had stubbornly insisted on the strict application of the Pact, including the ban of discretionary fiscal expansions, a severe confrontation with the Member States within the Council would have been very likely'. This echoes David Howarth's (2008: 42) assessment of the 2005 reform which, 'far from undermining the potential for Commission leadership, may increase it by decreasing the potential for member-government-Commission conflict'. The flexible and considered application of old and new rules in the wake of the Great Recession (to which I will return in Chapter 9) shows a Commission at ease with its changing role: that of the good cop.

The 2005 reform, with a more lenient reading of exceptional circumstances, increased the SGP's flexibility. In so doing, the reform legitimized the weak compliance with the SGP ex ante but hardly prepared for the storms ahead. Crucially, the flexibility introduced by the 2005 revision was not the type of flexibility needed to address serious unanticipated events (Larch et al. 2012: 5). First, the waiver provision of the reformed 2005 SGP stipulates that a deficit of more than 3 percent of GDP should not be considered excessive and hence may warrant an exemption of the rules, *if and only if* it stays close to the 3 percent threshold (TEU 126, 2–3). Concretely, the Regulation on speeding up and clarifying the implementation of the EDP (EC Regulation No. 1467/97) specifies that in order to fall under the escape clause, the deficit ratio must *always remain close* to the reference value. Second, an excess over the reference value must be temporary. In order for the excess to be considered temporary, the Commission's budgetary forecast must indicate that the deficit will fall below the reference value following the end of the unusual event or the severe economic downturn. Any deficit above 3 percent that is neither close to the reference value nor temporary should be considered excessive, irrespective of exceptional circumstances. Even though equipped with an escape clause, the SGP is 'too cumbersome and retrospective in its procedures to permit an early and aggressive response to a major slump' (Lane 2012: 568). When the economic crisis spread throughout Europe, the SGP lacked specific provisions for excessive stimulus spending which would lead public finances further away from the criteria of 'temporariness' and 'closeness'.

6.3.1 *Running Behind the Train*

From the very beginning of the Great Recession, it became apparent that the vast majority of member states considered EU rules to be void in extraordinary times.[3] Given the magnitude of the economic and financial crisis, many member states 'did not even see that their stimulus plans were at odds with EU legislation' (interview, April 2011). Francois Fillon, then Prime Minister of France, exemplifies this unawareness with his statement that 'the stability allows [deficit spending] because it foresees that in exceptional circumstances one can go beyond 3 percent' (*Financial Times*, November 4, 2008). The German Chancellor Angela Merkel and the French President Nicolas Sarkozy published a joint letter calling for stimulus programs across the EU, justified by exceptional circumstances as provided for in the SGP (Merkel and Sarkozy 2008). As laid out in the 'temporary and close' clause of the SGP, these readings are not correct. Member states engaged in national crisis exegesis that would essentially construe EU fiscal rules in ways compatible with domestic politics. As Chapter 5 has shown, even a country as vocally fond of rules as Germany is happy to postpone these rules in times of crisis. Comparative political economists working on contemporary Germany have dubbed the co-existence of strong rules and the pragmatic need for exceptions as 'management by exception' (Green and Paterson 2005).

Stimulus packages, according to Angela Merkel and Nicolas Sarkozy, were seen to be 'the responsibility of the national governments' (2008) and should be coordinated in the Council. The role of the Commission in fiscal policy coordination was not mentioned. This initiative speaks of a broader trend of 'executive leadership' in times of crisis. At the European level, interviewees from both the European Commission and the European Parliament (EP) complained about the 'return of intergovernmentalism' (interview, April 2011) and 'executive power grab' (interview, May 2011). In particular, members of the EP claimed to have felt ignored. The EP had no formal say in the adoption of the EERP; MEPs only formally voted on the plan in March 2009, by which point domestic stimulus efforts were well underway. In some member states (amongst them the United Kingdom, the Netherlands, France, Spain, and Germany), governments were in fact already preparing a second round of stimulus programs to follow the adoption of initial packages, before the ink on the EERP had dried.

The Council gave the impetus for the EERP back in October 2008 (Council 14368/08), which had called for the Commission to come up with a European action plan. Interview data with officials both within and outside the Commission suggests that the Commission was subject to political pressure to put forth a crisis framework that would allow for substantial stimulus policies (interview, March 2011; see also *Financial Times*, October 6, 2008). More specifically for the Directorate General of Economic and Financial Affairs (DG Ecfin), these pressures came both from member states and the Barroso cabinet (interview, March 2011). Describing the working relationship, one official of a Permanent Representation in Brussels stressed that 'since leadership of the Commission is staffed after all with ex-politicians from all over Europe, the Commission is very attuned to the needs of national policy makers' (interview, April 2011). Therefore the demands from member states 'did not fall on deaf ears' (ibid.). Barroso was eager to cast the Commission in a leadership role, embracing a new course for fiscal policy in times of crisis. Moreover, the Commission found itself in competition with a very active Council Presidency chaired by Sarkozy (interview, March 2011; Dehousse and Menon 2009) and was acutely aware of the demand for fiscal flexibility as evidenced by the EERP (2008) itself: 'At [difficult times], European governments and institutions need to show flexibility'.

Given these signals and the unilateral announcements of national stimulus plans, the Commission thought that 'it was running behind the train' (interview, April 2011; see also Puetter 2012: 172). With member states deciding unilaterally how to read and apply the SGP in times of exceptional crisis, the Commission saw a need to respond. According to one interviewee, without these national crisis responses, 'we [the Commission] would never have voluntarily recommended any fiscal stimulus [breaching the SGP] at all' (interview, March 2013). The EERP was therefore an attempt to 'get back behind the steering wheel' (interview, April 2011).

6.3.2 *An Unlikely Champion*

After decades of championing low deficits and debt levels, the Commission emerged as an unlikely advocate of stimulus policies throughout the EU, calling for a relaxation of the application of existing rules under the SGP. The embracing of Keynesian deficit spending was not only contested in some member states, but also proved a divisive issue within the European Commission. Members of DG Ecfin (in charge of all things economic governance) in particular 'had huge reservations' (interview, April 2011; Hodson 2012) about the design of the EERP; 'for years and years we [DG Ecfin staff] insist on consolidation and sound public finances and then we should come out and proclaim exactly the opposite?' (interview, April 2011). Another official pointed out that the EERP 'contradicted the philosophy of the Commission diametrically' (interview, May 2011). Martin Larch, from DG Ecfin, and his colleagues worried that the 'forced combination of accepting violations of the Pact on the one hand and insisting on the formal, although more flexible implementation of the EDP, on the other has not strengthened the already battered credibility of the surveillance framework' (Larch et al. 2012: 23). According to one Commission official, advocating fiscal stimulus policies was 'not something we [the Commission] would do lightheartedly, but in the light of the magnitude of the economic and financial crisis it became increasingly clear that we needed decisive state intervention to break the spiral of economic slowdown and job losses' (interview, April 2011). The Commission's policy turn can be seen as part of a broader picture of global crisis responses; in sharp contrast to the policies of the Great Depression where fiscal policy was not used extensively, fiscal policy (in the form of discretionary spending in addition to automatic stabilizers) was a crucial policy instrument of the Great Recession.

In tracing the Commission's fiscal crisis framework, it is helpful to turn to the public statements made by two, in this context key, figures: the Commission President José Manuel Barroso and the then Commissioner for Economic and Monetary Affairs, Joaquín Almunia. Barroso (2008b) was quick to suspend the SGP as early as September 20, arguing that the Commission could not go on with 'business as usual' as 'Europe's economy needs a boost to recover, to continue to grow and to provide employment'. Speaking at the European Parliament Plenary Debate only four days later, Almunia (2008a) still stressed the prescription that 'in budgetary policy, [the member states] must preserve [their] commitment to fiscal discipline and the rules of the Stability and Growth Pact'. Finding an ally in the European Central Bank (ECB), this assessment was echoed by Jean-Claude Trichet, who stressed that 'the Pact should be applied fully' (*Financial Times*, November 6, 2008). A senior ECB official explained the bank's thinking on stimulus spending as follows: 'At the time, we were cautious in saying well, there may be some in a better position fiscally, notably Germany and a couple of others, where we wouldn't necessarily object, but there were others who were in no position to open the purse and lavishly spend all sorts of discretionary spending programs' (cited in Farrell and Quiggin 2012). These evaluations are at odds with the outlook of President Barroso, who, on the occasion of the extraordinary Commission meeting of October 29, again stated that in the application of 'the Stability and Growth Pact, of course, there must be scope for fiscal and budgetary policy to be anti-cyclical in a downturn, to maintain demand and protect jobs' (Barroso 2008c).

With the announcement of the EERP, the view that applying the old rules 'would lead to a vicious recessionary cycle... [as] it would lead to falling purchasing power and falling tax revenues, to rising unemployment and the accompanying human misery, to ever wider budget deficits, ultimately to a risk of social instability' (Barroso 2008a) prevailed over more cautious voices. Throughout his remaining time at DG Ecfin until 2010, Almunia stressed the need to balance fiscal stimulus and fiscal sustainability on numerous occasions. Nevertheless, he publicly accepted that 'monetary policy alone cannot provide the full stimulus needed by the European economy... Realizing this... we proposed an ambitious economic recovery plan that brings together a fiscal stimulus to boost demand in the short term' (Almunia 2009).

Hence, the EERP was above all an institutionally strategic policy choice for the Commission. Crucially, the Commission considers the SGP as 'hard law'; that is, 'legally binding obligations that are precise' (Abbott and Snidal 2000). Based on this understanding, 'the problem was not whether countries actually needed stimulus policies, but that according to the [rules] it was simply not allowed. The EERP was an attempt to make the impossible possible' (interview, May 2011). The creation of the EERP and the survival of the SGP were deliberate political decisions that were taken, above all else, to justify preceding fiscal policy choices. The statistical insignificance of the EERP coefficient, well corroborated by qualitative data, should be viewed in this light.

6.4 Conclusion

This chapter has analyzed the effectiveness of rule-based incentives to motivate group-oriented behavior. Based on the empirical findings, domestic fiscal rules did not impact on the fiscal policy responses to the Great Recession. Similarly, the EU's fiscal agreements did not impact on fiscal policy choices. Yet ultimately, both procedures merely provided some background music; they hardly influenced the dancers. First, the majority of domestic fiscal rules were equipped with exceptionality clauses. Consequently, they neither imposed stern constraints on fiscal policy choices in times of crisis nor were able to facilitate coordination. And even where those escape clauses were not in place, policy-makers—in the mode of executive crisis management—loosened the rules to enable them to mitigate the economic fallout. Empirically, this is problematic for the strength of the Commission's FRSI. A lawful evocation of an escape clause did not show up as a change in the fiscal rules index. However, on the other hand, a suspension of existing rules, as in the case of the UK, did lead to a deterioration in the FRSI. The result in terms of fiscal outcomes may be similar. Put simply, a given score in the fiscal rules index in good economic times is not automatically equivalent to the same score in bad economic times when exceptionality clauses are evoked. To better investigate the impact of fiscal rules in times of crisis, we need an index that takes into account the evocation and scope of exceptionality clauses. The quasi-enforcement of the SGP, I contest, can be explained by its inconsequential nature. Here I disagree with political scientist David Cameron (2012) who claimed that the SGP imposed an important constraint. The SGP's intergovernmental appeals to exception mode meant that member states were able to construe it in ways that suited their domestic stimulus programs, irrespective of the fact that the rules at the time did not allow for substantial stimulus spending. In turn, the Commission put forth the EERP to make EU rules compatible with domestic fiscal policies and keep up the appearance of fiscal policy coordination.

The role of EU rules and agreements in shaping fiscal policy choices has been placed under scrutiny ever since the creation of the SGP; the history of the SGP matters. Accounts of collective action tend to be pessimistic with regards to the possibility of group-oriented behavior in the case of anonymous and infrequent interactions. The coordination of fiscal stimulus policies should be seen against a backdrop of a patchy first decade for fiscal policy coordination in the EU, which imparted the impression that agreements on fiscal matters were not binding. The choice of 'right' fiscal policies remains contested among EU member states and ultimately they responded to the crisis in a way that 'suited governments' (interview, April 2011), but which had 'nothing' (interview, April 2011) or 'very little' (interview, August 2011) to do with EU agreements. The vague commitments under the EERP and the generous implementation of the SGP further speak to the reluctance of sovereign policy-makers to coordinate fiscal policy in times of crisis. There is little evidence for 'a significant modification of national policies in recognition of international economic interdependence' (Wallich 1984: 85). Fiscal policy coordination in the EU is propped up by rules. Weak enforcement has plagued EU and domestic fiscal rules since their inception. And yet, EU fiscal policy coordination does not take place in an incentive-free environment. As Chapter 7 will demonstrate, unable and unwilling to sanction public finances amongst themselves, EU member states have willingly adopted an outsourcing strategy to deal with the so-called second-order free riding problem: how to motivate group members to contribute to the punishment of free riders.

Notes

1. The EERP barely qualifies as fiscal rule. For the sake of simplicity, the term is nevertheless used when grouping domestic fiscal rules, the EERP, and the SGP together.
2. These countries were selected based on their status as advanced economies and data availability from Ameco. Related summary statistics can be found in Table A6.1 in Appendix 4.
3. This was not only true for the fiscal rules but also more broadly for state aid law. Mirroring the unilateral design and implementation of the first stimulus spending in autumn 2008, the Commission felt ignored with respect to competition policy. Silvio Berlusconi, for instance, announced delightedly that 'State aid, which until yesterday was considered a sin, is now absolutely essential' (*Financial Times*, November 21, 2008). Undertaking the quick approval of state aid was not guided by the question of whether member states 'are throwing money out of their windows or whether a particular measure could have done more effectively, but solely whether or not this measure would have a distortional effect on the internal market' (interview, April 2011). In approving state aid, DG competition was not concerned with guiding fiscal policy or limiting wasteful public spending (interview, March 2011). Given that the Commission feared that the Council might decide to put state aid regulation on hold for the duration of the financial crisis, there was a palpable incentive within the Commission to act quickly and present a flexible framework (author interview, March 2011; see also *Reuters*, December 4, 2008). In so doing the Commission was conscious of not putting too many restrictions on the temporary crisis framework, out of fear that 'member states would not listen to it in the first place' (interview, March 2011).

7

Market Discipline

7.1 Meet the Bond Gods

The set of post-Great Recession consolidation policies, now labeled 'austerity', are frequently presented as a necessary evil to restore market confidence. Paul Krugman (2010) compared this strategy to 'the policy elite . . . acting like the priests of some ancient cult, demanding that we engage in human sacrifices to appease the anger of invisible gods'. The notion that policy-makers react to developments in the financial markets by offering their pound of flesh, notably via fiscal retrenchment, is widely accepted. Both the former UK Prime Minister David Cameron (2013) and the former French President Nicolas Sarkozy (cited in Debrun and Kinda 2016) have presented their budgetary consolidation plans in light of financial market pressure. Twenty years earlier, Bob Rubin, then Director of the National Economic Council, successfully lobbied US President Clinton to balance the books with a view of 'best not offend the Bond Gods' (Parenteau 2005: 140). 'In a world of globalized finance', so the underlying assumption goes, 'bond markets can discipline politicians just as effectively as an opposition party can, or even more so' (Johnson and Barnes 2015: 21). The power that the modern-day bond market has over sovereign states stands in stark contrast to its humble origins, where it was originally established to carve out a stable income for widows and orphans in the early nineteenth century.

This chapter will put the alleged power of so-called 'bond market vigilantes' to the test. Did market pressure keep government finances on the straight and narrow? What happens to market discipline in hard times? And what effect did Eurozone membership have? In answering these questions, I will scrutinize the potential of market discipline to act as an incentive toward collective action and its capacity to rein in free riding. In contrast to budgetary rules and the European Economic Recovery Plan (EERP) discussed in Chapters 1–6, market discipline offers both negative and positive incentives via a change in borrowing costs. Ideally, 'good' policies are rewarded and 'bad' policies punished. There is evidence that this diversification of incentives may increase government responsiveness. More importantly, I contest, market discipline is not subject to the so-called second-order free riding problem. Market discipline is provided from outwith the collective action group. Bond investors do not punish governments to prompt budgetary consolidation; market punishment is instead a by-product of risk pricing. Yet, as this chapter foregrounds, the outsourcing of incentive provisioning has profound and troubling implications, particularly for Eurozone member states.

7.1.1 *Bond Vigilantes and Deficit Cheerleaders*

It would be simplistic to characterize bond investors' attitude toward government debt as 'the lower, the better'. Debt burdens and economic growth both matter for debt sustainability and therefore have an impact on sovereign risk. There is evidence that investors take a more nuanced approach to issues surrounding stimulus programs and fiscal consolidation. Echoing the debate about the multipliers of retrenchment—that is, the question of whether fiscal belt-tightening can be growth-friendly—Joachim Fels (2015), global economic advisor at Pimco, the largest fixed-income investment fund in the world, chastised 'the erroneous belief that austerity would lift confidence and thus be expansionary'. In the words of a senior fixed-income manager, 'the dose makes the poison' (interview, February 2017). Some commentators even proclaimed the arrival of 'bond market deficit cheerleaders' (Collender 2010), urging the US government to increase its stimulus. Similarly, the view that 'saving-to-death did only bring more problems' is widespread (interview with German fixed-income manager, March 2015). Iain McMenamin, Michael Breen, and Juan Muñoz-Portillo (2015) demonstrate a broader distaste for austere budgets by bond investors. In their empirical analysis of announced Eurozone budgets between 1987 and 2012, the authors show that fiscal consolidation is associated with substantial interest rate increases. Austerity can harm sovereign risk (at least in the short term). As the former International Monetary Fund (IMF) Chief Economist Oliver Blanchard (2012) put it, 'financial investors are schizophrenic about fiscal consolidation and growth. They react positively to news of fiscal consolidation, but then react negatively later, when consolidation leads to lower growth'. Already prior to the Great Recession, investors were at times looking favorably at fiscal expansions. Paul McCulley (2001), then Managing Director at Pimco, came out in favor of fiscal stimulus in the wake of the 9/11 attacks, confessing that, 'Yes, I'm an unrepentant Keynesian'. When EU officials met with Pimco managers amidst the European Debt Crisis and asked what would sway their investment decisions, the answer was 'stability and growth' (interview, April 2014). Bond investors' preferences are attuned to the dichotomy of EU free riding. Both are essentially for the perceived creditworthiness of a sovereign. Public debt becomes riskier during periods of economic slowdown (Alesina et al. 1992). Bondholders are thus not automatically opposed to expansionary monetary or fiscal policies. A recent example of investors voicing support of stimulus spending took place in the wake of Brexit in May 2016. Bridgewater Associates, one of the world's largest hedge funds, has given the Bank of England's (BoE's) new stimulus package the nod of approval in a note circulated to clients; actions were 'appropriately aggressive' in trying to tackle the brewing storm facing the British economy.

In short, market participants may come out in favor of stimulus policies. This suggests a further motivation for the creation of the EERP. Layna Mosley (2000: 752) presents the use of the Maastricht convergence criteria as a case where governments influenced financial market behavior (cf. Schuknecht 2004: 19): by setting the deficit ceiling at 3 percent, policy-makers established the very criteria by which they were later judged (see also Kelemen and Teo 2014). So far the EERP has only been considered as an internal signaling device; important for conveying to other member states the need for stimulus policies and for creating a system of fiscal rules that was compatible with the economic fallout of the Great Recession. Yet, is it possible that the EERP was in part created to provide a 'judging yardstick' similar to that of the Maastricht criteria? Whereas interviewees pointed repeatedly and unprompted to the role of financial market participants in curbing government spending during the financial and economic crisis, one Commission official linked market discipline explicitly to the creation of the EERP: 'in times of crisis when there is big uncertainty on parts of the market and lack of information, having something like the EERP... played a positive role' (interview, March 2011). In a similar vein, consolidation policies are frequently portrayed as the sacrifice to appease angry bond gods. A Commission official defended the perceived need for fiscal consolidation as follows: 'but to put ourselves back in time, I don't think the markets were prepared to accept only small efforts' (interview, February 2015).

7.2 Market Discipline

The literature on market discipline considers, on the one hand, market signals as a response to fiscal policy changes, and on the other, governments' responsiveness to these signals. Further complicating the relationship between market punishment and government responsiveness is the fact that borrowers may anticipate an increase in borrowing costs and adjust policies accordingly. This anticipatory mechanism does appear to be at work, for example, in the UK's fiscal consolidation post-2010, despite low borrowing costs (Corsetti 2012); a strategy of pre-emptive obedience that has been vocally criticized by Martin Wolf, amongst others (*Financial Times*, May 27, 2010), who cautioned against 'giving the markets what we think they may want in future—even though they show little sign of insisting on it now'. The majority of empirical studies point to a significant reaction of market punishment to 'excessive' fiscal policy (Bernoth et al. 2004; Dewachter and Toffano 2012; Maltritz 2012). Here 'excessive' public finances are modeled as a determinant of a country's borrowing conditions (i.e. the market's risk pricing). This evidence is in line with a hypersensitive 'electronic herd' (Friedman 2000) of investors storming in or out of countries at the sign of policies they approve or abhor. Wolfgang Schäuble (2011b), the German Finance Minister presiding over the European Debt Crisis, urged fellow member states to consolidate public finances, arguing that '[markets] want to see action. Enough with words'. Yet despite a broad debate on government responsiveness to market pressure, empirical evidence as to its existence and its shape is comparatively scarce (see Chapter 2). This chapter considers market discipline as a collective action incentive in line with Olson's theory. I am therefore not analyzing whether or how strongly market participants react to fiscal policy outcomes, but testing the response of governments to market punishment.

7.2.1 *Quantifying Market Discipline*

The main source of market discipline considered in this chapter stems from bond yields in the primary market. A few words on the structure of the bond market: government bonds trade over the counter; both electronically and via voice brokers. Whereas equities only have a single issue, government bond issuers have many outstanding issues of varying maturity; currency (e.g. dollar denominated) and type (such as inflation-linked bond). The market is characterized by a primary dealer system. Primary dealers are financial institutions that are appointed by sovereign issuers to buy, promote, and distribute sovereign bonds. These primary dealers can be domestic but are usually international financial institutions. For instance, among Austria's primary dealers are the Royal Bank of Scotland and the domestic Volksbank Wien-Baden. Primary dealers are obliged to actively participate in the secondary market to facilitate liquidity—bonds purchased in the primary market are thus explicitly for reselling. Secondary-market trading among creditors does not transfer value to or from debtors. This is because the interest rate is fixed with the issuance of the bond; what varies is the price paid for the bond in the secondary market. Bond yields in the secondary market, although a powerful signal, must be translated into a directly meaningful indicator for governments to account for the pressure policy-makers face. First, I consider the current debt servicing costs (see Table 7.1 for summary statistics).[1] This variable is measured as the interest payments as a percentage of GDP (*Cost*).

Table 7.1. Selected summary statistics

Variable	Observations	Mean	Std. Dev.	Min.	Max.
Cost	81	2.18	1.29	0.13	5.94
Δ Interest	81	–0.001	1.74	–8.43	8.39

Note: Twenty-seven EU countries over the 2008–10 period.

Surprisingly, given the cast of myopic governments in the literature, a (variant of the) debt servicing variable is scarcely featured in studies on the determinants of fiscal policy. One exception is Hallerberg et al. (2009), who argue that the 'debt servicing costs capture the impact of interest payments as well as political pressures that might emerge from high levels of interest payments on governments'. Because of the substantial size of most government debt burdens, even small variations in bond prices may entail significant real costs for taxpayers, as well as political costs for governments. However, reactions of the financial markets translate only slowly into higher debt servicing costs, as higher interest rates are only to be paid for newly issued debt. The maturity structure of debt is crucial. The financial crises in Indonesia, Korea, Malaysia, Thailand, and Russia in 1997/8 were characterized by the fact that these countries had to roll over large amounts of short-term external debt, which made them particularly vulnerable to an abrupt change in market perceptions. Similarly, Mexico in 1994 faced default because it had nearly $29bn in dollar-linked short-term debt (tesobonos) maturing over the next year. Contrarily, the maturity of Greek debt in 2010 was the second longest among advanced economies (Cottarelli et al. 2010: 18). As a result, Greece was able to benefit from low pre-crisis rates in addition to the comparatively favorable rates of EU financial assistance; in 2012, Greece debt servicing costs stood at 5 percent of GDP. This is the same figure as in 2003, despite the fact that Greek debt levels had risen from 98 percent of GDP in 2003 to 157 percent in 2012. Similarly, Spanish debt servicing costs as a percentage of GDP were identical in 2012 and 2001 (3 percent of GDP). This figure is remarkable given that the public debt to GDP ratio had risen from 55 to 86 percent in the same period. For Belgium, Germany, the Netherlands, Austria, and Sweden, interest expenditure on debt *fell* continuously during the 1995–2013 period—including the financial and economic crisis years during which debt levels soared. Although the residual maturity of debt in the Eurozone converged prior to the financial and economic crisis, notably with high-debt countries seizing the opportunity to expand long-term financing at a cheaper cost (Wolswikij and de Haan 2005), there is still (and increasingly so) considerable variation in the average debt maturity structure of the government bond market (Lojsch et al. 2011). In addition to the debt servicing cost, I also test for an effect of changes in long-term bond yields; that is, changes in the interest rates on ten-year government bonds in the secondary market—a standard measure in the literature for sovereign risk.

The empirical model used is as follows:

$$\begin{aligned}\Delta \text{ fiscal outcome} = {} & \alpha + \beta_1 \text{L.GDP}_{i,t} + \beta_2 \text{L.debt}_{i,t} + \beta_3 \text{L.AS}_{i,t} + \beta_4 \text{Bailout}_{i,t} \\ & + \beta_5 \text{Election}_{i,t} + \beta_6 \text{Government}_{i,t} + \beta_7 \text{Opposition}_{i,t} \\ & + \beta_8 \text{Left}_{i,t} + \beta_9 \text{Cost}_{i,t} + \beta_{10} \text{Dummies}_{i,t} + \epsilon_{i,t}\end{aligned}$$

The econometric techniques used and tests carried out are identical to those described in Chapter 4 (namely, time-series estimation with standard errors corrected for groupwise heteroskedasticity and contemporaneous correlation across countries of the error terms corrected with panel-corrected standard errors). On the dependent variable side, I rely on the primary measures of fiscal policy outcomes only with interest payments filtered out. The two dependent variables used here are thus the change in the primary balance (Δ PB) and the change in the primary structural balance (Δ PSB).

7.2.2 *Endogeneity—Again*

The market discipline hypothesis has two sides. The first stipulates that financial markets react to fiscal policy outcomes; the second argues that policy-makers react to changes in financial market indicators. This twin logic means that causality is difficult to establish and raises concerns over simultaneity and, consequently, the endogeneity of the regressor and heterogeneous dynamic of the error term. Similar to the endogeneity tests in Chapters 1–6, I instrumented the interest rate variable with its t-1 lagged value. The instrument is correlated with the endogenous regressors and uncorrelated with the structural error term. I confirm that the instruments are neither weak instruments (Kleibergen-Paap rk Wald F-statistic) nor correlated with the error term (Hansen J statistics). The Kleibergen-Paap rk LM-statistic allows me to reject the null hypothesis that the equation is under-identified. I then test for endogeneity and conclude that the specified endogenous regressors can be treated as exogenous (see Table A4.1 in Appendix 4).

7.2.3 *Econometric Results*

Adding the interest variable to the main model, I find strong evidence for government responsiveness to market signals (Table 7.2). No impact is detected for long-term interest rates (measured as the change in interest rates on ten-year government bonds). This finding is qualified below with respect to Eurozone members; see Table 7.3. Overall the empirical results suggest that

Table 7.2. The impact of market discipline, 2008–10

	Δ PSB	Δ PB	Δ PSB	Δ PB
Cost	**2.436***** **(0.636)**	**1.232**** **(0.600)**		
Δ Interest			**0.061** **(0.096)**	**0.050** **(0.086)**
L. Δ GDP	−0.887*** (0.198)	−0.616*** (0.209)	−1.128*** (0.180)	−0.742*** (0.185)
L.Debt	0.101*** (0.037)	0.128*** (0.036)	0.185*** (0.038)	0.170*** (0.038)
Bailout	1.090*** (0.056)	0.959*** (0.065)	1.043*** (0.059)	0.936*** (0.064)
L.AS	2.309*** (0.483)	1.360*** (0.507)	2.769*** (0.463)	1.593*** (0.474)
Government	−25.334*** (8.100)	−23.381*** (6.249)	−17.236** (7.505)	−18.974*** (5.619)
Opposition	19.248*** (6.775)	17.383*** (5.641)	13.071** (6.430)	13.990*** (5.092)
Left	3.952*** (1.006)	2.873*** (0.689)	4.015*** (0.984)	2.851*** (0.678)
Election	−1.080*** (0.288)	−0.662** (0.306)	−1.346*** (0.311)	−0.802*** (0.311)
Constant	−16.176*** (3.942)	−14.225*** (3.845)	−13.996*** (3.885)	−13.056*** (3.880)
N	81	81	81	81
R2	0.914	0.920	0.905	0.914

Note: Standard errors are corrected for groupwise heteroskedasticity and contemporaneous correlation across countries of the error terms are corrected with panel-corrected standard errors. * Significant at the 5% level; ** at the 1% level; *** at the 0.1% level. Standard errors listed below coefficients. Time and unit dummies not shown to preserve space.

market punishment has constrained national governments in their fiscal response strategies. Higher borrowing costs reduce stimulus spending, while lower debt servicing costs spur on deficit spending. Similar to the finding that structurally adjusted fiscal policy—that is, discretionary policy—is more influenced by political factors than its non-adjusted counterpart (see Chapter 4), comparing the coefficients in both PSB and PB models indicates that market pressure had a stronger impact on discretionary fiscal policy. This makes sense intuitively: responsiveness should increase with the ability to take action. With a coefficient of 2.4, the impact of market discipline is far from negligible. Ceteris paribus, Estonia with debt servicing costs of 0.25 percent of GDP in 2008 would feel spurred to improve its primary balance by 0.25 percentage points. In 2010, with its debt at a mere 6.6 percent of GDP, debt servicing costs declined to 0.13 percent of GDP. On the other end of the spectrum, and of course all other things being equal, interest payments of 5.12 percent of GDP in 2008 in Greece are associated with a decline in the primary deficit of over 6 percentage points.

Table 7.3. Market discipline meets EMU, 2008–10

	Δ PSB	Δ PB	Δ PSB	Δ PB
Cost	**0.830**	**2.334****		
	(0.986)	**(1.039)**		
Cost_Euro	**2.107*****	**0.543**		
	(0.730)	**(0.693)**		
Δ Interest			**0.016**	**0.007**
			(0.073)	**(0.078)**
ΔInterest_Euro			**1.293*****	**1.161*****
			(0.347)	**(0.281)**
Eurozone	−2.856	−6.047***	−0.580	−0.292
	(2.078)	(1.978)	(1.124)	(1.279)
L. Δ GDP	−0.952***	−0.676***	−1.008***	−0.617***
	(0.222)	(0.211)	(0.195)	(0.182)
L.Debt	0.083**	0.104***	0.118***	0.114**
	(0.039)	(0.038)	(0.046)	(0.048)
Bailout	1.124***	1.081***	0.952***	0.856***
	(0.089)	(0.091)	(0.067)	(0.073)
L.AS	2.456***	1.443***	2.384***	1.195**
	(0.535)	(0.511)	(0.507)	(0.468)
Government	−26.613***	−23.448***	−14.848**	−16.841***
	(8.434)	(7.171)	(7.257)	(6.377)
Opposition	18.582**	14.336**	12.595**	13.879***
	(7.282)	(6.519)	(5.755)	(5.327)
Left	3.977***	2.172*	2.747**	1.671*
	(1.267)	(1.146)	(1.106)	(0.979)
Election	−0.945***	−0.311	−1.286***	−0.746**
	(0.289)	(0.293)	(0.298)	(0.307)
Constant	−13.174**	−11.510**	−8.133	−8.441
	(5.304)	(5.307)	(5.301)	(5.504)
N	81	81	81	81
R2	0.919	0.933	0.913	0.926

Note: Standard errors are corrected for groupwise heteroskedasticity and contemporaneous correlation across countries of the error terms are corrected with panel-corrected standard errors. * Significant at the 5% level; ** at the 1% level; *** at the 0.1% level. Standard errors listed below coefficients. Time and unit dummies not shown to preserve space.

7.3 Overcoming Group Latency

Again, fiscal rules, whether supranational or domestic, held little sway over public finances in times of crisis. They did not curb free riding. In contrast, market discipline prompted governments to implement smaller or larger stimulus packages, depending on the running costs of financing sovereign debt. This section will unravel the mechanisms through which market pressure operates. If rules did not matter, why did market discipline have an impact on fiscal policy outcomes? I discuss two key features. First, market discipline is not burdened by the so-called second-order free rider problems. Related to this feature, market discipline does not rely on decentralized incentives and therefore does not face internal cooperation problems. Second, market discipline in contrast to domestic fiscal rules or EU-level agreements relies both on punishing and rewarding, as the costs of borrowing go up or down.

7.3.1 *Second-Order Free Riding*

Within the EU, incentives toward fiscal policy coordination are one-sided. Breaching the Stability and Growth Pact (SGP) leads (on paper only) to sanctions. Compliance is expected but not rewarded. The choice of a pure punishment strategy for fiscal policy coordination in the EU makes sense if we think of Olsonian incentives as additional public goods that need to be provided by the group. This creates the problem of second-order free riding. Here, some group members do not contribute to the provision of incentives (reward or punishment). But if the incentive in question is able to induce group-oriented behavior, they are able to benefit from the provision by other group members. Instead of solving the initial collective action problem (e.g. why should group members not cross the picket line?), a new one appears (e.g. 'why should anyone beat up the persons who cross the picket line?') (Elster 1985: 146). Consider the following example: A first-order problem is that of littering. A second-order problem is that of disciplining others for littering. Would you confront the litterer if you knew her well? If you happen to be in an open-carry state? These underlying issues become tangible if we consider the diplomatic relationships in the Council where voting on the SGP takes place, the possibility of retaliation, and the high likelihood of future SGP breaches in times of sluggish economic growth.

The bias of the SGP seeks to minimize second-order free riding by making the provision of incentives (punishment) the exception and not the norm. Pamela Oliver's influential contribution (1980; see also Yamagishi 1986) scrutinizes how the use of a selective incentive to motivate others to act collectively is itself a form of collective action. The starting point is the idea that selective incentives must affect the decisions of all players in the situation. The cost of providing a given reward is an increasing function of the number that cooperate (the more cooperation, the more rewards are needed), but a decreasing function for punishment (the more cooperation, the less punishment is needed). As a result, negative incentives are cheaper to use the more successful they are at inducing cooperation. In the ideal scenario, punishment creates a situation where everyone cooperates and this negative incentive does not have to be used at all. Its only cost is that of a threat: 'Thus negative incentives are often less costly than positive ones when unanimous cooperation is sought' (ibid.: 1368). This is the case for fiscal policy coordination. All member states are expected to comply with the SGP, and all member states are expected to stimulate their economies, albeit to different degrees under the EERP. A similar logic holds for domestic fiscal rules, where usually all sub-sectors of the regional and federal governments are required to comply. In brief, a pure punishment strategy is more cost-efficient in the context of fiscal policy coordination. Alas, it is also less effective in bringing about collective action.

7.3.2 *Turkey's Christmas*

Given the reciprocal nature of sanctions in the Council, it is no surprise that no fines were ever agreed upon. Perhaps the most glaring example of the weak pre-crisis application of the SGP can be seen in the Council of Economic and Finance Ministers' (Ecofin's) decision in June 2007 to close an Excessive Deficit Procedure (EDP) against Greece despite 'what transpired to be widespread inaccuracies in the country's official statistics' (Hodson 2012: 58). For years Eurostat, the statistical agency of the European Commission, has refused to accept the official statistics coming out of Greece without much notice from EU officials or indeed from financial market participants. One Commission interviewee recalled the episode of Greece improbably recording a budget surplus, which led the then German Finance Minister Hans Eichel to proclaim a 'Helenic Wirtschaftwunder' (March 2011). Not for nothing was the head of the Greek National Statistical Service called 'the Magician'. This reluctance to escalate the EDP is even more pronounced in the wake of the European Debt Crisis. The politicized fiscal surveillance amongst EU member states has been frequently described by observers as 'turkeys deciding on the menu for Christmas' (Schelkle 2009: 835) and 'like asking the turkey what we have for Christmas dinner' (Eijffinger 2004). Particularly in the context of package deals and issue linkages, where trade-offs of benefits and costs are sought over different issues, voting on the deficit procedure quickly became a vote about more than just compliance with the SGP. Voting was regarded as a 'matter of diplomacy' (interview, June 2011). In the presence of counter-punishment opportunities, cooperators are less willing to punish free riders (Nikiforakis 2008). Given the web of cooperation within the EU, the scope for retaliation is large. But even within the SGP, head of governments may be likely to refrain from punishing countries, which have previously not punished them or are considered unlikely to punish them for transgressing in the future. In the case of market discipline, there is no immediate possibility for retaliation. Market participants are not group members. Although governments can restrict and, to a certain extent, shape borrowing conditions (for example, via financial repression), the relationship between sovereign borrowers and financial markets is not reciprocal.

The incentives offered by market discipline are not subject to second-order free riding. This is because market discipline is not a second-order public good. The main purpose of market discipline is not rewarding and punishing sovereign borrowers, or helping out at cozy Council meetings. Market discipline is instead a by-product of risk pricing. In other words, what is referred to in this book as market punishment is not the result of a normative or pedagogical agenda of bond investors. It is instead first and foremost the result of any portfolio model with standard preferences for risk and return. It follows that in contrast to punishment and reward options amongst members of a latent group, there are no additional costs for the production of market punishment and rewards.

7.3.3 *Enlisting Markets*

The notion that policy-makers can 'harness resources outside the public sector in furtherance of public policy' (Grabosky 1995) is not singular to the Economic and Monetary Union (EMU) project. A restructuring of the state alongside a privatization of hitherto state activity is commensurate not only with the Maastricht Agreements and EMU, but also with the broader perspective of the so-called Washington Consensus. By enabling market actors to discipline wayward debtors, EU member states outsource the punishment of free riders. Enlisting markets to do the jobs of governments is not a new feature of the market–state relationship. An early example of this practice can be seen in the 1793 UK Registration of Aliens Act, which required ship captains to report numbers, names, and occupations of foreign passengers to local port authorities upon arrival and introduced a fine for non-compliance. The UK Home Office's 'hostile environment' strategy enlists landlords and banks to run immigration status checks, thus pushing 'the mentality of border control into everyday social and economic life' (Davies 2018). Across the globe, today's transportation companies, such as airlines, are vital allies in governmental migration controls and face considerable costs for non-cooperation. From 'private military' to railroads, from electricity industries to internet-censorship, the list of 'public good tasks' outsourced to private markets is long and moot.

Market discipline was, and still is, considered to be a key ingredient for the functioning of the EMU (Padoa-Schioppa 2002; Cœuré 2013; see also Howarth and Quaglia 2016: 44f.). Although Eurozone member states are able to issue debt in their own right, they are limited in their policy options in the face of financial difficulties because they are no longer in charge of monetary policy. This has given rise to one of the 'founding fears' of the EMU, namely that governments would seek either monetary bailout from the European Central Bank (ECB) or a fiscal bailout from other member states (Cafruny and Ryner 2007: 151). Market discipline was thought to contribute to the EMU's fiscal constraint along the lines of what the SGP, the monetary financing prohibition, the banning of privileged access for the public sector to financial institutions, and the 'no-bailout clause' aimed to ensure: 'to the extent that market-imposed discipline leads to more prudent fiscal policies and helps prevent fiscal crises...it protects the citizens against having to pay for the profligacies of the governments of other states' (Schuknecht et al. 2009: 371). Indeed the incapacity of the SGP to discipline fiscally profligate states was seen as evidence that the EU 'may have to look to the market to sanction the inveterate debtors' (Artis and Corsetti 2005).

The underlying principle to turn market discipline into 'a sword to attack errant governments' (Dyson and Featherstone 1999: 674) has resonance both in policy-maker and academic circles. A survey of 263 randomly selected economists from the top 150 academic departments revealed that 69 percent rejected the proposition that governments should insulate themselves from market discipline (Chwieroth 2009: 94). Or consider Michel Camdessus (1997), then Managing Director of the IMF, who amidst the Asian Financial Crisis insisted that 'countries cannot compete for the blessings of the global capital markets and refuse their discipline'. The IMF's World Economic Outlook 1997, along similar lines, lauded the crises in the European Exchange Rate Mechanisms in 1992 and 1993 as examples that 'international financial markets can serve to "discipline" governments (either by raising default premiums or by forcing adjustments in exchange rates), encouraging the adoption of appropriate policies' (Gill 1998: 15).

7.3.4 *The Perils of Second-Order Free Riding*

Second-order free riding weakens collective action. This is a problem for the entire EU because markets are not reliable and efficient disciplinarians. Yet this problem is aggravated for Eurozone member states; monetary union empowers financial market discipline. The political discourse surrounding the European Debt Crisis has cast financial market participants as villains 'running riot' (Sarkozy 2011) and 'speculating on the debt that was taken on to save these very institutions' (Merkel 2010). Here, market participants are characterized as fickle and erratic; in the words of Susan Strange (1998: 10): 'Drunken sailors one minute; terrified rabbits the next'. The architects of the EMU were cautious about relying on market forces alone to discipline governments on the grounds that financial market participants are prone to herd behavior (Lux 1995). The Delors Report (1989: 20) comes out clearly against enlisting markets because instead of 'leading to a gradual adaptation of borrowing costs, market views about the creditworthiness of official borrowers tend to change abruptly and result in the closure of access to market financing'.

Developed countries' bonds, so the prevalent assumption prior to 2008 goes, are safe assets. This perception predates monetary union and is not EU-specific. As Nicola Anderson (1996: 2) pointed out more than twenty years ago, bond investors 'don't perceive default risk for developed country bonds'. The graph of converging Eurozone bond yields prior to 2009 has come to epitomize bond investors' fallacy. Missing from this visual depiction of a false sense of sovereign soundness are the likewise declining and—albeit to a lesser degree—converging spreads of Central and Eastern European countries. EU accession has stamped the 'seal of approval' on sovereign bonds across the EU (Gray 2013). A similar dynamic was already in play for countries that were part of the British Empire. These benefited from a 'good housekeeping seal of approval' (Ferguson and Schularick 2006: 283) and were able to borrow at lower interest rates than comparable economies outside the Empire.

To be sure, the introduction of the single currency did improve the perceived creditworthiness of participating member states. Yet other factors, like the EU enlargement and sustained period of low inflation during the so-called Great Moderation, made favorable borrowing conditions a phenomenon across (newly) developed market economies. The trend of continuously declining bond yields applies to Norway, New Zealand, Japan, Australia, Switzerland, and Canada. When financial panic started to set in during August 2007, policy-makers across the globe, not just the Eurozone, were caught by surprise. Indeed, demands for financial assistance appeared first outside of the single-currency zone. Analysts had warned that the new EU member states were burdened with vulnerabilities such as 'reliance on foreign savings, vulnerability to sudden stops in capital inflows, debt exposures, and banks' exposures to credit risk stemming from rapid credit growth much of which is foreign exchange indexed or denominated' (Schadler and Luengnaruemitchai 2007). The crises in Eastern Europe were testament to these vulnerabilities. In the boom years prior to 2007, capital attracted by the newly acquired 'EU Halo' flew into these countries and fueled substantial currency account deficits. In Bulgaria and Latvia accumulative currency account imbalances between 2000 and 2008 record levels close to Greece's −119 percent of GDP with −103 and −111 percent of GDP, respectively. Note that similar to the European Debt Crisis, this is not a story of myopic, time-inconsistent policy-makers' wasteful expenditure and excessive public borrowing.

7.4 Original Sin Revisited

Markets are known to behave in an irruptive and ill-tempered fashion. Depending on their political and economic profile, countries are more or less vulnerable to these financial market mood swings. Eurozone membership, as has been widely argued in the 'downgrading' literature on the EMU, intensifies market discipline. This is due to three main reasons. First, monetary union increases financial market integration and with it capital mobility; it opened the 'credit floodgates' (Pisani-Ferry 2014: 4). This, however, amplifies 'sudden stop' dynamics in the event of market turmoil. In particular the Eurozone's cross-border payments system, Target2, facilitates capital leaving a country (see Schelkle 2017). Second, monetary union takes away the policy tools of (unilateral domestic) debt monetization. I distinguish between two types of debt monetization: hard and soft. Soft debt monetization is a frequent policy of indebted states, whereby the burden of debt is reduced via inflation (printing money). The strict inflation target (below but close to 2 percent) of the ECB was meant to block this road. Given that defaulting is often an abrupt and unpredictable event for investors, markets favor debt monetization as means to reducing the burden of a high public debt: 'the high probability of a low impact event (a bit of inflation) is not equivalent to the low probability of a high impact event (default)' (Gros 2012: 42). Hard debt monetization refers to the purchasing of government bonds by the monetary authority. This was thought 'to exceed the current legal mandate of the ECB' (Lane et al. 2012: 61). The central bank of a sovereign state can issue the money with which to buy its own government's bonds, while sovereigns within the Eurozone cannot create money to buy their own debt. Eurozone member states thus no longer have access to a domestic monetary authority that can act as lender of last resort in times of crisis. Market participants may then be more wary of unsustainable fiscal policies because default risks are higher in the absence of debt monetization. This 'original sin' sentiment is echoed by a fund manager asked about the implications of monetary union in Layna Mosley's study on the relationship between government and financial markets after EMU: 'There is no default risk when the government runs its own printing presses, so the risks associated with bonds will change with EMU' (2003: 193).[2] The above distinction between unilateral domestic and coordinated debt monetization relates to the coordination challenge in a currency union. This is what Benjamin Cohen (2012) refers to, framing the Eurozone's 'original sin' in political terms:

> The euro is a currency without a country—the product of an international agreement, not the expression of a single sovereign power. Its success, therefore, is critically dependent on the continued co-operation of EMU's Member States, which can hardly be guaranteed for all time.

Third, exchange-rate adjustments are no longer set at the domestic level. This means that domestic devaluation is no longer possible and intensifies market discipline for Eurozone members. 'The euro is essentially a foreign currency for every Eurozone country', according to the economists Michel Aglietta and Thomas Brand (2015); '[it] binds them to rigidly fixed exchange rates, regardless of their underlying economic realities, and strips them of monetary autonomy'. Different exchange rates within the Eurozone, so the argument goes, would help to compensate for the inflation differentials. The merits of a flexible exchange rate have been praised ever since Barry Eichengreen and Jeffrey Sachs (1985) demonstrated that the time at which countries escaped from the Great Depression was largely determined by the speed at which they left the Gold Exchange Standard. Floating exchange rates, so the argument goes, can act as a shock absorber against a fall in demand and deflation that haunt the world economy in times of crisis (cf. Corsetti et al. 2010). First, exchange-rate depreciation leads to a real depreciation of the domestic currency. This counters the fall in net exports driven by the contraction of external demand. Second, it decouples and thus shields domestic prices from the global deflationary spiral. Lacking a flexible domestic exchange rate, Eurozone members are fully exposed to the breakdown of external demand. Furthermore, the fixed exchange rate of the Euro amplifies the transmission of a global great recession by anchoring domestic price levels to global deflationary processes. Contrast the experiences of Sweden, a Euro-outsider with a floating exchange rate, and Denmark, also a Euro-outsider, but with an exchange rate pegged to the Euro. As demand for Swedish products fell during the Great Recession, so did the demand for the Swedish krona. As a result the floating exchange rate depreciated and Swedish products became cheaper for foreigners and thus more competitive. The exchange rate then depreciated heavily, making products cheaper for foreigners. Denmark did not alter its Euro-peg. Denmark's deep and prolonged economic crisis may be partly explained by the fixed exchange-rate regime (Andersen and Malchow-Møller 2014). This is not to suggest that exchange-rate adjustments are a panacea and that 'exporting one's way out of misery' is an easy fix. In many instances, industrial reform—that is, structural reform by another name—would have to take place within or outside of a single currency. Furthermore, countries with floating exchange rates are vulnerable to global monetary cycles—the exchange rate can help in managing a crisis, but it requires managing itself (Mabbett and Schelkle 2014).

7.4.1 *Upgrading*

The downgrading literature on market discipline in the EMU, for the reasons discussed in section 7.4, assumes that monetary union strengthens market discipline, and leads to a deterioration of EMU member states' borrowing conditions. The upgrading literature claims that monetary union weakens market discipline, but improves EMU member states' borrowing conditions.

There is evidence that the forces of market discipline were weakened in the wake of monetary union. According to Barry Eichengreen (2010: 26), 'life for small European countries is more comfortable inside the euro area than outside', as being part of a liquid Eurozone-wide market in Euro-denominated bonds sheltered them from strong market discipline. Eurozone membership initially sheltered participating countries from financial sector turmoil in 2007 and 2008. The alleged absence of market responsiveness leading to debtor moral hazard has been widely indicted as the main culprit of the European Debt Crisis. Christian Fahrholz and Cezary Wójcik (2011) claim that 'markets have for many years been taking far too many risks by treating, for instance, Greek and German bonds in essentially the same way. This has led to a reduction in market discipline'. Along similar lines, the European Commission (2011a: 7) lamented the 'inconsistency' of market responsiveness in Eurozone member states as 'a notable feature of the period since the launch of the euro'. Michael Arghyrou and Alexandros Kontonikas (2012) find support for the 'convergence trade' hypothesis for the pre-2007 period, according to which market participants were assuming the best-case scenario of full convergence to German fundamentals, even for countries with a clear deterioration of their macro-fundamentals.[3] In the wake of Maastricht euphoria, markets were guided into 'the belief that entering into Euro would make everything fine' (interview at European Commission, March 2015). The liquidity risk premium, which reflects the risk that an investor might not be able to liquidate their investment within an expected time period, is reduced with EMU membership because of the deep Euro-denominated debt pool (Bernoth et al. 2004; Faini 2006). Market liquidity can be broadly defined as the ability to swiftly execute financial transactions, notably exit, at low cost with limited price impact. Conversely, markets with poor liquidity, according to Richard Prager (2012), a strategist at the bond investor BlackRock, are like 'a lobster pot: Easy to get into, but tough to crawl out of' (this metaphor is based on the belief that a lobster trap is difficult to escape. It is not; all but about a tenth of lobsters caught in a lobster trap are able to escape (Chesler 2017)). 'A common currency patches things up. Before monetary union you could tell a lot from the up and down of national currencies, just remember how often the lira [Italy's currency] was devalued', as one bond investor in Frankfurt pointed out (interview, August 2014). These findings suggest that 'markets may anticipate fiscal support for EMU countries in financial distress' (Bernoth et al. 2004: 18)—despite the no-bailout clause of the Maastricht Treaty which 'nobody took seriously' (fixed-income manager, interview, March 2015). The credibility of Art. 125 stands in contrast to the US's constitutional no-bailout commitment: 'With Detroit it was easy, it was [like Greece] a train wreck for a long time and then there is that bet: either help will come or it wouldn't come. But unlike in the Eurozone that was highly unlikely for constitutional reasons'. Muted market discipline in Europe fueled by bailout expectations, so the underlying assumption goes, would give rise to debtor moral hazard. The dynamics informing the upgrading view of EMU membership are also at play in the favorable borrowing conditions enjoyed by Eastern European satellite states during the Cold War. Western bond investors 'regarded credits to Eastern Europe as a sound investment, on the implicit assumption that, under the canons of social internationalism, the Soviet Union would ultimately bail out its junior partners in case of repayment difficulties' (Miller 2003: 110).

7.4.2 *Up or Down*

In sum, whereas the upgrading view would see a diminished force of market discipline, the downgrading view predicts that governments will be more responsive to market signals under monetary union. To test which assumption played out during the Great Recession, I interact the variables *Cost* and *Interest* with a Eurozone dummy. If Eurozone membership strengthened market discipline, we should see a positive and statistically significant coefficient for the interaction term. The results are presented in Table 7.3. Both debt servicing costs as a percentage of GDP and changes in long-term interest rates led to an improvement of public finances; crucially, this effect is stronger for Eurozone member states (the key variables here are jointly significant at the 1 percent level). The findings suggest that Eurozone governments are more responsive to market signals, supporting the downgrading view of existing studies. In fact, for Eurozone members market punishment is exerted both through debt servicing costs and changing bond yields. The correlation of interest payments and stimulus packages provides further evidence for this. The two scatterplots in Figure 7.1 visualize the relationship between market pressure, as felt by interest payments, and fiscal stimulus packages for the years 2009 and 2010. For Eurozone members, high debt servicing costs are associated with a decrease in stimulus programs (rho = 0.28, N = 27), whereas for non-Eurozone EU members the relationship is the reverse, with high market pressure being correlated with more, not less stimulus spending (rho = –0.55, N = 32). These findings are in line with a previous study (Rommerskirchen 2015), which analyzes the dynamics of market discipline for all twenty-seven EU member states between 1996 and 2012. In this study I demonstrated evidence in favor of both market reaction to excessive deficits and government responsiveness to market signals. Notably, both mechanisms are found to be stronger for Eurozone member states. Taken together, these findings suggest that for both the years leading up to the crisis and during the Great Recession, EU policy-makers consolidated public finances in response to higher debt servicing costs. Crucially, governments' responsiveness is stronger within the Eurozone. This challenges the common wisdom of weak market discipline in monetary union and rampant debtor moral hazard. Instead, policy-makers retained an awareness of the potentially heightened constraints of Eurozone membership.

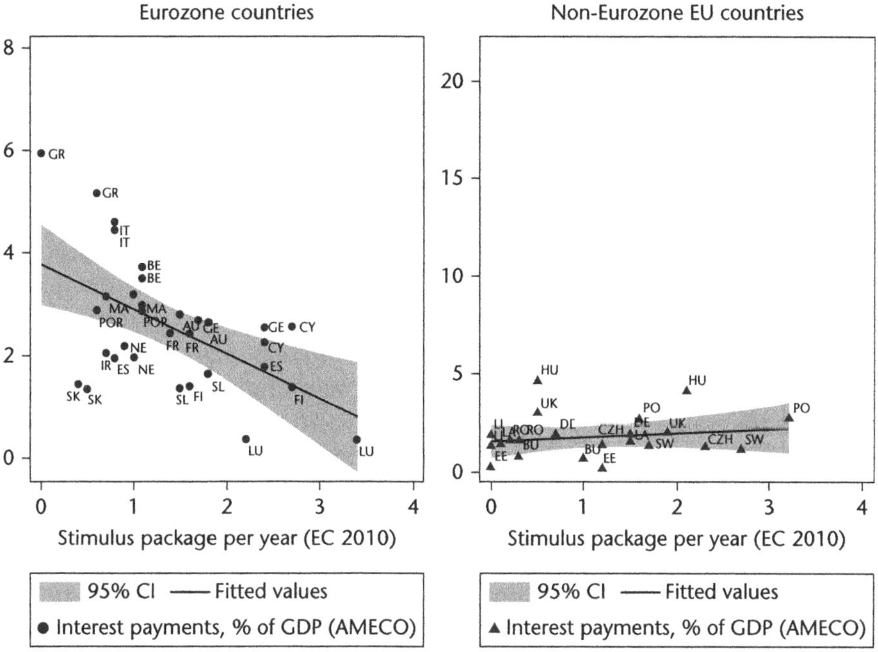

Figure 7.1 Interest payments and stimulus spending (2009–10)

7.5 Conclusion

Free riding is rife in the European Union. But it is not the type of first-order free riding that policy-makers publicly chastised. Instead, fiscal policy coordination is burdened by a serious internal enforcement problem. The argument presented here is different from the usual decrying of a lack of enforcement in fiscal policy coordination. I do not argue that the lack of enforcement is a problem because it invites member states to engage in rampant fiscal free riding. Instead I contest that without internal enforcement, fiscal policy coordination has come to rely on market discipline with dire consequences for its members. Policing free riders has been deliberately left to financial markets. Bond investors are arguably comfortable with this role; 'of course investors should play a role [in guiding politics], if you are worried about your money you can act accordingly' (US fixed-income analyst, interview, October 2013), 'market discipline is the ultimate corrective' (German fixed-income manager, interview, March 2015).

Market discipline, both in the form of debt servicing costs as a percentage of GDP and as a percentage of public debt, constrains fiscal policy. Crucially, this constraint is stronger for Eurozone member states. Monetary union increases market discipline. This is because of the absence of both strong and soft unilateral domestic debt monetization and the (again unilateral domestic) use of exchange-rate adjustments. The European Commission's Robert Kuenzel and Eric Ruscher (2013: 4) contest that 'underpinning the prevailing pre-crisis attitude of "benign neglect" towards wider macroeconomic vulnerabilities may have been a tacit belief that the main disciplining role should fall to financial markets'. I argue that there is nothing 'benign' about this division of labor.

For all EU member states, not just Eurozone countries, this creates an inferior system of collective action. And yet the appeal of market discipline to punish and reward fiscally wayward states has survived the Great Recession largely unscathed. It seems that the brunt of 'immoral' market behavior has been borne by hedge funds with fierce rhetoric surrounding the EU regulatory efforts in the wake of the financial crisis (Quaglia 2011).[4] Derogatorily labeled 'vulture funds', they have a reputation for disloyal investment and their trading is, albeit at times exaggeratedly so, associated with numerous sovereign debt crises from 1996 in Peru, to 1998 in Russia, to 2001 in Argentina, to 2010 in Greece. Singling out this particular investor group, policy-makers across the political spectrum continue to defend the use of a hired gun to intimidate public policy. It would be a mistake to relegate support for market discipline to the corner of the European Commission or Germany and its 'Stability Culture' allies. Even actors that are usually vocal critiques of market forces, such as members of the European Parliament across party wings, came forth endorsing market discipline (interviews, March 2011 and February 2015). More cautious backers of second-order free riding cite the time-tested excuse of 'there is no alternative', pointing to endemic enforcement failures in the first decade of the SGP. I will contest this assumption in Chapter 9; there are alternatives.

The fact that market discipline may both be too strong (after 2009) and too weak (before 2009) for policy-makers' tastes is well known. But it is not only the (lacking) strength of bond market pressure that poses a problem for EU fiscal policy coordination; markets do not necessarily incentivize group-oriented behavior. Bond market pressure does imperfectly correspond to free riding. Instead they are prone to react in an untimely and disproportional fashion. In delegating the task of discipline to markets, governments do not retain control over their 'agents'. Trichet's letters to the Spanish and Italian governments discussed in Chapter 2 are one example of policy-makers attempting to loosen or tighten the screws of market discipline. And yet they lack the firm grip and ultimate control to make market discipline work. This, then, bears little resemblance to Olson's criterion of 'selective and separate' for successful incentives.[5] A further problem lies in financial markets' limited capacity to sanction growth free riding. Although markets reward economic growth (and are thus not automatically against stimulus policies), there is little evidence that they care about whether growth rates are achieved via free riding, as evidenced by the EU's surplus countries' very favorable treatment by bond investors.

The common wisdom suggests that governments in the developed world need to pay very close attention to only a few macroeconomic headline indicators, but are free to pursue a wide range of ideological choices in microeconomic policy within the confines of the 'golden straightjacket' (e.g. Mosley 2003; Rodrik 1997). The emergence of strong market discipline in developed economies post-2008 put existing assumptions of credit risks into question—'old market assumptions have broken down' (*Financial Times*, June 9, 2010). As one US bond investor explained, 'we simply couldn't image that there would be credit risk for sovereign debt in Europe' (interview, October 2013). This suggests that the past crisis years have revealed 'a new paradigm of financial market behavior in developed countries, one in which policy-makers find their "room to move" is significantly constrained' (Phillips 2012: 4). Bond investors now scrutinize areas of politics and policies, which they previously left untouched. In the words of a US bond analyst, 'I'm still an economist, although to some extent I now consider myself a political economist' (interview, September 2013); a German fixed-income manager repeated this new identity unprompted: 'I'm actually a pure macro-economist, but the crisis has made me a political economist' (interview, March 2014). European policy-makers are once more befuddled by the 'ubiquity of unintended consequences' (Pierson 1996) that continues to overrun European integration. Rawi Abdelal and Mark Blyth (2015: 41) relate the episode of the anticipated downgrading of France in January 2012 which had a knock-on effect on the rating of the European Financial Stability Facility (EFSF) whose rating is contingent on that of its subscribing members. This compromised the EFSF's ability to backstop the EU's fragile banks and contain the ongoing crisis. This episode echoes the announcement of Jean-Claude Trichet in 2010 that the ECB would phase out acceptance of BBB-rated bonds, which fueled the bond market crisis in Greece. By endorsing second-order free riding, policy-makers have created disciplinary incentives whose form they struggled to control, as has become painfully obvious during the European Debt Crisis. Lacking a cohesive response, their haphazard efforts to contain the crisis remind me of Goethe's Sorcerer's Apprentice: 'Spirits that I've cited, My commands ignore.'

Notes

1. The independent variable measuring the 'market punishment effect' (e.g. change in interest rates/debt servicing costs) is included only in its linear form; the square of

the same variable is not included. I tested for the inclusion of the quadratic transformations as well as the log transformation of *Interest* to account for the potentially non-linear relationship between interest penalties and fiscal outcomes. Government reaction to higher interest rates is likely to display non-linearities in the sense that the severity of the punishment may increase borrowers' responsiveness. If, however, a certain threshold is reached at which the solvency is put into question, then it is possible that market punishment may lead to deterioration in the budgetary position. Testing the misspecification of the functional form, the regression equation specification tests (see Ramsey 1969) reject the use of quadratic, cubic, and log forms of the variable *Interest*. As such, I model market punishment as a linear relationship.

2. Governments around the world have defaulted despite having their own printing presses (Mosley 2004). Since 1997, nineteen sovereign states have defaulted: Mongolia, Venezuela, Russia, Ukraine, Pakistan, Ecuador (twice), Turkey, Ivory Coast, Argentina, Moldova, Paraguay, Uruguay, Dominica, Cameroon, Grenada, Dominican Republic, Belize, Seychelles, and Jamaica.
3. Convergence of bond yields should not be equated with the absence of market discipline; although market pressure was low prior to 2008, member states were not treated equally by market participants (Hallerberg and Wolff 2008).
4. Hedge funds are largely unregulated, alternative investment vehicles known for leveraging (buying securities using borrowed money) and short selling (selling securities in the expectation their prices would fall).
5. Olson considers the proportionality of the contribution toward the collective good vis-à-vis the benefits that the collective good incurs (1965: 30, 35)—but not the proportionality of punishment beyond his criteria of 'selective and separate'.

8

Exit Stimulus

8.1 The Consolidation Years

Starting in 2009, the term 'exit strategy' entered the EU dictionary of fiscal policy coordination. It described the ending of stimulus spending in combination with fiscal consolidation. Originally the term 'exit strategy' was predominately used to describe tactics to withdraw troops from war-zones (Safire 1995). Similarly, in pre-crisis EU communications it showed up in reference to humanitarian crises, disaster relief, and emergency assistance. Debates about suitable 'fiscal exit strategies' have featured heavily in EU policy, starting with EU economies still in recession and the European Debt Crisis yet to escalate. While the stimulus debate of the Great Recession years was dominated by a new concern over growth free riding, the Consolidation Years of 2011–14 sought to re-establish an old hierarchy. Worries that free riding member states would benefit from the expansive fiscal policies of other EU member states without having to pick up the tab turned into worries that free riding member states would not consolidate public finances and thus endanger the economic stability of the entire union—a concern that quickly gained traction amidst the spiraling European Debt Crisis. The Economic Policy Brief of May 2009 (Ecfin 2009b) was already proclaiming 'the European Commission is intensifying its efforts to help governments overcome the crisis and prepare an "exit" strategy for the longer term'. In June 2009 the European Council cautiously concluded that 'it is important that consolidation keeps pace with economic recovery. There is a clear need for a reliable and credible exit strategy'. Another stab at agreeing on the size and timing of fiscal consolidation was made over lunch at the Council of Economic and Finance Ministers (Ecofin) meeting in Göteborg with two economists giving talks on the topic. Both Jean Pisani-Ferry and Francesco Giavazzi presented a nuanced case, arguing that 'the exit must not be rushed or we risk a relapse into another recession' (von Hagen et al. 2009), and that fiscal consolidation should be gradual (Giavazzi and Pagano 2009). Ecofin agreed on the principles according to which a withdrawal of discretionary spending starting in 2011 at the latest was only required 'provided that the Commission forecasts continue to indicate that the recovery is strengthening and becomes self-sustaining'. Similar to the call for fiscal expansion under the European Economic Recovery Plan (EERP), consolidation was to be gauged according to the 'specificities of country situations'. Likewise, the numerical pace for consolidation 'beyond the benchmark of 0.5% of GDP per annum in structural terms' was relativized by applying only to 'most Member States', without a definition or clarification of this category. According to the then Portuguese Finance Minister, 'every country will have to define its exit strategy in its own due time. I don't think that we can have a precise, or a common schedule' (*Reuters*, October 1, 2009). Although simplistic slogans like the title of the German Finance Minister Schäuble's opinion piece ('Why austerity is the only cure for the Eurozone') were part of the policy discourse, EU official analysis and EU recommendations were predominantly nuanced. The vague endorsement of exit strategies reflected the underlying tensions over the appropriate fiscal policy design within member states, described by a participating Commission official as 'fierce discussion between the austerity and the consolidation camp' (interview, February 2015), echoing John Maynard Keynes' dispute with officials of the British Treasury in 1924. History, as is so often the case, provided seemingly cautionary tales for both camps cherry-picking the 'received wisdom about the mistakes of their predecessors' (Eichengreen 2014: 1). On the one hand, a premature exit before the underlying recovery had set in was blamed for extending the crisis in the US in the second half of the 1930s, leading to a double-dip recession. On the other hand, the late exit from discretionary public spending after the first oil crisis in the 1970s was argued to have led to inefficient allocation of resources and high inflation (see Pollin 2012).

Within the austerity debate, an economic variable called a 'multiplier' took centerstage. The fiscal multiplier refers to the change in real GDP that is produced by a shift in the fiscal stance. For example, a multiplier of 1.5 means that €1 in government-spending cuts reduces GDP by €1.50; a multiplier of 0.5 means a €1 increase in spending only increases GDP by 50 cents. Fiscal multipliers matter for fiscal expansion and fiscal consolidation alike. And yet as Giancarlo Corsetti (2012: 2) put it, 'from a theoretical perspective, however, there is no such thing as the multiplier. Instead, fiscal multipliers are likely to depend on a number of factors which vary both across countries and time'. The multiplier debate took place in two acts. First, during the Stimulus Years the discussion turned around how much extra stimulus spending would stimulate the economy. Then the question turned to the potential harm or good done by fiscal belt-tightening to economic growth. Key proponents of fiscal consolidation are associated with the so-called Bocconi school. The work of its most influential figure, Alberto Alesina (2010), on the benefits of 'expansionary austerity' appears to have informed EU policy responses to the European Debt Crisis directly (Helgadóttir 2016). Recent economic research has highlighted that fiscal multipliers vary across economic environments. There is evidence that fiscal multipliers increase during times of financial crisis or recessions, particularly with interest rates at or near the zero lower bound (Helgadóttir 2016; Perotti 1999; Auerbach and Gorodnichenko 2012; Ilzetski et al. 2013). Fiscal retrenchment hurts more amidst market panic than in economically rosy times. There is further evidence that for some countries austerity could become 'self-defeating' (Delong and Summers 2012). According to this scenario, debt-to-output ratios would increase rather than decrease: austerity would bring about more pain than gain. This is not an ivory-towered debate. By way of example, consider the public disagreement between George Osborne, then UK Chancellor, and the then chief economist of the International Monetary Fund (IMF), Oliver Blanchard, on the speed and size of fiscal consolidation (and the underlying multiplier which matters for both) (*Reuters*, April 20, 2013).

In this chapter I analyze the state of collective action in the Consolidation Years (2011–14). The analysis therefore moves away from the Great Recession and enters the territory of the EU's 'slow burning crisis' (Seabrooke and Tsingou 2018). To do so I start with an overview of fiscal policy developments. Next, the questions answered in this chapter parallel those in Chapters 1–7: What are the drivers of fiscal policy outcomes? Was free riding rampant? Did fiscal rules impact on fiscal policy? Or was market discipline, again, a key determinant of public finances?

8.2 The Austerity Delusion

Already at the turn of the twenty-first century Europe was said to suffer from a 'fiscal regime of austerity' that would lead to the demise of the welfare state (Pierson 1996). In the wake of the Great Recession there is now a widespread perception that the EU is in the grips of an austerity delusion (Blyth 2013; Armingeon 2012b; Schaefer and Streeck 2013). Asked about where the perception of EU austerity came from, interviewees from the Commission seemed puzzled: 'frankly, I really don't know', 'that is a mystery to me' (interviews, April 2015). Yet a mystery this is not. Fiscal consolidation was on the menu very early on—the important difference is that few countries ordered or were made to order it.

Many accounts of 'austerity Europe' have focused on the discourse of fiscal consolidation and not the actual policies. Mark Blyth (2013), for instance, nimbly dissects the flawed ideology of austerity. Similarly, Schmidt and Thatcher's edited volume (2013: xvi) focuses 'on the resilience of neoliberal ideas in policy and political debates rather than the consequences of neoliberal prescriptions, how neoliberal ideas may be put into practice, or whether policy outcomes are, in fact, neoliberal'. The dialectics and politics of fiscal consolidation are not the same, and rarely have been. Frequently initial announcements of fiscal consolidation plans do not live up to implemented policy actions (Devries et al. 2011). Post-crisis publications like the Organisation of Economic Co-operation and Development's (OECD's) Fiscal Consolidation Survey (2011), which presented self-reported consolidation plans, further created a divide between analysis based on retrospective and prospective fiscal policy. The fiscal consolidation talk was a misguided attempt at restoring market confidence and appeasing the taxpayers of creditor countries. This has created the impression that austerity was the only game in town. German policy-makers, spearheaded by the then Finance Minister, were leading the consolidation chorus. But Berlin's fiscal policy once again did not live up to its rhetoric, contrary to Dan Drezner's assertion (2014: 268) that 'Germany followed through on its austerity pledge'. Although its budget balance is improving, the German government has not implemented wholesale fiscal tightening, as, for instance, the stable levels of public expenditure or investment show. In the words of a member of the Juncker cabinet: 'Germany has not really consolidated much and if you look at the rest of Europe it's not happening much either' (interview, March 2015). According to Werner Eichhorts and Anke Hassel (2015: 3), 'Germany has not continued any austerity strategy in economic or social policy, beyond sticking to fiscal constraint and the debt brake. On the contrary, since the financial crisis hit Europe, the government has responded with policies promoting growth and expansion'. This would of course not be the first time that 'medicine dispensed abroad was, in important respects, not really the same stuff...drank at home', echoing Josef Stiglitz's assessment of the United States' recommendations summarized under the Washington Consensus heading (2004: 23).

Designing exit strategies, national and EU policy-makers were once again misreading the economic outlook, mirroring their initial misperception of the looming crisis in 2007/8—recall the Commission President proclaiming in early 2008, 'Let's be clear, it's not time to run for the lifeboat' (Barroso 2008a). Hindsight is a thing of beauty. Similarly, the dissonant calls for fiscal exit strategies came at a time when the storm was hardly weathered. Endorsing consolidation, fiscal policy was set for a premature withdrawal. Herein the EU fiscal policy recommendations followed the premature interest rate increase by the European Central Bank (ECB) in 2010. Fiscal consolidation plans were set too soon, period. Yet those plans were revised, suggest gradual adjustment, and, perhaps most crucially, are not perceived as binding where they are not linked to lending conditionality. Those criticizing the EU for advocating consolidation fail to demonstrate that EU communication had an impact on fiscal retrenchment. In the words of a Council official: 'Nobody in the current climate [referring to the European Debt Crisis] reads the opinions on the stability program as we moved from exit strategy to survival strategy' (interview, April 2011). Market pressure and the threat thereof, not the Stability and Growth Pact (SGP) or EU agreements, moved some countries to consolidate prematurely. The European system first and foremost is to blame for *not* sheltering member states from this pressure, not for endorsing fiscal consolidation.

I wish to put the charge of austerity illusion into perspective. My argument here is not one of Mussolini making the trains run on time—in fact, he didn't (Evans 1954). To be clear, Germany's communication has persistently been wrong-headed and hypocritical. Something is off if an official feels compelled to clarify that 'we [the German government] are not the consolidation Taliban', as the German Deputy Finance Minister Thomas Steffen did in spring 2012 (*Reuters*, April 26, 2012). The demands for fiscal consolidation in the program countries, above all Greece, were misguided and deeply harmful. Indeed, interviewees consistently differentiated between program countries (experiencing the 'ultimate nightmare' (interview, May 2011)) where 'the rules of the game change completely' (interview, March 2015) and EU member states without financial assistance programs. Yet outside of intergovernmental program austerity, the evidence for dramatic spending cuts is far more irregular and EU calls for consolidation much less influential than warnings of an 'austerity delusion' suggest.

Looking at the changes in the primary structural balance (a standard measurement for consolidation), the EU member states' consolidation averaged 3 percent of GDP over a five-year period—above the 0.5 percent envisioned in current rules. However, if we exclude program countries, this drops to 2 percent of GDP, or 0.4 percent per annum. This experience is broadly in line with other developed economies. There is, however, considerable variation in the consolidation effort, from an actual expansion of −1.4 percent of GDP (Denmark) to a consolidation of +10.5 percent of GDP (Greece). Since 2013 fiscal consolidation in Europe has on average petered out. As of 2013, twelve countries pursued (mostly moderately) expansive fiscal policies as indicated by negative changes in the structural balance. In this country group are Germany, Austria, Italy, Spain, and France. For the years 2014 and 2015 the change in the primary structural balance was negative (expansive) for the EU as a whole. European post-crisis consolidation stands out neither by historical nor contemporary standards. The considerably larger consolidation efforts of program countries are, albeit painful and in this form counterproductive, not an anomaly under intergovernmental borrowing conditionality. On average, IMF programs target a fiscal adjustment of about 1 percentage point of GDP across all types of arrangements during the first year of the program, with 'large' fiscal adjustment (defined here as more than 3 percentage points of GDP over a two-year horizon) taking place in close to one-third of all cases. Greece's improvement of its structural balance of 10 percentage points from 2010 to 2016 is below the adjustments of Algeria (20.5 percent), Denmark (15.1 percent), Jordan (13.5 percent), and Sweden (14.1 percent).[1] What we see then in EU program countries is the same consolidation conditionality that has played out before in other debtor countries. The over-zealous lending conditions of the Institutions, formally known as the Troika, are set to repeat the mistakes of numerous IMF bailouts. Consider the example of Asian countries amidst the 1997 Asian Financial Crisis who 'have had to sign agreements that look more like Christmas trees than contracts, with anywhere from 50–80 detailed conditions covering everything from the deregulation of garlic monopolies to taxes on cattle feed and new environmental laws' (Kapur 1998: 123). For comparison, the lending conditionality in Greece covered motorway revenues, licensing of a casino, water tariff policy, supply chain agreements in the tobacco industry, and the funding of political parties, to name but a few (EC 2018).

A tension between the prioritization of and relationship between economic growth and economic stability was manifest in EU fiscal policy coordination ever since its inception. Given the ongoing challenges to consolidate both goals, the EU has come a long way. Whereas the SGP was single-mindedly concerned with achieving low budget deficits, the economic governance landscape of 2016 strives to balance both interdependent policy goals. The recommendations for fiscal consolidation are not imposing a hard doctrine of austerity that depicts fiscal consolidation as the harbinger of growth. In the words of former EU President Barroso (2013): 'The Commission . . . will never propose a policy that is only based on the correction of the deficits'. The post-reform application of newly created or modified institutional tools suggests that Barroso's statement amounts to more than the strategic appeasement of an audience weary of painful austerity measures. The post-2008 flexibility was endorsed by then Ecofin Commissioner Oliver Rehn (2012): 'contrary to the misleading impression . . . that the EU fiscal framework forces all Member States into a "one-size-fits-all" consolidation straightjacket, the Stability and Growth Pact is not stupid'. Fiscal space is important in this regard. The concept is now firmly established in EU economic governance. In line with its application during the Great Recession and a backing of stimulus spending depending on a country's room to move, 'Member States with more fiscal space—particularly Germany' are urged to 'take measures to encourage domestic demand, with a specific emphasis on investment' (Public Finances in EMU 2014). Outside of 'drunken' lending conditionality (Jacoby and Hopkin 2017), I find little support for the claim that the Commission 'made austerity a point of pride' (Sandbu 2017: 198). As this book has discussed the European

Commission, though far from a unified actor, it has come to embrace flexible, anti-cyclical fiscal policy. This position has only increased with the new Juncker Commission (Peterson 2017). The institution is then hardly a henchman of the German austerity doctrine, as Paul Krugman with his moniker of a 'Rehn of Terror' suggests. Across EU institutions there is what Deborah Mabbett and Waltraud Schelkle (2014: 1) identify as a 'resistant to the prescription of austerity'. Even Mario Draghi suggested a looser fiscal stance in his high-profile Jackson Hole speech in the late summer of 2014 (*Financial Times*, September 2, 2014). These are not the programs and policies of institutions cobbled into submission by Germany's misguided austerity demands.

The endorsement of an expansive aggregate fiscal stance for the Eurozone, most recently found in the Five Presidents' Report of June 2015, is furthermore evidence of this twin notion of free riding, and makes for a more nuanced reading of Commission recommendations beyond 'fiscal water-boarding' (Varoufakis 2017). Fiscal stance measures the impulse of governments' discretionary decisions on public finances, defined as the change in the general government's primary structural balance. The concept of fiscal space was central to the EU goal to achieve a fiscal expansion of 0.5 percent of GDP at the Eurozone level in 2017, which would have amounted to an additional fiscal stimulus of around 50 billion Euros, comparable to the Great Recession's EERP, on an annual basis. This endorses means-tested fiscal policy. This idea further resonates with the ECB, an institution that has found itself out of breath at the coalface of stabilizing the Eurozone and promoting growth (van de Riet 2017). By considering fiscal policy in aggregate terms with both stability and growth clearly in mind, fiscal policy coordination has come a long way indeed. Nevertheless, Commission officials are frustrated that 'those who do not have fiscal space want to use it; those who have fiscal space do not want to use it' (European Commission 2018). I will test this claim in section 8.3. Did countries with more fiscal space engage in less fiscal consolidation? Or, put differently, was deficit reduction in line with member states' fiscal room for maneuver?

8.3 Consolidation and Fiscal Space

A reminder on definition: Fiscal space refers to 'the capacity of a government to provide financial resources for a desired purpose, subject to the constraint that the fiscal position is sustainable, both over the medium and long-term' (Heller 2005). To investigate the relationship between fiscal space and fiscal consolidation, I focus on the Consolidation Years 2011–14. The motivation for this timeframe is twofold. 2011 is the year the EERP officially ended and thus a suitable starting point. 2014 marks the year when Jean-Claude Juncker took over as Commission President, promising 'a new start for Europe' and marking a shift in the rhetoric on fiscal consolidation. Incidentally, this time-frame is also comparable with the Stimulus Years (2008–10) analyzed in Chapters 1–7. I created a fiscal space indicator using the same methodology as in Chapter 5. Specifically, I built sub-scores based on the Macroeconomic Imbalances Procedure's (MIP's) scoreboard which contains ten indicators covering both the public and private sector. Please refer to Table A8.1 in Appendix 4 for a discussion on the construction of the fiscal space indicator. I find evidence that member states' fiscal consolidation, measured by a change in the primary structural balance, was broadly in line with domestic fiscal space. This is suggested by a strong correlation of −0.46 (N = 28, 2011–14) which is graphically represented in Figure 8.1. The smaller a country's fiscal space, the larger its consolidation efforts. Denmark and Sweden, among the countries with large fiscal space, did consolidate less than Greece or Cyprus, whose fiscal space was very narrow. Following our framework of free riding, these findings offer some evidence that growth or stability free riding during the Consolidation Years was not rampant. And yet these descriptive statistics based on simple correlations are only able to tell us so much about the drivers of fiscal policy outcomes. It is also not clear why the outlier countries (whose country dot is far removed from the correlation line in Figure 8.1) exceeded or undershot in relation to their fiscal space without controlling for other factors. In sections 8.4 and 8.5 I will thus consider the determinants of consolidation

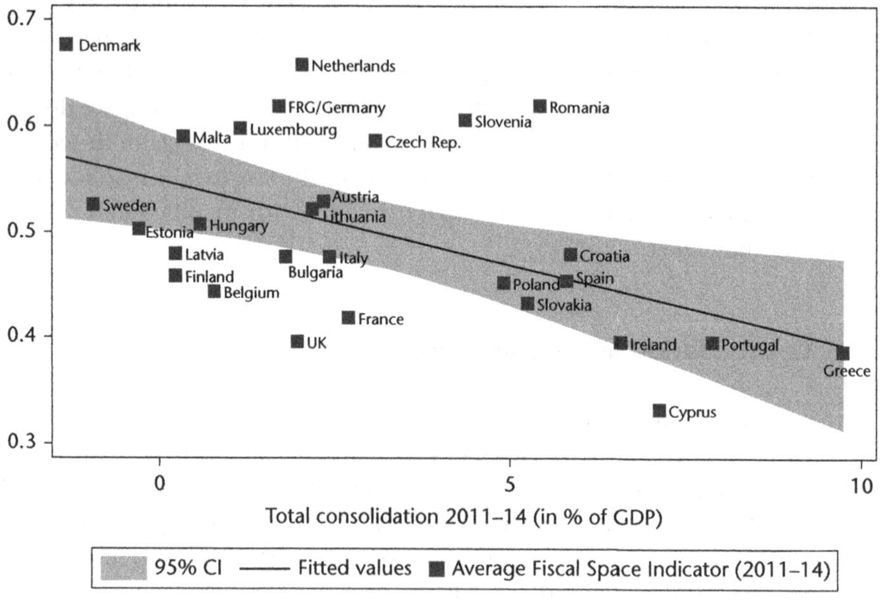

Figure 8.1 Fiscal consolidation and fiscal space

in greater detail, focusing on the two sets of incentives we encountered in Chapters 1–7; namely, fiscal rules and financial market pressure.

8.4 Drivers of Fiscal Consolidation

The following investigation seeks to shed some light on the question of what drove fiscal policy outcomes. I follow the same methodology used in Chapters 1–7; namely, pooled ordinary least squares (OLS) estimation with robust standard errors. Summary statistics are presented in Table 8.1.

I have previously argued that the Stimulus Years were not marked by path-dependent fiscal policy, but instead saw policy-makers using discretionary and non-discretionary budget measures to boost the economy in times of crisis, independent of the fiscal policy outcomes of previous years. This finding does not seem to apply to the Consolidation Years. For the period 2011–14 the addition of a lagged dependent variable (thus capturing path dependency) improves our goodness of fit measurement markedly in the cyclical models. The goodness of fit measure jumps from 0.63 to 0.73 (where changes in the primary balance are the dependent variable) and from 0.66 to 0.78 (where it is changes in the budget balance). For the structurally adjusted models I detect no evidence of path dependency, which gives us some confidence in the appropriateness of these indicators as capturing discretionary fiscal policy outcomes and not merely path-dependent budgeting over which policy-makers may have little agency. In this chapter I thus include a lagged dependent variable in the cyclical models (excluding the lagged dependent variable does not alter the results).

Table 8.1. Selected summary statistics

Variable	Observations	Mean	Std. Dev.	Min.	Max.
Δ PSB	110	0.77	1.33	−1.82	5.51
Δ SB	110	0.75	1.26	−1.59	6.25
Δ PB	110	−0.66	3.44	−12.48	10
Δ BB	110	−0.67	3.50	−13.08	9.6
L. Δ GDP	110	0.94	2.63	−9.1	7.6
L.Debt	110	66.93	35.18	6.1	177.4
L.AS	110	0.03	0.78	−2.55	2.20
Government	110	0.59	0.25	0.18	1
Opposition	110	0.51	0.19	0.21	1
Left	110	0.22	0.42	0	1
Election	110	0.27	0.45	0	1
Rule	108	0.84	1.13	−0.99	3.32
Interest	110	2.44	1.34	0.1	7.3
Costs	108	4.21	2.97	1.16	22.5

Note: Twenty-eight EU countries over the 2011–15 period.

Table 8.2. The drivers of fiscal consolidation, 2011–14

	Δ PSB	Δ SB	Δ PB	Δ BB
lag. dep. variable			−0.500***	−1.098***
			(0.078)	(0.146)
L. Δ GDP	−0.178	−0.203	0.211	0.400
	(0.119)	(0.114)	(0.237)	(0.214)
L.Debt	−0.005	0.007	0.133**	0.028
	(0.020)	(0.019)	(0.041)	(0.034)
L.AS	0.257	0.193	0.913	0.291
	(0.346)	(0.332)	(0.661)	(0.596)
Government	2.546	2.302	−2.480	−0.624
	(1.554)	(1.565)	(2.162)	(1.729)
Opposition	2.192*	2.072*	−2.775	−1.528
	(0.964)	(0.900)	(2.147)	(1.802)
Left	−0.065	−0.388	2.049*	0.541
	(0.359)	(0.354)	(0.898)	(0.772)
Election	−0.406*	−0.306	−0.229	−0.146
	(0.192)	(0.186)	(0.372)	(0.308)
Constant	0.021	−0.813	−15.161**	−7.844*
	(2.227)	(2.138)	(4.742)	(3.852)
N	110	110	110	110
R2	0.552	0.548	0.759	0.843

Note: Standard errors are corrected for groupwise heteroskedasticity and contemporaneous correlation across countries of the error terms are corrected with panel-corrected standard errors. * Significant at the 5% level; ** at the 1% level; *** at the 0.1% level. Standard errors listed below coefficients. Time and unit dummies not shown to preserve space.

Two interesting findings of the baseline model in Table 8.2 to highlight relate to the political business cycle and government debt burdens. First, election years led to a reduction in discretionary fiscal consolidation. Fiscal consolidation is of course not a popular policy and governments facing the electorate might thus be less likely to engage in fiscal belt-tightening (cf. Guichard et al. 2007; Hübscher 2015). Jean-Claude Juncker, then as Prime Minister of Luxembourg, referred to the unpopularity of austerity by pointing out that 'we [politicians in government] all know what to do; we just don't know how to get re-elected after we have done it'. The findings presented here suggest that governments were wary of the 'Juncker curse'. Hübscher and Sattler (2017) show that governments associate significant electoral risk with consolidations because electorally vulnerable governments strategically avoid consolidations toward the end of the legislative term in order to minimize electoral punishment. In this calculation of potential electoral costs, it does not necessarily matter whether voters actually punish incumbent governments.[2] There is some evidence that governments that reduce budget deficits are *not* systematically voted out of office (Buti et al. 2009). Second, the results indicate that consolidation is hindered by high opposition fragmentation. This is in line with the findings from the 2008–10 period, where high opposition fragmentation was shown to lead to an increase in stimulus spending.

A highly fragmented opposition, so it seems, brings discretionary spending up and reduces consolidation efforts. The impact of opposition fragmentation is again in line with the 'common pool argument' (Hardin 1982) of many fishers depleting the oceans.

8.4.1 *Rules and Consolidation*

To test whether fiscal rules provide an Olsonian incentive to curb free riding in the context of fiscal consolidation, I included the variable *Rule*, based on the European Commission's Fiscal Rules Index. In line with the findings of Chapter 6, it perhaps does not come as a surprise that domestic fiscal rules are not a statistically significant driver of fiscal consolidation across model specifications; see Table 8.3.[3] Interacting the fiscal rules score with a Eurozone

Table 8.3. Fiscal consolidation and domestic fiscal rules, 2011–14

	Δ PSB	Δ PSB	Δ PSB
Rule	**−0.165**	**−0.401**	**−0.216**
	(0.160)	**(0.266)**	**(0.253)**
Rule*Eurozone		**0.290**	
		(0.274)	
Rule*PC			**−0.014**
			(0.085)
Eurozone		0.829	
		(0.804)	
PC			2.005**
			(0.727)
L. Δ GDP	−0.143	−0.130	−0.017
	(0.126)	(0.123)	(0.119)
L.Debt	−0.005	−0.007	−0.012
	(0.020)	(0.021)	(0.019)
L.AS	0.169	0.199	−0.141
	(0.353)	(0.352)	(0.345)
Government	2.420	2.586	2.152
	(1.524)	(1.552)	(1.415)
Opposition	1.889	2.088*	1.632
	(1.015)	(1.012)	(0.962)
Left	−0.063	−0.110	0.119
	(0.357)	(0.365)	(0.351)
Election	−0.411*	−0.409*	−0.361*
	(0.190)	(0.192)	(0.180)
Constant	0.027	−0.720	0.724
	(2.280)	(2.741)	(2.130)
N	108	108	108
R2	0.557	0.566	0.599

Note: Standard errors are corrected for groupwise heteroskedasticity and contemporaneous correlation across countries of the error terms are corrected with panel-corrected standard errors. * Significant at the 5% level; ** at the 1% level; *** at the 0.1% level. Standard errors listed below coefficients. Time and unit dummies not shown to preserve space.

membership and a program country (*PC*) dummy, I confirm that the role of fiscal rules is not conditional on these features. The intuition behind this test is that the role of fiscal rules in spurring fiscal consolidation might be stronger in the context of lending conditionality or the constraints of monetary union. The fact that both the fiscal rules' variable and corresponding interaction terms are statistically not significant suggests that this is not the case. Fiscal rules did not impact on discretionary fiscal policy outcomes during the Consolidation Years.[4]

This book has provided no evidence that fiscal rules matter for budgetary outcomes, whether in times of stimulus or consolidation. Nevertheless, EU member states and institutions continue to dedicate energy toward promoting and upholding fiscal rules, which to a large extent have been aspiration rather than coercive in nature. These rules are predominantly focused on stability free riding. On the plus side, EU rules have been a comparatively 'easy fix', especially as they continue to require no Treaty change. These piecemeal reforms amounted to proposals for what the Commission had aimed for over a long time and what German negotiators thought would fly well with the 'Stability Culture' narrative of crisis management. They offered a narrow profession of faith when other aspects of the economic catechism remained discordant. Critiques of these reforms argue rightly that they take attention away from needed policy responses (notably banking union; see Jones 2015) and contribute to the ongoing 'morality play' of EU crisis (Matthijs and McNamara 2015; see also Fourcade et al. 2013). The washed-out fiscal rules chorus, however soothing it may sound to some members, furthermore distracts from the real innovation of the post-crisis reform packages in fiscal policy coordination. This lies, so I argue, in the creation of the so-called MIP. It marks a departure away from a single-minded focus on stability free riding, toward a more balanced appraisal of stability and growth free riding. Specifically, the MIP established a scoreboard to provide an early-warning signaling device for potentially harmful macroeconomic imbalances in member states. Crucially, the MIP is both broad and flexible. It is 'not a numerical exercise' (Commission interview, February 2017). Assessing the functioning and impact of the MIP, the 'scoreboard is the least interesting aspect' (ibid.). According to another Commission official, 'strictly speaking [the scoreboard] is not needed at all. The indicators are there purely to legitimize the Commission's right to dig into issue areas that are sensitive nationally' (interview, February 2017). Although this procedure should be interpreted against a global recognition of the threat of imbalances, and the role that imbalances have played in the International Financial Crisis of 2007/8, the challenge of rebalancing has particular salience for the EU, and particularly for the Eurozone (see Chapter 3).

8.4.2 *Consolidation and Market Discipline*

'If you give the blood of your own people, the markets will calm down' (Ban 2016: 200)—this was the belief of the then Spanish Prime Minister Zapatero, according to one of his advisors. This belief was further motivated by a discussion Zapatero had with the then US Vice President Joe Biden, who 'with a cruelty that I've never encountered said that the only way to get market confidence is to take decisions that make you suffer really hard... that you are credible in a given set of circumstances if you subject your citizens to difficult tests and if unions openly reject your policies—in brief, if there are tears and suffering' (Zapatero 2013: 102, quoted in Ban 2016: 200). Spain is an example of a broader trend. Sue Konzelmann (2012: 29) reproves that 'in the aftermath of the 2008 financial crisis, economic policy has been increasingly dictated by financial market traders, with their own interests at heart'. The set of post-Great Recession consolidation policies are frequently presented as a necessary evil to restore market confidence. A positive reading of this is that de-politicized bond market pressure can discipline governments and bring about positive reforms, enabling 'sound' economic fundamentals (cf. Helleiner 1996: 324). Jens Weidmann (interview in Atkins and Sandbu 2011), German Bundesbank President, echoed this textbook defense of market discipline by suggesting that 'recent experience has shown that market interest rates do play a role in pushing governments towards reforms'. Chapter 7 has presented evidence for market discipline, in the form of debt servicing costs, impacting on stimulus outcomes—the higher the cost of borrowing, the lower the stimulus spending. This section will consider whether the forces of market discipline also impacted on fiscal consolidation. Put differently, was austerity driven by bond market pressure?

In answering this question I will include the same market discipline variable as in Chapter 7, namely the current debt servicing costs which measures as the interest payments as a percentage of GDP (*Cost*). In addition, I consider the role of bond yields (*Interest*) as well as changes in these variables (in addition to levels). Model specification and estimation techniques are identical to section 8.4.1.

There is evidence that market discipline spurred fiscal consolidation. Figure 8.2 illustrates this relationship with a plot of the average debt servicing costs as a percentage of GDP and the total consolidation efforts (measured as the cumulative change in the primary structural budget deficit) of 2011–14. Furthermore, as Table 8.4 indicates, changes in borrowing costs, total borrowing costs, sovereign bond yields, and total bond yields all impacted on the size of fiscal consolidation. An important difference between the drivers of fiscal policy outcomes of the Great Recession (2008–10) vs. the Consolidation Years (2011–14) emerges with respect to the effects of Eurozone membership.

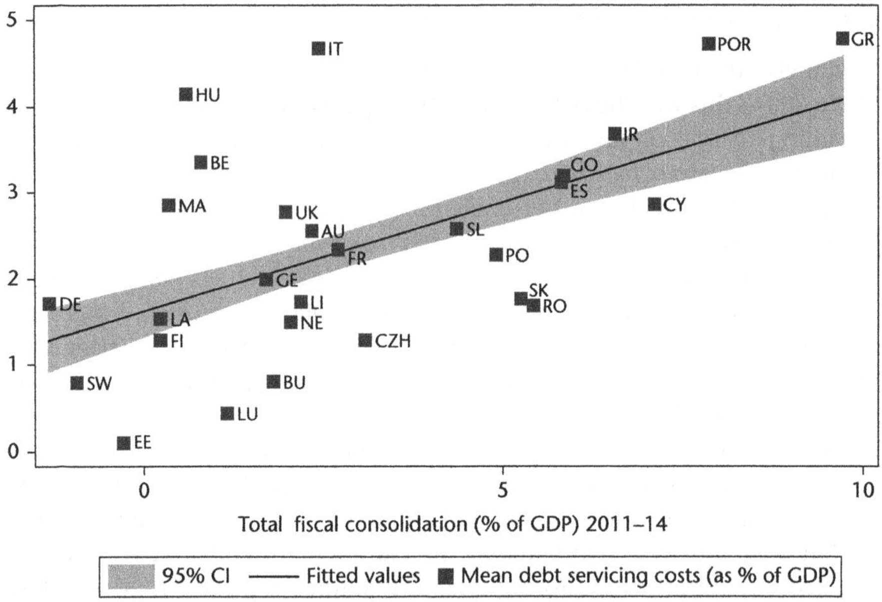

Figure 8.2 Fiscal consolidation and debt servicing costs

In Chapter 7 I presented evidence for the downgrading view of monetary union according to which Eurozone governments are to be more responsive to market signals. This finding does not hold for the Consolidation Years. I have argued that the finding of stronger market discipline in monetary union challenges the common wisdom of rampant moral hazard. Instead, policy-makers retained an awareness of the potentially heightened constraints of Eurozone membership and thus reacted more strongly to financial market signals. The fact that during the 2011–14 period markets seem to constrain EU and Eurozone member states alike needs further qualification. My interpretation is *not* that with the financial assistance programs in five Eurozone countries, market discipline can no longer be an adequate deterrent (cf. Lane 1993). Eurozone member states still respond to market discipline; there is simply no longer a difference between the responsiveness of Eurozone and non-Eurozone members to bond market pressure.

Before the eruption of the European Debt Crisis there was a common perception that bond market discipline in advanced economies was a thing of the past. With the re-emergence of financial market turmoil in Eurozone bond markets, the actual pressure of market discipline (in the form of higher yields and borrowing costs) met the *threat* of (further) market panic. The emerging fault line shifts from Euro-insider/Euro-outsider to debtor/(potential) creditor country (cf. Dyson 2014; Otero-Iglesias 2012; Moschella 2017). Controlling for both program country status and Eurozone membership with a

Table 8.4. Fiscal consolidation and market discipline, 2011–14

	Δ PSB	Δ PSB	Δ PSB	Δ PSB
Cost	**0.929*****			
	(0.239)			
ΔCost		**0.803***		
		(0.382)		
Interest			**0.321****	
			(0.113)	
ΔInterest				**0.201****
				(0.072)
L. Δ GDP	−0.232*	−0.189	−0.047	−0.195
	(0.117)	(0.117)	(0.123)	(0.127)
L.Debt	−0.030	0.008	0.004	0.006
	(0.019)	(0.020)	(0.019)	(0.019)
L.AS	0.419	0.185	0.266	0.402
	(0.329)	(0.336)	(0.346)	(0.356)
Government	1.393	2.089*	0.818	0.984
	(0.777)	(0.903)	(1.100)	(1.051)
Opposition	1.297	2.294	0.567	0.595
	(1.454)	(1.569)	(1.541)	(1.574)
Left	−0.229	−0.245	−0.020	−0.122
	(0.354)	(0.354)	(0.340)	(0.345)
Election	−0.311	−0.341	−0.460*	−0.438*
	(0.183)	(0.183)	(0.191)	(0.192)
Constant	−0.211	−1.093	−1.578	−0.407
	(2.000)	(2.229)	(2.250)	(2.090)
N	110	110	106	106
R2	0.596	0.582	0.608	0.604

Note: Standard errors are corrected for groupwise heteroskedasticity and contemporaneous correlation across countries of the error terms are corrected with panel-corrected standard errors. * Significant at the 5% level; ** at the 1% level; *** at the 0.1% level. Standard errors listed below coefficients. Time and unit dummies not shown to preserve space.

binary dummy,[5] there is evidence that while the former led to an increase in fiscal consolidation (+1.7), being a member of the Eurozone had no impact on discretionary fiscal policy outcomes (see Table 8.5). The dummy 'program country' used here does not capture the full spectrum of 'market panic vulnerability'. As David Woodruff argues (2016), in threatening to refuse to act as lender of last resort for government bonds, the ECB was able to (openly) demand consolidation and reform even in non-program countries. The example of Italy stands out here and highlights the power of the ECB. Any discussion of the role of market discipline remains incomplete without considering the role of European institutions in amplifying or muting market pressure, chief amongst them the ECB. This is true irrespective of whether one considers the ECB as a 'hero or as an ogre' (Schmidt 2016: 32, f4; see also Högenauer and Howarth 2016).

The challenge remains to 'find a way to channel market discipline in a positive way' (Hallerberg 2011: 129). I argue that the program to harness

Table 8.5. Eurozone membership and program countries, 2011–14

	Δ PSB	Δ PSB	Δ PSB
Eurozone	**0.921**		**0.760**
	(0.896)		**(0.793)**
PC		**1.903****	**1.881****
		(0.637)	**(0.633)**
L. Δ GDP	−0.176	−0.075	−0.075
	(0.118)	(0.117)	(0.117)
L.Debt	−0.002	−0.013	−0.011
	(0.020)	(0.019)	(0.019)
L.AS	0.256	0.010	0.012
	(0.345)	(0.349)	(0.348)
Opposition	2.260*	2.064*	2.122*
	(0.972)	(0.908)	(0.915)
Government	2.616	2.307	2.368
	(1.548)	(1.446)	(1.442)
Left	−0.041	0.103	0.121
	(0.361)	(0.358)	(0.360)
Election	−0.428*	−0.357	−0.376*
	(0.195)	(0.185)	(0.188)
Constant	−1.219	0.719	−0.313
	(2.608)	(2.094)	(2.455)
N	110	110	106
R2	0.555	0.590	0.592

Note: Standard errors are corrected for groupwise heteroskedasticity and contemporaneous correlation across countries of the error terms are corrected with panel-corrected standard errors. * Significant at the 5% level; ** at the 1% level; *** at the 0.1% level. Standard errors listed below coefficients. Time and unit dummies not shown to preserve space.

market discipline should be replaced by an attempt to shield member states from it. And yet there is a surprisingly resilient consensus on the role of market discipline in guiding public finances. The 'Deauville deal' is perhaps the most noted episode of this continuing endorsement of market discipline. Reached allegedly on the beach of a French seaside resort, the deal between Angela Merkel and Nicolas Sarkozy formalized private sector involvement in future debt relief or restructuring. This agreement sought to ensure that 'markets should provide some ex ante discipline for fiscal excesses' (Brunnermeier et al. 2016: 29). As a result, interest rates on peripheral countries' debt increased markedly and disproportional of said 'excess'. Consensus on market discipline spans institutions and political affiliations. Commission officials in particular came out readily in its defense: 'market pressure is the only way to go, the only really effective pressure on government action' and 'it's essential, we couldn't operate without it' (interviews, February 2015). One member of the Permanent Representation of a EU member state that had run afoul of bond investors poetically suggested that (without detectable irony) 'they are the moral guardians sitting at the top of the hill, they give an indication to member states as to whether they are on the right track' (interview, March 2015). Despite the tremendous upheaval of the debt crisis, EU policy-makers were unable to agree on how to discourage discrimination in sovereign risk pricing. On the contrary, the German Finance Minister Wolfgang Schäuble (2011b) launched into a full-hearted defense of market discipline at an EU summit that conveniently ignored the fact that bond yields do not only react to fiscal recklessness:

> But we must not simply abandon interest rates as a disciplinary mechanism. Governments need the markets. Markets tell governments things that governments don't want to hear. And they force governments to do the right thing, although too often too late and too suddenly. For this reason, I am convinced that we cannot do away with the threat of higher interest rates for spendthrift states.

The frustration of German officials regarding China's active buying of troubled governments' debts in 2011, on the grounds that these purchases would undermine the market discipline it was trying to impose on these governments, is telling in this regard (Otero-Iglesias 2012). Schäuble's endorsement of market forces shows a striking persistence of Europe's neoliberal policy support for 'depoliticized' monetary union (see McNamara 1998: 175; Dyson and Featherstone 1999: 786). At some point the reform architects at the EU level considered including bond yields in the macroeconomic imbalances' risk factor scoreboard. The idea was dropped because of the impracticality of deciding on an upper and lower threshold (interview, February 2017). And yet the persisting weakness of the reformed economic governance architecture, in combination with an explicit endorsement of financial market pressure, suggests that EU policy-makers are prepared to continue to rely on market discipline as a means to limit free riding.

8.5 Consolidation

This chapter has considered the determinants of fiscal policy outcomes during the Consolidation Years (2011–14). As governments ended stimulus efforts and implemented fiscal consolidation in an attempt to reduce budget deficits, these years brought the duality of the EU's free riding challenge into bold relief. Germany and Greece epitomize both sides. On the one side, Greece, cast as the archetypal stability free rider, a country with severely limited fiscal space, was forced to slash its budget. On the other side, Germany, well accustomed to accusations of growth free riding, faced complaints of premature budgetary retrenchment although it had considerable fiscal space. Despite these heated charges of free riding, the findings of this chapter confirm that member states' fiscal consolidation was by and large in line with domestic fiscal space. Those with limited space consolidated public finances more than those member states with larger fiscal space. This finding suggests that there was no first-order collective action failure in EU fiscal policy consolidation. Proponents of fiscal rules would credit the strictures of the SGP or newly created debt brakes for bringing about proportional consolidation. Yet there is no evidence (based on both interviews and the statistical material analyzed in this chapter) that these rules mattered for fiscal policy outcomes. The outsourced Olsonian incentive lies in financial market pressure—this holds for the Stimulus Years and the Consolidation Years alike. Financial markets held considerable sway over public finances, and this market discipline is now felt across the EU, as the equal responsiveness of Eurozone and non-Eurozone governments to bond market pressure suggests. Within these two groups there is naturally variation. A prominent emerging fault line runs between program (debtor) and those who fear the threat of market panic on the one hand, and credit countries who remain largely insulated from the vagaries of international capital markets on the other. This cleavage has broader implications for the future of European integration. It is visible not only in the sometimes toxic political discourse on financial assistance and fiscal consolidation, but also with respect to broader attitudes toward the EU. Public opinion regarding the benefits of EU membership shows a growing center–periphery divide with anti-EU parties across Europe emerging as one of the few 'crisis beneficiaries' (see Matthijs 2014). On the eve of the Great Recession, the average level of EU citizens' trust in the EU stood at 57 percent. By 2012 this level had fallen to 31 percent (and it stayed there for the next two years, after which it slowly recovered, but has yet to reach pre-crisis levels). As of autumn 2017 the majority of EU citizens *do not trust* the EU (48 percent vs. 41 percent, Eurobarometer Interactive 2018). This drop is, unsurprisingly, particularly strong for program countries. Compared to 2007 levels, trust in the EU fell by 21 percentage points in Greece (by 2010), 45 percentage points in Spain and 31 percentage points in Portugal (both by 2012), and 51 percentage points in Cyprus (by 2013).[6] Erik Jones, Dan Keleman, and Sophie Meunier (2016: 1011) worry that the piecemeal reforms of the past years have contributed to this trend because 'the perception that the EU is constantly in crisis and in need of reforms to salvage the union is undermining popular support for European integration'. Who would argue that muddling through, or governing by market panic (Woodruff 2016), has served Europe well?

Notes

1. This comparison is based on from the Monitoring of Fund Arrangements (MONA) of the IMF, which contains information about conditionalities, program goals, and monitoring.

2. Electoral costs are not the only costs of fiscal consolidation. See, for instance, the work on the link between fiscal adjustments and riots (Passarelli and Tabellini 2013).
3. To address the potential endogeneity of fiscal rules I use an instrumental variables estimation technique with the fiscal rules indicator instrumented by its t-1 and t-2 lag. I confirm that instruments are neither weak instruments (Kleibergen-Paap rk Wald F-statistic) nor correlated with the error term (Hansen J statistics). The Kleibergen-Paap rk LM-statistic allows me to reject the null hypothesis that the equation is under-identified (passing the critical value of 10). I then test for endogeneity and conclude that the specified endogenous regressors can be treated as exogenous for all dependent variable models (with p-values ranging from 0.11 to 0.64 for the corresponding null hypothesis).
4. The results also hold for the cyclical fiscal policy measures (changes in the budget balance and the primary budget balance).
5. The Eurozone dummy takes the value 1 if a country is a member of the Eurozone, and 0 otherwise. The program country dummy takes the value 1 if a Eurozone country receives financial assistance from the EU in that year (Greece, Ireland, Portugal, Spain, and Cyprus) and 0 otherwise.
6. The benchmark years chosen are the years when countries first applied to the EU for financial assistance.

9

Free Riding Beyond Hard Times

This book has sought to contribute to the wide literature on economic policy coordination by foregrounding the challenges of fiscal policy coordination in hard times. Fiscal policy during the Great Recession was not coordinated; member states adopted largely unilateral fiscal crisis responses. In so doing, national governments showed little concern for EU-level agreements or EU-wide stability and growth. Yet despite this lack of coordination, which would represent 'a significant modification of national policies in recognition of international economic interdependence' (Wallich 1984: 85), I find no strong evidence for first-order free riding, drawing on multiple methods. Looking ahead, the legacy of the crisis years is already shaping the future of fiscal policy coordination. The two main aspects of change are purview and pliancy. First, fiscal policy has ceased to be defined in narrow 'low-deficit' targets and instead is set to encompass a twin notion of free riding: growth free riding and stability free riding. Second, fiscal policy coordination has become more flexible and as a result more adaptive to the challenges of sound public finances in the twenty-first century. These developments are in principle welcome to keep fiscal free riding at bay. While the institutional architecture for collective action has been strengthened, there is little reason to be optimistic as to the containment of endemic second-order free riding; that is, the EU's inability to sanction free riders internally. Member states continue to rely on market discipline as the imperfect enforcer of rules they are unable to bring to bear amongst themselves. This chapter will reiterate the key findings of the analysis before addressing policy challenges ahead and suggesting avenues for future research.

9.1 Key Findings

As the economic and financial fallout of the Great Recession upended the belief that advanced economies enjoyed some type of superior inoculation against deep crisis, the EU sought to coordinate the fiscal responses of its member states. Part of this response was the European Economic Recovery Plan (EERP) which I presented in Chapter 2. This crisis plan appealed for countercyclical policies amounting to a total of 1.5 percent of EU GDP. After decades of championing low deficits and debt levels, the European Commission emerged as an unlikely advocate of stimulus policies throughout the EU, calling for a relaxation of the application of existing rules under the Stability and Growth Pact (SGP). The crisis framework laid out in the EERP presented an attempt to coordinate not fiscal constraint but, for the first time, fiscal expansion. With the declaration that '[w]e sink or swim together', the EERP (2008) provides a clear economic rationale for the coordination of fiscal response strategies—interdependence.

The basic argument in favor of fiscal policy coordination, outlined in Chapter 3, is found in the need to internalize the externalities arising from spillover effects. Fiscal policy is considered a matter of common concern and its coordination emerges as a means to achieve better outcomes. The challenge for fiscal policy coordination during the Great Recession was then to prevent two types of free riding behavior. The first type, growth free riding, involves benefiting from other countries' expansive fiscal policies—it is about spending 'too little'. The second type, stability free riding, considers the hazard of too much fiscal expansion, which might threaten the stability of the Eurozone in particular and the EU more generally—it is about spending 'too much'.

Prior to 2008, fiscal policy coordination was seen as a means to prevent stability free riding and, more concretely, to prevent monetary or fiscal bailouts. This changed during the Great Recession. On the one hand, the economic fallout prompted a Keynesian moment in the EU, as well as across the developed and emerging market world. This brought the coordination of stimulus packages, and consequently concerns over growth free riding, to the top of the EU fiscal policy agenda. On the other hand, the recession of 2008 and, even more forcefully, the European Debt Crisis have brought the so-called 'Sound Money paradigm' into bold relief. Macroeconomic stability could no longer be reduced to low inflation rates and low deficit levels. This led to a reappraisal of what sound fiscal, and more broadly sound macroeconomic, policy could comprise. The old schism between good fiscal policy (low deficits) and bad fiscal policy (high deficits) has come under attack. Indeed, the notion of growth free riding was institutionalized alongside a strengthening of stability free riding provisions with the Six Pack.

Fiscal policy coordination is marred by a classic collective action problem; it pays to be egoistical. In other words, member states have an incentive to under- or overstimulate their economies, despite a common interest in coordinated policies. Given the focus on free riding, Mancur Olson's treatise on collective action (1965) provides the theoretical foundation of this book.

Building on Olson's premises on collection action failure, I developed three research questions that guided the empirical investigation. These cover the EU's group latency, incentives for collective action, and free riding behavior. As a first step, I examined whether, in terms of fiscal policy coordination, EU member states form a latent group for which collective action is inherently challenging. The existence of group latency is said to render the provision of separate and selective incentives necessary in order to motivate group members to contribute to the production of the collective good in question. Hence, as a second step, I analyzed the evidence for and against fiscal free riding during the Great Recession. Successful collective action/rampant free riding would suggest effective/ineffective selective incentives to curb or boost public spending. Thus as a third step, I investigated the workings of different incentives, identified in fiscal rules/fiscal policy agreements and market discipline. Here the focus was on whether these incentives mattered for public finances in times of crisis.

9.1.1 *Group Latency*

Chapter 4 set out to examine the determinants of fiscal policy outcomes and tested whether the EU can, in terms of fiscal policy coordination, be considered a latent group. In so doing, I analyzed time-series cross-sectional data from the then twenty-seven EU member states over three years (2008–10). This is a comparatively small sample and findings are further interrogated vis-à-vis qualitative materials, notably interview data. I focused on a range of fiscal policy measures, from bespoke summaries of stimulus packages to statistically less ambiguous headline indicators of public finance, namely the (primary) budget balance and (primary) structural balance. The empirical analysis confirmed that the deficit bias attributed to contemporary public finances was stronger during the Great Recession. Political factors have shaped public finances markedly. I argued that fiscal policy outcomes were not apolitical products of the harsh economic logics of compulsion, but a complex result of intervening political features: '[public] policies seldom, if ever, represent a definitive solution to a problem' (Majone 1975: 270). Faced with a common shock, member states not only responded to the economic imperative of crisis management, but also identified different solutions to similar problems. These were co-determined by the political landscape: namely, the electoral calendar, political fragmentation, and executive partisanship. The diversity of political conditions has implications for the latency of the EU member states and in turn the coordination of fiscal policy choices. Member states without election years falling in the 2008–10 period, for example, were more likely to implement smaller stimulus programs than those where policy-makers faced the electorate imminently. Conversely, right-leaning governments were more likely to have designed larger stimulus plans than their left-leaning counterparts. This suggests that being part of a latent group meant that member states may have either under- or overstimulated their national economies, depending on their political profile.

9.1.2 *Free Riding*

Latent groups are a hotbed for free riders. Thus, building on the findings of group latency, Chapter 5 tested whether fiscal policy coordination was marred by free riding. Specifically, both stability and growth free riding behavior were investigated. The central claim of this chapter is that accusations of stability or growth free riding are not borne out by factual evidence. I showed that despite their greater ability to free ride, larger and more open economies implemented larger stimulus programs. To better distinguish between growth and stability free riding, I considered fiscal response strategies vis-à-vis a country's fiscal space; that is, a country's room for public spending without undermining fiscal sustainability. This allowed me to ask whether countries stimulated *too much* in relation to their small fiscal space (stability free riding) or *too little* in relation to their large fiscal space (growth free riding). In so doing, I constructed a new composite indicator based on the EU's Excessive Imbalances Procedure (EIP) and correlated its score with member states' fiscal crisis responses. Results show that, by and large, member states stimulated their economies in line with their fiscal room for maneuver as laid out in the EERP. These findings are contrasted with the political discourse of late 2008 and 2009, when accusations of growth free riding were widespread. Accusations of beggar-thy-neighbor politics were rife; first-order fiscal free riding was not.

9.1.3 *Incentives*

According to Olson, latent groups need incentives. As I did not find evidence for first-order free riding, I asked in Chapters 6 and 7 which incentives may be credited for this. Specifically, I analyzed two types of incentives to keep first-order free riding in check, whether stability or growth free riding: fiscal rules and market discipline. The empirical findings suggest that domestic fiscal rules, such as debt brakes, did not impact on the fiscal policy responses to the Great Recession. Similarly, EU-level fiscal agreements, the SGP and the newly created EERP, did not impact on fiscal policy choices. First, the majority of domestic fiscal rules were equipped with exceptionality clauses. As a result, they did not impose stern constraints on fiscal policy choices in times of crisis. And even where those escape clauses were not in place, policy-makers loosened the rules to enable them to mitigate the economic fallout. Second, the role of EU rules and agreements in shaping fiscal policy choices has been found wanting ever since the creation of the SGP in the late 1990s. I argued that in terms of fiscal policy outcomes, the EERP was meaningless; member states essentially adopted stimulus programs as they saw fit with little concern for EU-level agreements or EU-wide aims for stability and growth. It would be a mistake to assume that just because member states predominantly resorted to an increase in public expenditure to combat recession, these policy choices were driven by EU-level incentives. Instead, discretionary stimulus spending as a response to the economic downturn seems to have been a default option for developed, and to a lesser extent emerging, market economies.

The vague commitments under the EERP and the generous implementation of the Excessive Deficit Procedure (EDP) further speak to the reluctance of sovereign policy-makers to coordinate fiscal policy in hard times. In this book I argued that the efforts of fiscal policy coordination during the Great Recession were unsuccessful. And yet these efforts did matter—not for fiscal policy outcomes, but for the European institutions' promotion of collective action. Despite its deficient steering power for public finances in times of crisis, the EERP was a meaningful policy choice for the Commission. The EERP both excused non-compliance with the SGP and upheld the appearance of fiscal policy coordination. These efforts during the Great Recession furthermore paved the way for a more comprehensive, flexible system of economic governance, which recognizes the challenges of both growth and stability free riding.

In contrast to fiscal rules and intergovernmental agreements, the incentives provided by market discipline (measured as interest payments and bond yields) are found to have an impact on fiscal crisis responses. Importantly, this effect is stronger for Eurozone member states. Adopting the common currency, I argued, increases market discipline. This is because of heightened capital mobility, the absence of both hard and soft unilateral domestic debt monetization, and the (again unilateral domestic) use of exchange-rate adjustments. In contrast to budgetary rules and EU-level agreements, market discipline offers both stick and carrot, via a change in borrowing costs. Key to the disciplinarian success of market discipline is the fact that it is not faced with the second-order free riding problem (Oliver 1980), i.e. it is not a decentralized incentive provided within the collective action group. Markets do not punish governments primarily to prompt budgetary consolidation—market punishment is a by-product of risk pricing.

Yet markets punish governments neither in a linear nor a proportional fashion. The near-absence of market discipline in the first decade of the Economic and Monetary Union (EMU) and the sudden soaring of bond spreads in 2009 speak to this. The track record of financial market participants to price sovereign risk punctually and correctly is far from perfect, with bond investors' surprise at the UK's EU referendum in June 2016 being a recent example. Further compounding the deficiency of markets as fiscal policy sheriff is the fact that markets react far more to stability free riding than growth free riding. Although markets clearly care about economic growth, and thus are not automatically averse to stimulus policies, imbalance-fueling growth strategies are often left unsanctioned. The risk premium on Dutch sovereign bonds, for instance, is not damaged by its 10 percent export surplus—if anything, it is treated as a positive sign of a competitive economy. Along similar lines, investors have on occasion effectively paid money to the German government for being able to lend money to Berlin by accepting (near-)negative interest rates. Internal EU-level incentives were all but absent to prevent growth free riding. I argue that, particularly in hard times, policy-makers do not need further incentives to stimulate their economies. This view of public finances is in line with a vast literature on the determinants of government expenditure and the political business cycle. Again, in the words of one interviewee: 'Do you really think anybody needed to tell Germany to help its car industry?' Growth free riding—that is, spending 'too little' vis-à-vis a country's fiscal space—was thus kept at bay by governments' natural propensity for state intervention—a propensity that is amplified in times of crisis, as Chapter 4 suggested. Put bluntly, governments like to spend money and in hard times they have a strong(er) mandate to do so.

Relying on market discipline gives rise to the so-called second-order free riding problem. Building on the literature of collective action failure, we know that latent groups need incentives to overcome the standing temptation of free riding. Second-order free riding refers to members not contributing to the provision of these incentives. The evidence presented in this book suggests that stability and growth free riding were kept at bay. And yet I argue that second-order free riding continues to pose a risk. Even in the absence of growth or stability free riding, markets have been empowered to compensate for weak rules and procedures whilst being poorly correlated with free riding in the first place. Put differently, volatile and procyclical market punishment continues without member states' fiscal policies necessarily being at odds with EU collective action goals. By analogy, a nightclub owner would be unlikely to endorse a bouncer who erratically harasses customers. EU member states continue to enable financial market pressure.

9.1.4 *The Consolidation Years*

Chapter 8 considered what drove fiscal policy outcomes during the Consolidation Years (2011–14). Echoing Chapter 5, the findings suggest that notwithstanding heated charges of free riding, member states' fiscal consolidation was by and large in line with domestic fiscal space. This means that those with limited space consolidated public finances more than those with larger fiscal space, and vice versa. There is little evidence for first-order collective action failure in EU fiscal policy consolidation. Proponents of fiscal rules would credit the strictures of the SGP or newly created debt brakes for bringing about consolidation. I argue instead that these rules did not matter for fiscal policy outcomes. Instead, the outsourced Olsonian incentive lies in financial market pressure—this holds for the Stimulus Years and Consolidation Years alike. Financial markets held considerable sway over public finances. But market discipline is not felt equally across the EU. A prominent emerging fault line runs between programs (debtors) and those who fear the threat of market panic on the one hand, and credit countries who remain largely insulated from the vagaries of international capital markets on the other.

9.2 Containing First-Order Free Riding

Fiscal policy goes to the heart of politics. It is 'by definition political to its core' (Hallerberg 2004: 2). Setting—or perhaps more to the point, respecting—upper and lower limits for public finances is a formidable task for EU member states, no matter how urgent or compelling the underlying logic of interdependence may be in suggesting a need for (greater) fiscal policy coordination. Fiscal policy outcomes do not emerge in a political vacuum, but are instead best described by a host of factors emerging from the interplay of politics and economics. Economic conditions in Europe set the scene for fiscal policy coordination (see Chapter 4). The past crises have revealed the limits of applying this motto to an 'ever closer' economic and monetary union and laid bare the destabilizing effects of a diversity found in macroeconomic imbalances. Economic diversity is increasing: growth developments in the EU are continuing to diverge. Yet this disparity points to more than just different economic growth trends; it is indicative of vastly different political challenges facing EU policy-makers in times of enduring financial instability and fiscal consolidation. The obvious division line separates debtor (program) and creditor countries, in addition to old parameters (Eurozone and non-Eurozone, north and south, core and periphery, old and new member states). Different country groups have vastly different, even diametrically opposed, views on the scope and directionality of fiscal policy coordination, as well as the importance of and remedy for growth or stability free riding. Given persistent divergences and heterogeneity between EU economies, it is unlikely that the latency of EU member states will decrease in the near future. Building on Olson (1965: x), member states would be well advised to look for 'innovative institutional arrangements well matched to their local circumstances' in order to make diversity work. EU members have set out to reform economic governance and complemented the institutional arrangement in place to boost not only fiscal but also economic policy coordination more broadly. Key here is that these arrangements should adopt in-house enforcement, instead of outsourcing this task to financial markets.

9.2.1 *SGP 3.0*

The SGP, together with the EU's entire economic governance edifice, was renovated in the years after the Great Recession under the Six Pack, the Two Pack, and the Fiscal Compact. The aim of these updates and piecemeal reforms was to strengthen and broaden fiscal policy coordination under the SGP with its remaining 3 percent deficit and 60 percent debt levels (see Chapter 2). Commentators have highlighted the renewed possibility of sanctions under the EDP with the newly introduced reversed majority voting. Yet for now, there is little reason to assume that 'SGP 3.0' (Larch et al. 2012) will exert more substantial pressures. The recent experience of the EDP shows that member states are cautious not to escalate the procedure and avoid moving it up to the newly introduced reverse majority voting (Hodson 2013). Reverse majority voting is not extended to all decisions taken by the Council. The key decision to place a country under EDP in the first place continues to be governed by the old qualified majority process. Furthermore, it is not only governments in the Council that have opted for a soft reading of the SGP; the Commission has also come out as a champion of its increased flexibility, shying away from recommending sanctions. Pierre Moscovici, the new Commissioner for Economic and Financial Affairs, justified the decision not to sanction France and Italy on the grounds that the Commission's aim was to encourage deep reform and not apply penalties 'willy-nilly' (*Financial Times*, February 25, 2015). It is telling that the highest escalation of the EDP to date had little to do with public finances. In the case of Hungary, the Council decided to freeze its EU structural funds in 2012 because Hungary did not take the necessary steps to correct its excessive deficit. Yet this move was primarily concerned with the democratic values of the EU, which were considered under threat by the nationalistic Orban government, rather than with fiscal policy coordination. This episode also suggests that in the future 'sanctions cannot be ruled out, if a country is playing rough' (interview, February 2017).

Since (re-)opening a wave of EDPs in 2008–9, the delayed deadlines for correcting excessive deficits have been set and generously (re-)revised, and rightly so. The flexible and cautious application of the SGP during the Great Recession and beyond bears little resemblance to Martin Sandbu's assertion (2017: 110) that the 'EU enthusiastically wielded the excessive deficit procedure'. What enthusiasm? The new SGP is comfortable with the appeals to exception mode that has started to dominate fiscal policy coordination since 2008. In the words of Moscovici: 'It's clear we need to take into account some circumstances, structural reforms, investment, natural phenomena, earthquakes, fight against terrorism, all the work, and integration of refugees. This explains why the pact is no more a rigid, stupid, pro-cyclical tool' (*Reuters*, October 28, 2016). The corollary of this practice may well be that 'peer pressure' erodes further as member states congratulate themselves on actions taken. This poses risks for three reasons. First, while this should not be problematic in times of economic distress (when deficit reduction may well be procyclical), problems are likely to emerge in the subsequent years when anti-cyclical measures call for stronger fiscal consolidation. Second, although a lack of peer pressure does not take away from the wanting substance of the SGP, it risks spilling over into areas of economic policy coordination which can play a more positive role in facilitating collective action, notably the Macroeconomic Imbalances Procedure (MIP). And third, the lack of peer pressure reinforces the existing justification of the delegation to financial markets in the face of internal enforcement failure. One Commission official described the arc of peer effects as 'from peer sanctions, to peer pressure and now we have peer support' (interview, April 2013). There is a common perception that the post-2008 reforms have led to stricter and sterner economic governance as an institutionalization of fiscal discipline (e.g. Henning 2017: 4). My interpretation is different. Instead of strong and inflexible, EU rules are floppy and weak. The first is to be welcomed; flexibility and contingency are an asset. The second feature, however, is problematic as it gives rise to second-order free riding.

9.2.2 *Goodnight SGP*

Flexible or not, the SGP is no safeguard against instability or the need to bail out other member states. Fiscal policy coordination, with its focus on low deficit and debt levels, failed to address the causes of both the economic and financial crisis of 2007 and the subsequent European Debt Crisis. Charles Wyplosz (2013) attempts to rescue the 'sound fiscal policy' paradigm by redefining fiscal discipline: 'the Sovereign Debt Crisis is the result of a lack of fiscal discipline broadly defined to include adequate banking supervision'. This definition is decidedly unhelpful; the attempt to bring the experience of the debt crisis under the mantle of the SGP risks confounding financial markets and public finances; that is, the causality between fiscal policy outcomes and financial sector stability. Mark Blyth (2013) has perhaps most vocally and rightfully argued against the hazards confusing the high costs of bank bailouts with irresponsible fiscal policies. Granted, sound fiscal policy is ultimately impossible without a sound financial sector. Yet the real threat to macroeconomic stability was found in the financial-fiscal feedback loop, not in corybantic policy-makers seeking to buy electoral favor. Repeated attempts to thrust fiscal policy into the limelight of crisis recall the old joke about the International Monetary Fund (IMF) acronym ('It's mostly fiscal')—EU fiscal policy coordination can do better than that. Ultimately, then, the SGP has not fulfilled its purpose and should be disbanded. This is neither a radical nor a novel suggestion (Enderlein 2004). In principle, low budget deficits are desirable. The problem is rather that the SGP signals an unwarranted hierarchy of policy goals with deficits below 3 percent at the top.

Disbanding the SGP can be done relatively straightforwardly. The MIP establishes the bridge between macroeconomic imbalances and fiscal sustainability. In contrast to the SGP, it is not skewed toward a single indicator, nor is it 'a numerical exercise' (interview, February 2017). In an accompanying document (European Commission 2011b), the Commission emphasizes that 'the sustainability of public finances will not be assessed in the context of the MIP given that this issue is already covered by the SGP'. The artificial separation of macroeconomic imbalances and fiscal sustainability is impractical. In the Commission's justification of the choice of indicators, accompanied by a comprehensive review of the literature, the link between each indicator and fiscal sustainability, default, and crisis incidences is meticulously presented (ibid.). Currently the scoreboard includes the general government sector debt as a percentage of GDP, with a threshold of 60 percent. By complementing this indicator with a (structural) deficit measure, the MIP is able to replace the SGP. The European Semester recommendations already read like a more sensible and nuanced version of the EDP. Resolving the SGP into the MIP would uphold the idea of fiscal restraint in context, while at the same time increasing the profile of these new processes. The SGP can and should go gently into that good night.

9.2.3 *After the Great Moderation*

Of all the new processes for macroeconomic surveillance and coordination, the MIP has the strongest potential to address both stability and growth free riding. Despite this potential, in its current form it is tilted toward stability free riding and predominantly targets deficit countries with the current account balance thresholds at 6 percent for surplus countries and 4 percent for deficit countries. However, it is worth considering that when MIP indicators were designed, it was estimated that *no country* would breach the 6 percent current account surplus in the foreseeable future (interviews, March 2011 and February 2017). Consequently, the decision of the European Commission to launch an in-depth review against Germany in November 2013 came as a surprise to many, not least to German officials who thought the surplus target would leave them with enough of a margin—a prerequisite for agreeing to the threshold in the first place. The Commission's conclusions were predictably guarded: 'Germany is experiencing macroeconomic imbalances, which require monitoring and policy action' (COM (2014) 150 final, March 5, 2014). This language is a feature of the MIP application across countries; in the first 2012 round of the MIP review, no country (not even Cyprus, where a banking crisis erupted the following year) was found to have excessive macroeconomic imbalances. The phrasing of country reports ('very serious' instead of 'excessive') suggests a cautious approach, so as not to alert financial markets and signal credit risks. In times of market crisis it became inappropriate 'to call a spade a spade' (interviews, March 2015 and February 2017). Likewise, the Commission's debt sustainability analysis has adopted a cautious approach: 'for the short-term classification [of sovereign risk] we are extremely careful; for the time being it is all low risk. I don't know what would happen if we had one country flagging high risk in the short term' (interview, February 2017). This brings to mind Jean-Claude Juncker's comment on why he lied about organizing a secret crisis meeting with a few select member states, the European Central Bank (ECB), the European Commission, and Greece in 2011. This lie was justified by not wanting to spook the markets; 'if the going gets tough, you have to lie' (*FAZ*, May 10, 2011). This points to the performativity of EU crisis management, but also of EU-level risk assessments where 'recommendations and findings in and of themselves shape events' (interview, February 2017). The in-depth review of the German economy nevertheless makes for a very different reading than that of the previously identified surplus countries Sweden and the Netherlands. In its review the Commission (COM 2014) dissects Germany's surplus position, pointing to subdued domestic growth, inefficient allocation of domestic resources, a lack of investment, labor costs, and 'the adverse effects on the functioning of the domestic economy and of the euro area'. The final imbalances report on Germany is not only almost twice as long as the other seventeen country reports, but lists more contributors than the in-depth reports for France, Spain, the Netherlands, and Ireland combined—this review is not a perfunctory exercise.

Regardless of how individual countries respond to being admonished by the MIP, any attempt (however limited) to address broader governance problems is to be welcomed. At the EU level this represents a substantial shift and broadening of the debate on macroeconomic policy coordination; 'politically the MIP has established a dialogue where we look at both sides of the coin' (interview, March 2015). Perhaps less audible outside of the country, the discussion about imbalances and Germany's contributing role in destabilizing the Eurozone is now an important part of the political debate within Germany (Rommerskirchen and Snaith 2017; Johnston 2016: 180f).

9.2.4 *In Defense of Sanctions*

Sanctions are naturally not popular. The MIP, though still in its infancy, has the potential not only to provide a broad review of economic policy surveillance, but also to support the twin notion of free riding. To matter, though, the MIP must not shy away from using clear language and applying its tools, including sanctions. Note that sanctions apply not for the initial violation of rules, but in the event of a member state not acting upon recommendations to rectify a macroeconomic imbalance. Fining Germany under current rules (up to 0.1 percent of a country's GDP) would add over €3bn to the EU budget of about €130bn—which would roughly represent the sum allocated to its Youth Employment Initiative between 2014 and 2020. This is money that could be well spent along the lines of what the EU's Structural Funds already do. Currently sanctions under the MIP only apply to Eurozone member states. Yet imbalances can pose risks for the EU as a whole, not just the Eurozone, as the events of 2008–9 suggest. In relative terms (percent of GDP) the current account deficits of Greece and Portugal do not look dissimilar to Latvia or Hungary and the current account surplus of Denmark is comparable to that of Germany.

In contrast to the erratic lottery of market discipline, internal sanctions can be applied in a targeted, linear, proportional, and transparent fashion. Market discipline is a by-product of risk pricing. It is not a function of first-order free riding and yet it has been enlisted to sanction collective action. Critics of fines complain that these fines were counterproductive by taking money away from government when it is most needed, akin to kicking somebody down on the ground (Buiter et al. 1993). First, this criticism does not consider the alternative costs of market discipline. The past experience of Greece, Spain, Portugal, Italy, Ireland, or Cyprus clearly suggests that the economic costs of market panic by far exceed those of EU-level sanctions. Markets are procyclical and erratic; EU rules needn't be. Second, sanctions in times of economic distress are highly unlikely because of exceptionality provisions and the discounting of hard times. Imposing sanctions on Portugal and Spain, despite being in clear breach of the rules, was considered 'immoral' given the burden of adjustment both countries had experienced in the previous years. Even Wolfgang Schäuble, dubbed 'Europe's foremost ayatollah of austerity' (*Economist*, February 7, 2015), came out advocating leniency—a signal interpreted by some members of the Council to better 'not be holier than the pope' (interview, April 2015). Germany's austerity bark lacks bite outside of program conditionality.

EU rules need to matter in good times. In the words of a senior Commission official, 'we need something that also that works when we are out of crisis and when the recommendations are less popular than saying "let's stimulate".

We need something that works on the downside and on the upside' (interview, February 2017). So rules must not enforce procyclical austerity as is feared or alleged, but instead focus on countercyclical stabilization. This furthermore counteracts the likely absence of market discipline in rosy economic times. Sanctions offer an incentive for collective action. They can encourage countercyclical policies which may not be recognized or even disincentivized by procyclical bond investors.

9.3 Market Scapegoats

In times of fiscal consolidation, financial markets offer a scapegoat for unpopular policy choices. Austerity politics are presented as the forced response of a state that has become a residual authority sandwiched between financial market pressure and the conditionality of EU financial assistance. Austerity measures in peripheral Eurozone member states, so the common lament goes, 'have been dictated too much by market sentiment instead of being the outcome of rational decision-making processes' (De Grauwe and Ji 2013). Consequently, fiscal consolidation is the price for restoring market confidence (Altman 2013) and squeezes governments 'between what markets want and what populations will accept' (Schwarzer 2012). Scholars with otherwise different perspectives seem to agree on the power of markets: 'international investors... unrelentingly police sovereign commitments to austerity' (Schaefer and Streeck 2013: 20) and 'austerity, however, has not been imposed by policymakers, but by the capital markets' (Sinn 2014: 4). These concerns echo the hyper-globalization thesis of the relentless demands of globalization and mobile capital 'threatening, diluting or eroding the powers of the state' (Sbragia 2000: 243; see also Horsman and Marshall 1994). This narrative of the powerless state faced with 'the enemy [of] the world of finance', as the former French President Hollande (quoted in Bamat 2018) put it, is politically convenient. Extending Schäuble's (2011b) logic, financial markets not only 'tell policy-makers what they don't want to hear', but also what other member states cannot or do not want to enforce. Not wanting to forgo the disciplinarian effects of sovereign risk pricing, policy-makers risk amplifying the constraints of market discipline with considerable costs for national economies and the E(M)U project as a whole.

Without internal enforcement (that includes the use of sanctions), fiscal policy coordination will continue to rely on market discipline. This has, and is likely to continue to be, disadvantageous for many of the EU's member states. Policing free riders has been deliberately left to financial markets, specifically bond market investors. Instead of enlisting bond investors as enforcers of fiscal discipline, the interdependence of EU membership, and particularly the vulnerabilities of Eurozone membership, need to be addressed. A clear commitment to internal collective action and its enforcement can provide an impetus for reducing the sovereign risk that markets react to, thus also mitigating market discipline. Ever since the dawn of financial globalization, policy-makers in the developing and developed world have sought to (re)define the relationship between global capital markets and government autonomy (Weiss 1997; Jessop 2002; Mosley 2003). For EMU policy-makers this challenge is complicated by the unique status that being part of 'the last utopia of the 20th century' (Pisani-Ferry 2014: 19) confers. In Chapter 6, I showed that the constraints of market discipline are higher inside EMU than outside. Chapter 8 suggested that in the wake of the Great Recession market discipline is now felt across the EU, with program (debtor) countries facing the brunt. Containing market discipline is not doing away with gravity. There is nothing natural about the current set-up of collective action, and neither is it condemned to be an immutable, permanent feature of EU policy coordination. In so arguing I take issue with one Commission interviewee's defenses of market discipline, namely that 'nothing better has been found' (interview, March 2015).

9.3.1 *Gimme Shelter*

Market discipline is not the result of a normative or pedagogical agenda of market participants. Bond yields do not rise because investors want to punish governments. First and foremost, bond yields are the result of any portfolio model with standard preferences for risk and return which covers both push and pull factors. Put crudely, market discipline is therefore primarily concerned with supply and demand, not crime and punishment. Investors are not out to discipline governments but to make a return on an investment. In contrast to EU members, financial markets are not working toward a reduction of free riding. This applies not only in the context of growth free riding (where account surpluses are not sanctioned), but also to stability free riding; for some investors searching for yield, risk tolerance matches the promised return. Investment decisions are guided by the question of 'is the price right?' (given the underlying sovereign risk) and not by considerations of whether EU rules are respected or whether governments are free riding. Given that the preferences of EU policy coordination and bond investors do not align well, it is problematic to enlist bond markets with the task of enforcing collective action. On these grounds, proposals to shelter EU members from the vagaries of financial markets (particularly where they relate to 'sudden stop' dynamics) are to be welcomed.

Various suggestions on a common issuance of sovereign bonds (for a review see Curzio 2011) laid out plans to tame market discipline. This effectively seeks to channel market discipline despite the fact that there is little evidence that market participants are reliable judges. Eurobonds thus continue the tradition of outsourcing discipline as a way to contain moral hazard. I am skeptical that Eurobonds are 'the most potentially efficacious alternative solution to the euro's woes' (Matthijs and McNamara 2015: 230) and that they can achieve the desired outcomes (stable and low borrowing costs combined with limited deficit spending) in both good and bad times. In good times, Eurobonds are unlikely to offer an incentive for 'responsible borrowing' as yields are likely to be comparatively low for both mutually guaranteed and domestic bonds. Member states are then facing little disincentive (in the form of higher borrowing costs) for issuing sovereign bonds outside of the agreed mutually covered allocation. In bad times, governments may breach the debt limits guaranteed by Eurobonds. Existing proposals predominantly replicate the existing arbitrary ceiling of 60 percent, arguing that 'eurobonds would only be available for responsible borrowing' (Delpla and Von Weizsäcker 2011). A charitable explanation of the repurposing of idiotic thresholds would be that linking a newly and fiercely contested proposal to an established and (particularly from reluctant creditor countries) widely embraced procedure would help to overcome political resistance. Still, these proposals, in so doing, are linked to a simplistic and wrong view of what constitutes sound public finances and implicitly risk favoring a narrative that blames irresponsible public finances. All EU program countries had debt levels that (often due to the costs of bank bailouts) exceeded the suggested 60 percent threshold. In times of crisis, sovereign borrowing is then likely to take place outside of the umbrella of Eurobond protection and bound to attract prohibitively high interest rates. Even where an extension of coverage was agreed, along the lines of existing 'exceptionality provisions', this is sure to attract political controversies and divisions. Extended Eurobond borrowing would be presumably subject to the same conditionality and political uncertainty that undermine the ability of financial assistance under the European Stability Mechanism (ESM) to calm market participants. Niels Thygesen (2010), the new chair of the European Fiscal Board, is wrong to applaud this ambiguity in the Eurozone's rescue mechanisms in order to let investors impose discipline on national governments. Ambiguity has contributed to the escalation of the crisis.

9.3.2 *Destroying the Doom Loop*

The proposals on Eurobonds, albeit rightly identifying the need to insulate member states from (excessive) market discipline, risk perpetuating the 'sound public finances' view of the E(M)U. Again, the Eurozone crisis is not so much a crisis with fiscal as with financial causes. This means that shelter from markets is most needed where it relates to financial sector instability and not fiscal union or debt mutualization (see also Sandbu 2017; Jones 2015). The banking union project launched in June 2012 recognizes this diagnostic and seeks to address the 'doom loop' of weak sovereignty and weak banks (Howarth and Quaglia 2016). The interconnection between governments and banks has been a painful feature of the crises following 2008, with bank bailouts burdening public coffers and suspicions of sovereign creditworthiness weakening the position of domestic banks who were among the key holders of their sovereigns' bonds. Academics have long recognized the need for European banking supervision and, more importantly, resolution (Folkerts-Landau and Garber 1992; Vives 2001; Goodharta and Schoenmaker 2009). Banking union originally aimed at cutting the ties between bank failure and sovereign debt distress by creating a joint pool to deal with the costs of bank resolution, a so-called fiscal backstop. The current EU banking union sets up a system where (most) banks are supervised together by member states and treated similarly under shared banking resolution rules. But the third pillar, a meaningful fiscal backstop, is absent. Beyond a shared €55bn fund, a mere one-five-hundredth of the assets of European banks, bank bailouts continue to be national (Jones 2015). In the event of a banking crisis, this will inevitably resemble bringing a knife to a gunfight. To complete a banking union alongside what has existed in the USA since 1933, the ECB's lender of last resort ability must be boosted. This means governments agreeing to buy into the scheme by offering fiscal backing and standing ready to indemnify any ECB losses. Such policy initiative aimed at the banking sector would go a long way to mitigate market discipline, addressing the fiscal vulnerabilities of EU member states and, by implication, the collective action challenge within fiscal policy coordination.

9.3.3 *Market Discipline Meets the ECB*

It is not fiscal rules or even the partial mutualization of debt that is necessary for the survival of the Euro, but the ability and willingness of its central bank to step up. Indeed, Charles Wyplosz (2011: 16) muses that 'the EFSF [European Financial Stability Facility] is a sideshow that provides the ECB with an excuse not to act as lender of last resort'—the lender of last resort referring to the ultimate source of credit for a given country's financial system. Extending this political economy production of *The Lady Who Swallowed a Fly*, there are arguably two sideshows: the Fiscal Compact for the ESM and the EFSF and, more importantly still, banking union for ECB action. Since 2009 the ECB has taken numerous initiatives to fight liquidity problems affecting financial institutions and ensure a smooth transmission of monetary policy, notably through intervention in secondary sovereign markets. In July 2012 the ECB president Mario Draghi (2012a) held a speech addressing investors in London with by-now-famous words scribbled in the margins: 'The ECB is prepared to do whatever it takes to preserve the euro—and believe me it will be enough'. The desired effect of the ECB's 'wagon of fat' moment was almost instantaneous. In Spain, for example, the interest rate on ten-year government bonds fell from 7.62 to 6.75 percent within a week of Draghi's promise and to 5.27 percent by the end of 2012, with similar effects observable throughout the Eurozone (Hodson 2013). Subsequently the ECB has become the *de facto* lender of last resort with the launch of 'outright monetary transactions' (OMT) that put a backstop to the European Debt Crisis. These transactions, which allow for the purchase of government bonds in the secondary market, are essentially a financial assistance mechanism. Similar to the ESM, OMT countries are subject to strict conditionality and approval is subject to a similar procedure (with support needed from the EU and IMF).

In the short run, Draghi's pledge has assuaged market discipline; the No-Bailout Clause is no longer credible, if it ever was. That does not mean, however, that market discipline will cease to be harmful. First, collective action clauses in newly issued Eurozone government securities signpost the road toward private sector involvement (debt restructuring) in the event of crisis.[1] Second, current bailout arrangements, whether they involve member states or the ECB, remain uncertain. Their credibility is contingent on the political ability and willingness to assist other member states in crisis. It seems that bond investors are aware of this component and that 'the political will could change with the next election' (fixed-income manager, interview, March 2014). According to one US investment analyst, '[the] crucial thing is the position of a pro-European sentiment. If you see Golden Dawn and Beppe Grillo, Ukip, to really gain traction, getting 25–30 percent, maybe joining coalitions, that would be to me a sign that the political landscape is changing' (interview, October 2013). Bond yields for crisis countries in the periphery have not fallen uniformly and market participants continue to distinguish between member states' credit risk. Financial assistance is likely to be a permanent and resilient feature of EU economic governance. To contain market discipline, monetary and fiscal bailout must be allowed to remain in the toolbox of policy-makers. Bailouts are of course neither a novel nor distinct feature of the EU or even Eurozone membership. The same goes for the moral hazard (Vaubel 1983; Breen 2013). From inter-state debt relief in the United States in the 1970s to the rise of the IMF, the politics of modern-day financial assistance have played out at the global level. With the ESM and the yet-to-be-completed banking union, the EU has created two crucial pillars to address members' financial and fiscal risks in-house. In so doing, EU member states have just started to wake up to the reality of their interdependence. When the Greek bailout was first discussed, fears of moral hazards were cited as an objection, namely that financial assistance would encourage future governments (in Greece and elsewhere) to engage in similarly reckless actions. Given the disastrous experience of the Greek bailout programs, it is hard to imagine a country willfully running excessive deficits by banking on bailout from fellow member states. This is hardly an attractive prospect (cf. the 'co-payment' dimension of this in Schelkle 2017). Given the predominantly non-fiscal nature of the Eurozone crisis, member states in need of a bailout are hardly farmers who just bought fire insurance and are now playing with matches.

9.4 Macroeconomic Policy Coordination Goes Global

As I mentioned in Chapter 2, interdependence between countries is ubiquitous in the contemporary global economy. Consequently, collective action problems underpin multilateral macroeconomic coordination efforts beyond the borders of the EU. Dan Drezner claims that the institutions of global governance (particularly the G20, the IMF, and the World Trade Organization (WTO)) succeeded in coordinating crisis responses and thus prevented an outright escalation of the global financial crisis. Particularly, the G20 as a forum for coordination on issues spanning the political gamut from finance to climate change to global health has received much scrutiny. Some argue that G20 efforts had little policy significance (e.g. Helleiner 2014; Rommerskirchen 2015; Rommerskirchen and Snaith 2017), while others hold it up as a major boost for cooperation (e.g. Cooper and Thakur 2013; Kirton 2014). This book joins ranks with the 'system worked' literature with its assessment of EU first-order free riding, but reaches a damning verdict regarding second-order free riding. If and how EU member states resolve the political and economic tensions resulting from growing imbalances will be watched with interest by spectators across the globe. Tensions between surplus and deficit countries are of course not limited to the EU. At the time of writing this book, developments between China and the US in the context of bilateral trade imbalances are a particular cause for worry. More broadly, global macroeconomic imbalances continue to create the conditions for boom and bust cycles to wreak havoc. Demonstration means with which to cope with economic interdependence in a peaceable way have been the root of European integration from its humble beginnings. Getting EU rebalancing right would be a high achievement indeed.

Future research in this area should focus on two areas. First, more rigorous empirical work is needed on the relationship between first- and second-order free riding in international economic cooperation. While the literature is so far focused on scrutinizing collective action success or failure, a more comprehensive assessment of the origins and consequences of second-order free riding in the global economy is missing. As the web of agenda items for economic policy cooperation at the global level grows, the task of disentangling the processes of coordination will increase in complexity—and so will the benefits of greater understanding. Second, more comparative work is needed to establish a framework to assess collective action failure/success across countries and across time. 'Better than the Great Depression?' has been a frequent yardstick for policy of the Great Recession (e.g. Kahler 2013: 30; Drezner 2014; Brainard 2015). It is of course above all fortunate that scholars lack global economic crises for a more suitable comparison—even at the expense of comparative insights. Other accounts of success for multilateral cooperation frequently relate to notions of 'what ifs', where calamitous counterfactuals serve as interrogative foils. Financial system breakdown and trade and currency wars were—and in future crises will continue to be—substantial threats to peace and prosperity. Designating these outcomes as markers of failures speaks to the low expectations that dominate scholarship on global collective action problems. This risks a bias toward a heroic verdict on collective action in hard times.

9.4.1 *Crumbling Consensus*

The Great Recession upheaved thinking in macroeconomic policy-making and spelled the end of the Great Moderation period. Prior to 2008, a broad consensus on the merits of prioritizing low inflation and low deficits was secured by the apparent stability of the pre-crisis decades in the developed world. The crisis threw the fallacies of this paradigm into stark relief, illuminating systemic risk in corners of the economy that lay beyond the conventional boundaries of macroeconomic policy regulation and coordination. Faced with the limitations of existing governance strategies in predicting, let alone preventing, the economic fallout, policy-makers across the globe sought more nuanced and integrated guidelines on macroeconomic management. Yet to some this was only another blow to a system that was already torn and tattered well before Lehman Brothers collapsed (Helleiner 2014). Yet the notion of the Washington Consensus remains prominent in International Political Economy scholarship. Other alternatives have been thrown on the wall—yet so far refuse to stick (Babb 2013; Ramo 2004). For the EU, the lack of policy consensus has thrust the logic of consequences to the fulcrum of policy coordination. In contrast to most international cooperation, EU collective action has the ability to bite. With a more comprehensive governance structure to address both growth and stability free riding, the new mode of coordination has become more complex and as a result open for contestation. This is a good thing. The absence of fiscal policy consensus requires a deliberative mode of coordination. Arguably these recent developments, although gaining momentum during the crises, do predate the events studied in this book. After all, 'the EU has long been considered a consensus-generating machine par excellence' (Menon 2008: 1). Based on the evidence presented in this book, I speculate that fiscal policy coordination in the EU will be possible without strong policy consensus. As Webb (1995: 259) reminds us, 'the historic record suggests, the possibilities for coordination are greater when government leaders disagree among themselves about what policies to pursue'.

Ascertaining whether Webb remains correct in this assessment, and if so why, will be an intriguing issue for future research. The research avenue charted here is not confined to the EU or to fiscal policy issues. First, the EU's monetary policy consensus that Kathleen McNamara (1998) diagnosed in the run-up to the EMU has eroded during the European Debt Crisis and the ECB's (re)interpretation of the rules on the go. This internal discord surrounding the ECB's roles of financial and Eurozone stability and keeping to its inflation mandate has become visible with the resignations of Axel Weber from the Bundesbank and Jürgen Stark from the ECB's executive board. Debates on the role of the ECB will continue for the foreseeable as the ECB is poised to remain in a 'more political' role, not least in the context of banking union where it will supervise national banks. Looking beyond the EU, Alex Cukierman (2013) sees this contestation playing out across central banks and predicts further upheaval in the policy consensus in the years to come. Second, at the international level, the paradigms underpinning financial sector cooperation have likewise come under attack. Some commentators claim that the crisis has propelled a new consensus around the notion of macro-prudential ideas in international regulatory policy communities to the forefront (e.g. Baker 2013), while others argue that consensus-building has been incremental and is not leading to meaningful reform (e.g. Helleiner 2011). One interesting question to address here is whether strong structures of cooperation like those found in the EU can mitigate the lack of consensus. A coordination mode of deliberation and contestation takes time—a key ingredient of which the G20 notably has little, with a diverse cast of issues from anti-corruption and climate change to Ebola competing in the calculus of attention (interview, March 2015). Future research will be able to tell us what this shattering of policy consensus means for future collective action and whether economic policy coordination will remain a space void of concord.

9.5 Black Box Market Discipline

Market discipline has been made the linchpin of EU collective action. Yet instead of the market being 'a talisman' (Jabko 2006), it has been its curse. The experience of the European Debt Crisis has upended the common wisdom about market discipline in developed market economies. For the first time since the 1970s, developed countries—generally thought able to borrow as much as they wished—needed official financial assistance to repay their existing debt. In particular, the turmoil of Eurozone members has thrown existing views into bold relief as the adoption of the Euro was thought by many to provide governments with more 'room to move'; to strengthen their economies and therefore state capacity. The experience of market discipline in developed economies post-2008 put existing assumptions of credit risks into question—'old market assumptions have broken down' (*Financial Times*, June 9, 2010). In the words of a senior fixed-income manager, 'we are witnessing the rediscovery of tail risk in developed country bond markets' (interview, February 2017)—more accurately, market participants are not merely witnesses of this but key promoters. Axel Weber (2016), the former head of the German Bundesbank, argued that investors in industrialized countries are facing 'the unprecedented situation [of] mature country risk'. An important question that Weber's assertion throws up is whether Mosley's (2003) influential portrait of 'strong but narrow' market pressure in the developed world still holds. The evidence presented in this book suggests that the answer is no. A more comprehensive answer to this question calls for an updated analysis of market discipline in the twenty-first century. In revising Mosley's seminal thesis, future research may well avoid binary camps such as developed and developing economies—recent evidence suggests that these distinctions are becoming increasingly fluid and ultimately obsolete.

In this book I have treated market discipline as an amalgamated source of pressure (measured as bond yields or debt servicing costs). Yet more research is needed to differentiate between bond investors' evaluation practices of sovereign risk and capacity for loyalty. Discussion of financial markets, like the treatment of other markets, tends to lump together actors with distinct, possibly even opposing, characteristics. Labels such as 'electronic herd' (Friedman 2000), 'bond gods' (Krugman 2010), or 'Marktvolk' (Streeck 2014) do not do justice to the different evaluation and investment practices of financial market participants. And yet within the academic literature there is a growing body of research that suggests important differences between bond investors (Andritzky 2012; Hardie 2011; Wellhausen 2015). With the addition of new data on the make-up of government bond investors (Arslanalp and Tsuda 2012; Merler and Pisani-Ferry 2012), the opportunity exists for more rigorous testing. This research agenda calls for a probe into the mechanisms and micro-foundations of market discipline by opening up the black box of financial markets and investigating how different types/classes of bond investors respond to policy and influence those policies in turn. An analysis here should consider not only the behavior of bond investors (that is, the determinants of specific investor groups' sovereign risk pricing), but also governments' responsiveness to market discipline, and whether responsiveness is contingent on its investor base. Across the globe, market discipline continues to exert pressure on national governments. For some countries, like the US or Germany, bond investors are easy bedfellows; for others, like the recent economic collapse of Venezuela or the ongoing Greek saga, market pressure is brutal. In the context of the EU, market discipline is actively courted and empowered. It is high time we come to terms with who these investors are, what they want, and how governments react to them, given the prominent role of bond investors as fiscal policy sheriffs in the EU and beyond.

Note

1. From July 2013 onwards standardized and identical collective action clauses (CACs) are included in all new Eurozone government securities with a maturity above one year. CACs allow creditors to change the terms of payment (such as extensions of maturity or interest rate cuts). This decision can be reached by qualified majority which aims at overcoming the so-called 'holdout creditor problem' that has, for example, plagued debt restructuring in Argentina.

APPENDIX 1

Operationalizing Fiscal Space

Among the most prominent proxies for fiscal space is the ratio of public debt to GDP. It is much less problematic for countries with a balanced budget and low debts, so the argument runs, to stimulate the economy by increasing demand through increased spending than it is for countries with high debts and deficits. For countries with high public sector debt to GDP ratios, a lack of fiscal space not only restricts the government's ability to implement discretionary fiscal policies, but also weakens the effectiveness of fiscal stimulus spending (Baldacci et al. 2009). Accordingly, there should be a negative relationship between the debt burden and the stimulus measures adopted. Aizenman and Jinjarak (2010) construct a variable for the '*de facto* fiscal space' of a country, measured as the inverse of the tax-years it would take to repay the public debt. Alternative methods construct a sustainability indicator comparing the current and future debt levels to identify the fiscal gap (Buiter 1985). Problematically, these indicators are based on long-term projections, which are necessarily subject to wide margins of error (Balassone and Franco 2000).

In its annual publication on public finances in the Economic and Monetary Union (EMU), the European Commission presents a fiscal space indicator composed of five variables: 1) the initial public debt, 2) the contingent liabilities vis-à-vis the financial sector, 3) the expected revenue shortfalls stemming from the unwinding of the real estate and construction boom, 4) the current account position, and 5) the share of discretionary expenditure in the government budget. A large government debt, high contingent liabilities, potentially high tax revenue shortfalls, and a large share of non-discretionary expenses are expected to reduce a country's fiscal space and thus enter the composite indicator with a negative sign. Yet the meaningfulness of the indicator is questionable because some of the scores obtained do not accurately reflect a country's fiscal sustainability—for example, according to this study, Bulgaria has a larger fiscal space than Germany and Finland, and Romania has more room for maneuver than Sweden and Finland.

There are two main reasons for the apparent miscalculation of the European Commission indicator. First, the standardization method of the indicator relies on z-scores.[1] This 'rewards' exceptional behavior. A very good performance in a few sub-indicators leads to a higher value for fiscal space than a lot of average scores. The low debt burdens in Romania and Bulgaria, for example, are likely to lead to an overestimation of the country's fiscal space. On a related note, it may be asked whether debt levels and payments of social benefits are a good indicator of a country's fiscal space. The debt crisis has brought the old levels of debt sustainability (usually set at 60 percent of GDP, in line with the Maastricht criteria) into bolder relief. Spain and Portugal faced financing difficulties, despite their economies being 'widely seen as fundamentally solvent' (Gros 2012: 37). Eastern European countries in particular have low debt burdens, which do not indicate high fiscal room for maneuver. Furthermore, the inclusion of social benefits is likely to introduce a bias in the indicator. First, by focusing merely on social benefits rather than social transfers in kind, the measurement is hardly complete. Public expenditure in kind is a substantial part of the costs of the welfare state. More problematically, the link between the size of the welfare state and fiscal sustainability is dubious. On the one hand, Nordic countries are in particular famous for their generous social benefits without this negatively impacting their fiscal space. On the other hand, the comparative paucity of welfare state provisions in Eastern European countries should not be seen as a predictor of fiscal sustainability.

One way to correct the bias of sub-indicators would be to omit the best and worst sub-indicator scores from inclusion in the index or by assigning differential weights based on the importance of the sub-indicator scores. Second, given the high complexity of the estimation of a country's fiscal space, it may be advantageous to create a larger set of sub-indicators from which to construct the fiscal space score. Seeking to obtain an appropriate indicator, I introduce new sub-scores based on the EU's Excessive Imbalances Procedure (EIP) and use a different weighting strategy based on factor analysis.

In the first instance, factor analysis is able to reveal how different variables change in relation to each other and how they are associated. Specifically, factor analysis transforms correlated variables into a new set of uncorrelated variables. In so doing it groups together individual indicators which are collinear to form a composite indicator that captures as much as possible of the information common to individual indicators. Bear in mind that the weighting corrects for the overlapping information between two or more correlated indicators and is not a measure of the theoretical importance of the associated indicator. I follow the procedure described in OECD (2008) and begin with the full set of ten variables of the EIP. These are again:

1. Three-year backward-moving average of the current account balance as a percentage of GDP, with a threshold of +6 percent of GDP and −4 percent of GDP;
2. Net international investment position as a percentage of GDP, with a threshold of −35 percent of GDP;
3. Five years' percentage change of export market shares measured in values, with a threshold of −6 percent;
4. Three years' percentage change in nominal unit labor cost, with thresholds of +9 percent for Eurozone countries and +12 percent for non-Eurozone countries;
5. Three years' percentage change of the real effective exchange rates based on Harmonized Index of Consumer Price (HICP) and Consumer Price Index (CPI) deflators, relative to thirty-five other industrial countries, with thresholds of −/+5 percent for Eurozone countries and −/+11 percent for non-Eurozone countries;
6. Private sector debt in percent of GDP with a threshold of 160 percent;

7. Private sector credit flow in percent of GDP with a threshold of 15 percent;
8. Year-on-year changes in house prices relative to a Eurostat consumption deflator, with a threshold of 6 percent;
9. General government sector debt in percent of GDP with a threshold of 60 percent;
10. Three-year backward-moving average of unemployment rate, with a threshold of 10 percent.

The first step is to derive a set of eigenvectors and their associated eigenvalues, restricting myself to those components that are associated with an eigenvalue greater than one (as suggested by, for example, Jolliffe 1986). Next I checked the correlation structure of the data to ascertain that correlation between the indicators is indeed strong. This is confirmed by the results of the Kaiser-Meyer-Olkin measure of sampling adequacy (0.78). The second step is to generate the factors. Following existing practice, I retain only factors whose eigenvalue is greater than one (Dunteman 1989: 22–3), which leaves me with three factors. In the third step I compute the rotation of factors to minimize the number of individual indicators that have a high loading on the same factor. Rotation changes the factor loadings and hence the interpretation of the factors. Next I construct the weights from the matrix of factor loadings after rotation using the square of factor loadings, which represents the proportion of the total unit variance of the indicator, which is explained by the factor. The weights listed in the last column of Table A8.1 in Appendix 4 represent the final weight to be used for the fiscal space composite indicator. These weights are then applied to the fiscal space sub-indicators based on the Macroeconomic Imbalances Procedure (MIP) scoreboard. For the composite indicator the individual scores are transformed into fuzzy sets ranging from 0–1. The findings related to the fiscal space indicator hold true if equal weights are used for the construction of the composite indicator to reflect the uncertainty about the origin of fiscal sustainability.

Note

1. Z-scores are a standardization method which converts indicators to a common scale with a mean of zero and standard deviation of one.

APPENDIX 2

Data Definitions and Sources

Δ BB: Change in the budget balance (Source: Ameco 2018).

Δ PB: Change in the primary budget balance (minus interest payments) (Source: Ameco 2018).

Δ SB: Change in the structural budget balance (Source: Ameco 2018).

Δ PSB: Change in the primary structural balance (Source: Ameco 2018).

Δ GDP: Real GDP annual growth rate in percent (Source: Ameco 2018).

Δ DEBT: Change in general government gross public debt as a share of GDP in percent (Source: Ameco 2018).

BAILOUT: Direct costs (recorded as an increase in debt) of financial sector interventions in percent of GDP (Source: Eurostat 2012).

AS: Size of automatic stabilizers as percent of GDP. Calculated as the change in the output gap multiplied by the revenue-to-GDP ratio (used as a proxy of the semi-elasticities of the budget balance) (Source: Ameco 2018).

GOVERNMENT: The sum of the squared seat shares of all parties in the government. In the case of 'other' parties, Herfindahl divides the number of 'other' seats by the number of 'other' parties and uses this average for the size of the 'other' parties. Independents are calculated as if they were individual parties with one seat each. (Source: Keefer 2010).

OPPOSITION: Calculated in the same manner as the Herfindahl government. (Source: Keefer 2010).

LEFT: A 0–1 dummy, coded 1 if a left government is in power. Variable is based on EXECRLC in Keefer (2010) which records the party orientation of the executive with respect to economic policy. Left: for parties that are defined as communist, socialist, social democratic, or left-wing.

ELECTION: A 0–1 dummy, coded 1 if an election was held in that year (Source: Keefer 2010).

RULE: Standardized fiscal rules index. The fiscal rules index measures the strength of fiscal rules based on their legal basis, coverage, strictness of monitoring and enforcement, and media visibility (Source: European Commission 2012).

INTEREST: Debt servicing costs, interest expenditure as percent of GDP (Source: Ameco 2018).

EU: A 0–1 dummy, coded 1 for EU membership.

Eurozone: A 0–1 dummy, coded 1 for Eurozone membership.

PC: A 0–1 dummy, coded 1 for EU financial assistance program country.

APPENDIX 3

Research Interviews

A key asset underpinning the arguments of this book are fifty-three interviews with bureaucrats and policy-makers working on EU economic governance in addition to eighteen interviews with financial market participants.

On the policy side, interviews were conducted at the European Commission, the European Council, the European Parliament (EP), Permanent Representations of the Member States to the EU, and the International Monetary Fund (IMF). The decision to interview broadly across different institutions is based on the 'fragmentation of responsibilities' (Hodson and Maher 2001: 645) of fiscal policy coordination. All institutions of the EU contribute to fiscal policy coordination to various degrees: 'Perhaps the most intractable aspect of [fiscal] coordination is that it is caught in a political no-man's-land between the member states and the supranational level' (Ardy et al. 2006: 114). Although not all are equally powerful, it is nevertheless not possible to single out one institution as the main locus for fiscal policy coordination. The European Council is responsible for setting the main policy orientations and manages a plethora of committees and policy coordination processes under its ambit. Here I interviewed members of the DG Economic and Regional Affairs. The EU's Committee of Permanent Representatives, or COREPER, is responsible for preparing upcoming ministerial meetings of the Council and has long been a major player in the EU system (see Lewis 2005). Interviews here offer a bridge to national perspectives on fiscal policy coordination. I paid particular attention to and succeeding in interviewing representatives of both Eurozone and non-Eurozone countries, new and old member states, program and non-program countries, as well as small and large countries. Interviews with eleven Permanent Representatives were conducted with staff of representatives' economic and financial affairs division or their functional equivalent, and in one case with the Permanent Representative to the EU.

Within the Commission, the Directorate General of Economic and Financial Affairs (DG Ecfin) is responsible for fiscal policy coordination. It monitors performance and compliance, acting as the representative of the EU interest, and as such is present at most Council and Committee meetings. The Commission's power in fiscal matters is perhaps greatest with respect to the Stability and Growth Pact (SGP), notably because of its reports that form the basis of the Council of Economic and Finance Ministers' (Ecofin's) assessment of national stability programs and the fact that the EDP is triggered by a recommendation from the Commission. Eurostat has the role of regulator of member states' fiscal accounting, watching over the accounting of budget deficits or public debt. Interview material from the Commission's statistical agency was especially helpful for Chapter 4 which identifies appropriate measurements of fiscal policy choices. During the Great Recession the Commission President José Manuel Barroso played an active role in the orchestration of stimulus policies, as Chapter 6 describes. One senior and two junior members of his cabinet were therefore interviewed as well. In President Juncker's cabinet, one junior and one senior member were interviewed as well. What is more, I interviewed members of the DG Competition's newly created Task Force Financial Crisis, as well as its general state aid division. This decision was motivated by the fact that fiscal policy choices during the Great Recession were potentially at odds with EU state aid rules. What is more, said Task Force is active in the country programs of EU member states receiving financial assistance and its members are very well informed about various reform proposals relevant to this study.

The European Parliament is excluded from most coordination procedures and has no say in the implementation of the SGP and fiscal policy coordination more broadly. Members do, however, have access to information via shared documents and hearings. Specifically, I interviewed members of the Committee on Economic and Monetary Affairs, who work on matters of fiscal policy coordination. Finally, I also conducted interviews at the IMF. During the debt crisis the IMF has gained importance for fiscal policy coordination in the EU, notably through its role in the Troika, surveilling, and (some would say) directing fiscal and macroeconomic policies in Greece. This development caused Hodson (2013: 1) to proclaim that 'the IMF emerged as a *de facto* decision-making body of the EU'. But even before 2010, the IMF was an active commentator on national and EU-level fiscal policy. These interviews incorporate an outsider's perspective.

Requesting, although perhaps not securing, interviews with EU officials is remarkably easy. A publicly available directory lists personnel according to their unit (hence responsibility) and contact details. To identify suitable interviewees from the financial sector I pursued three main strategies. First, whilst researching this book I consulted various reports from and news items featuring bond investors. Here I took note of relevant contacts. Second, via Morningstar's, an investment research and management firm reporting on the industry, I searched for key institutional players in the sovereign bond market and consulted their web presence to identify fixed-income managers and staff in related positions such as bond analysts. Third, I used LinkedIn, a business and employment-oriented social networking service, to search for financial market participants on the fixed-income/bond side with the available job search function. Although LinkedIn does not provide email addresses, in most instances names proved sufficient when matched with the company-specific email formula (e.g. firstname.lastname@firm.com). I also trialed LinkedIn's premium service which lets you send messages to members (similar to Facebook's internal messaging service), yet found that response rates were even lower, possibly because of the straightforward and built-in option to reject the interview request by clicking 'not relevant'. In the end I conducted eighteen interviews with institutional investors, fixed-income managers, and market analysts in Germany (Frankfurt, Berlin, and Cologne), the United States (Chicago and New York), and Belgium (Brussels).

Response rates to interview requests vary across time and interviewees. During the first year of interviewing EU policy-makers and officials in the spring of 2011, my response rate (the number of accepted interviews relative to interview requests sent) was 42 percent. In the two subsequent interview rounds in 2015 and 2017, my response rate increased to 70 percent. Four reasons for this notable change may be considered. First, the fact that I conducted the first interviews as a PhD student may have dissuaded busy EU officials from participating. Second, 2011 was an exceptionally hectic year for EU fiscal policy coordination, particularly for contacted EU officials working at the coalface of all things economic governance. Third, it is not impossible that I improved interview requests—better emails simply got better results. The high response rate here stands in contrast to that of my interview requests with financial market participants, where merely 35 percent of requests resulted in a successful interview.

Interviews took place almost exclusively at the interviewee's place of work. For the EU interviews this meant, with few exceptions, interviewees' offices next to walls with crayon drawings and report-clad desks. In the case of financial market participants in all but one interview, this meant a conference room. Here the mise-en-scene conveyed information primarily about the company, not the interviewee—like Toblerone bars on the conference room table and the cufflinks of my interviewee embossed with the Swiss equilateral cross.

The vast majority of the information gathered during the interviews was explicitly 'not for attribution' (e.g. Goldstein 2002); that is to say, it could be used and quoted provided that the individual would be granted anonymity. Five interviews were conducted over a series of email exchanges; six were conducted over the phone; and the remainder were face-to-face. The interview length varied from 30 to 150 minutes. In deciding how many interviews to conduct, this research was guided primarily by 'thematic saturation': continuing to interview so long as the evaluation of fiscal policy coordination continued to be markedly modified or added to substantially by the interviews. The interviews were relatively unstructured in form to capture more qualitative aspects of the challenges and dynamics of fiscal policy coordination. As such, the semi-structured interviews were based around a range of questions depending on the interviewee's job description, responsibilities, and (in some cases) previous expertise, covering subjects as appropriate. These open-ended questions allowed respondents to organize their answers outside of what Joel Aberbach and Bert Rockman (2002: 674) call 'the straightjacket of close-ended questions'. Using semi-structured in contrast to fully structured interviews furthermore complements the quantitative evidence of this book, and offers a deliberate counterweight to the unsubtle generalization inherent to quantitative analysis, particularly in the context of binary variables.

This analysis usually draws on individual interviews when exemplifying general tendencies or corroborating previous findings from other sources. In addition to exercising critical judgment about the information provided by interviewees (of which aspects might be colored by judgments and prejudices), I confronted them with different positions or apparent incongruities. What is more, interview material has not only been checked for consistencies and conflicting evidence, but also cross-referred to written documents where possible. For the purpose of minimizing potential methodological problems of elite interviewing, interviewees have been selected to control for known political, national, and institutional divides in EU politics, and an effort was made in the selection of interviewees to cover each country and to ensure a fair distribution in terms of age, background, and nationality.

APPENDIX 4

Supplementary Tables

Table A4.1. Hausman test for endogeneity of various variables (p-values)

Variables	Δ PSB	Δ SB	Δ BB	Δ PB
Endogeneity of macroeconomic variables[a]	0.07 **	0.05 **	0.11	0.07 *
Endogeneity of elections[b]	0.55	0.45	0.72	0.18
Endogeneity of fiscal rules[c]	0.34	0.57	0.39	0.17
Endogeneity of market discipline[d]	0.98	0.14	0.74	0.3

Note: The H0 hypothesis of the Hausman test is that the coefficient estimates of the standard regression model and the instrumental variables model are both consistent and do not differ. Therefore, if we fail to reject H0, endogeneity is thought not to be a problem. [a] The two macroeconomic variables, GDP growth and the change in public debt, are instrumented using the lags of these variables as well as US GDP growth and public debt. [b] Election years are instrumented using the constitutionally determined term duration. [c] Fiscal rules are instrumented using the lagged variable. [d] Market discipline is instrumented using the lagged variable as well as US interest payments on debt.

Table A5.1. Weights for the EIP indicators based on factor analysis

	Factor loading			Squared factor loading*			
	F1	F2	F3	F1	F2	F3	Weight**
Current account balance	0.61	0.46	0.19	**0.13**	0.11	0.02	**0.09**
Investment position	0.55	0.24	0.52	0.1	0.03	**0.16**	**0.06**
Export market shares	−0.68	−0.25	0.43	**0.16**	0.03	0.11	**0.1**
Nominal unit labor cost	0.15	−0.84	0.03	0.01	**0.36**	0	**0.16**
Real effective exchange rates	−0.66	−0.31	0.32	**0.15**	0.05	0.06	**0.1**
Private sector debt	0.69	−0.39	0.08	**0.17**	0.08	0.01	**0.1**
Private sector credit flow	0.38	−0.1	0.61	0.05	0.01	**0.21**	**0.07**
Changes in house prices	−0.22	0.67	0.49	0.02	**0.23**	0.14	**0.1**
General government debt	0.32	0.19	−0.69	0.04	0.02	**0.27**	**0.1**
Unemployment rate	−0.69	0.4	−0.2	**0.17**	0.08	0.02	**0.1**
Explained Variance	2.84	1.94	1.73				
Explained Variance/Total	0.44	0.3	0.26				

Note: * Scaled to unity sum. ** Final weights rescaled to sum up to 1. Explained Variance is the variance explained by the factor. Explained Variance/Total is the explained variance divided by the total variance of the factors. Weights are squared factor loadings multiplied by the Explained Variance/Total.

Table A6.1. Descriptive statistics of key variables for non-EU countries* (2008–10)

Variable	Observations	Mean	Std. Dev.	Min.	Max.
Δ PSB	18	−1.47	2.49	−8.1	2.2
Δ SB	18	−1.44	5.82	−21.4	10
Δ PB	18	−1.99	3.33	−8.16	3.8
Δ BB	18	−2.33	3.55	−8.2	2.5
L. Δ GDP	18	0.01	3.41	−6.6	6
L.Debt	18	91.29	56.51	28.49	210.25
Government	18	0.71	0.28	0.26	1
Opposition	18	0.54	0.25	0.33	1
Left	18	0.28	0.46	0	1
Election	18	0.39	0.5	0	1

* Norway, Canada, USA, Iceland, Japan, and Switzerland.

Table A8.1. Weights for the EIP indicators based on factor analysis, 2011–14

	Factor loading				Squared factor loading*				
	F1	F2	F3	F4	F1	F2	F3	F4	Weight**
Account balance	0.458	0.421	0.061	0.676	0.065	0.104	0.002	**0.456**	**0.11**
Invest. position	0.774	0.306	–0.290	0.093	**0.188**	0.054	0.069	0.008	**0.15**
Export market shares	0.376	–0.306	–0.191	–0.136	0.043	**0.054**	0.036	0.018	**0.02**
Unit labor cost	0.250	–0.658	0.583	0.036	0.019	**0.254**	0.029	0.001	**0.11**
Exchange rates	0.664	–0.212	–0.447	–0.258	0.138	0.025	**0.164**	0.066	**0.05**
Private sector debt	0.541	–0.101	0.292	0.378	0.092	0.005	0.070	**0.142**	**0.04**
Credit flow	–0.023	0.733	0.438	–0.212	0.003	**0.315**	0.191	0.044	**0.15**
Change in house prices	0.543	0.346	0.416	–0.508	0.092	0.070	0.142	**0.258**	**0.07**
Government debt	–0.809	–0.186	0.178	0.115	**0.206**	0.020	0.025	0.013	**0.17**
Unemployment	–0.694	0.398	–0.273	0.012	**0.151**	0.092	0.061	0.001	**0.13**
Explained Variance	0.318	0.176	0.122	0.101					
Explained Variance/Total	0.443	0.245	0.170	0.140					

Note: * Scaled to unity sum. ** Final weights rescaled to sum up to 1. Explained Variance is the variance explained by the factor. Explained Variance/Total is the explained variance divided by the total variance of the four factors. Weights are squared factor loadings multiplied by the Explained Variance/Total.

Bibliography

Abbott, K. W., & Snidal, D. (2000). Hard and soft law in international governance. *International Organization*, 54(3), 421–56.

Abdelal, R., & Blyth, M. (2015). Just who put you in charge? We did: credit rating agencies and the politics of ratings. In Alexander Cooley and Jack Snyder (eds.), *Ranking the World: Grading States as a Tool of Global Governance*. Cambridge: Cambridge University Press, 39–59.

Aberbach, J. D., & Rockman, B. A. (2002). Conducting and coding elite interviews. *PS: Political Science & Politics*, 35(4), 673–6.

Acharya, V. V., & Steffen, S. (2015). The 'greatest' carry trade ever? Understanding eurozone bank risks. *Journal of Financial Economics*, 115(2), 215–36.

Afonso, A., & Strauch, R. (2007). Fiscal policy events and interest rate swap spreads: evidence from the EU. *Journal of International Financial Markets, Institutions and Money*, 17(3), 261–76.

Aglietta, M., & Brand, T. (2015). II/La stagnation séculaire dans les cycles financiers de longue période. *CEPII: L'économie mondiale* 2016, La Découverte, Paris, 24–39.

Aizenman, J., & Jinjarak, Y. (2010). De facto fiscal space and fiscal stimulus: definition and assessment (No. w16539). National Bureau of Economic Research.

Alesina, A. (2010, April). Fiscal adjustments: lessons from recent history. In Ecofin meeting, Madrid, April (vol. 15, pp. 1909–40).

Alesina, A., & Bayoumi, T. (1996). The costs and benefits of fiscal rules: evidence from US states (No. w5614). National Bureau of Economic Research.

Alesina, A., & Ardagna, S. (1998). Tales of fiscal adjustment. *Economic Policy*, 13(27), 488–545.

Alesina, A., & Wacziarg, R. (1998). Openness, country size and government. *Journal of Public Economics*, 69(3), 305–21.

Alesina, A., De Broeck, M., Prati, A., & Tabellini, G. (1992). Default risk on government debt in OECD countries. *Economic Policy*, 7(15), 427–63.

Allard, J., Catenaro, M., Vidal, J. P., & Wolswijk, G. (2013). Central bank communication on fiscal policy. *European Journal of Political Economy*, 30, 1–14.

Almunia, J. (2008a). EMU@10: successes and challenges after 10 years of Economic and Monetary Union, Foreword by Commissioner Almunia. Brussels.

Almunia, J. (2008b). European Parliament Plenary Debate. Situation of the world financial system and its effects on the European economy. September 24, 2008.

Almunia, J. (2009). Commissioner Almunia calls for a stronger EU foreign economic policy. Brussels.

Alt, J. E., & Lowry, R. C. (1994). Divided government, fiscal institutions, and budget deficits: evidence from the states. *American Political Science Review*, 88(4), 811–28.

Altman, R. (2013). Blame bond markets, not politicians, for austerity. *Financial Times*, May 8.

Ameco (2018). Macro-economic database, European Commission. Available from: https://ec.europa.eu/info/business-economy-euro/indicators-statistics/economic-databases/macro-economic-database-ameco_en.

Andersen, T., & Malchow-Møller, N. (2014). Denmark's fixed exchange rate regime and the delayed recovery from the Global Financial Crisis: a comparative macroeconomic analysis (No. 10/2014). Department of Business and Economics, University of Southern Denmark.

Anderson, C. M., & Putterman, L. (2006). Do non-strategic sanctions obey the law of demand? The demand for punishment in the voluntary contribution mechanism. *Games and Economic Behavior*, 54(1), 1–24.

Anderson, N. (ed.) (1996). *Estimating and Interpreting the Yield Curve* (vol. 6). New York: John Wiley & Sons.

Andritzky, M. J. R. (2012). Government bonds and their investors: what are the facts and do they matter? (No. 12–158). International Monetary Fund.

Antonio, S., Symansky, S., Blanchard, O., & Cottarelli, C. (2008). Fiscal policy for the crisis. *IMF Staff Position Note*, 29, 2008.

Ardy, B., Begg, I., Hodson, D., Maher, I., & Mayes, D. (2006). *Adjusting to EMU*. Houndmills, Basingstoke; New York: Palgrave Macmillan.

Arestis, P., Mccauley, K., & Sawyer, M. (2001). The future of the Euro: is there an alternative to the Stability and Growth Pact? (No. 63). Public policy brief//Jerome Levy Economics Institute of Bard College.

Arghyrou, M. G., & Kontonikas, A. (2012). The EMU sovereign-debt crisis: fundamentals, expectations and contagion. *Journal of International Financial Markets, Institutions and Money*, 22(4), 658–77.

Armingeon, K. (2012a). The politics of fiscal responses to the crisis of 2008–2009. *Governance*, 25(4), 543–65.

Armingeon, K. (2012b). The politics of austerity: what political parties can do and what markets want. Presentation at the 2012 Meeting of the American Political Science Association. New Orleans, August.

Arslanalp, S., & Tsuda, T. (2012). Demand for government debt of advanced economies: a new database. IMF Working Paper.

Artis, A., & Corsetti, G. (2005). Market sanctions will replace pact. *Financial Times*, March 24.

Atkins, R., & Sandbu, M. (2011). FT interview transcript: Jens Weidmann. *Financial Times*, November 13.

Auerbach, A. J., & Gorodnichenko, Y. (2012). Measuring the output responses to fiscal policy. *American Economic Journal: Economic Policy*, 4(2), 1–27.

Axelrod, R. (1984). *The Evolution of Cooperation*. New York: Basic Books.

Ayuso-i-Casals, J. (2010). National fiscal governance reforms across EU member states: analysis of the information contained in the 2009–2010 Stability and Convergence

Programmes. European Commission, Directorate-General for Economic and Financial Affairs, Publications.

Babb, S. (2013). The Washington Consensus as transnational policy paradigm: its origins, trajectory and likely successor. *Review of International Political Economy*, 20(2), 268–97.

Baker, A. (2013). The new political economy of the macroprudential ideational shift. *New Political Economy*, 18(1), 112–39.

Balassone, F., & Franco, D. (2000). Public investment, the stability pact and the 'Golden Rule'. *Fiscal Studies*, 21(2), 207–29.

Baldacci, E., Gupta, S., & Mulas-Granados, C. (2009). How effective is fiscal policy response in systemic banking crises?. *IMF Working Paper: How Effective is Fiscal Policy Response in Systemic Banking Crises?*, 9(160), 1–26.

Ballabriga, F., & Martinez-Mongay, C. (2002). *Has EMU Shifted Policy?* (No. 166). Directorate General Economic and Financial Affairs (DG Ecfin), European Commission.

Bamat, J. (2017). François Hollande: The French president who was anything but 'normal'. *France24*. Available from: https://www.france24.com/en/20170405-france-president-francois-hollande-five-years-not-normal-look-back.

Ban, C. (2015). Austerity versus stimulus? Understanding fiscal policy change at the International Monetary Fund since the great recession. *Governance*, 28(2), 167–83.

Ban, C. (2016). *Ruling Ideas: How Global Neoliberalism Goes Local*. Oxford: Oxford University Press.

Barroso, J. M. (2008a). *A European Economic Recovery Plan*. Press Conference. Brussels, November 26.

Barroso, J. M. (2008b). From financial crisis to recovery: a European framework for action. Remarks by President Barroso after the extraordinary Commission meeting of October 29, Brussels.

Barroso, J. M. (2008c). The European Union in the 21st century and the role of the Commission. CEPS - Karamanlis Foundation International Conference. Brussels, November 4.

Barroso, J. M. (2009). State of the union: delivering a 'Europe of results' in a harsh economic climate. *JCMS: Journal of Common Market Studies*, 47(s1), 7–16.

Barroso, J. M. (2013). Austerity and growth debate: what President Barroso actually said at the Brussels Think Tank Dialogue. MEMO/13/368.

Bartels, L. M. (2014). Ideology and retrospection in electoral responses to the Great Recession. In Larry Bartels and Nancy Bermeo (eds.), *Mass Politics in Tough Times: Opinions, Votes and Protest in the Great Recession*. Oxford: Oxford University Press, 185–223.

Baum, C., Schaffer, M., & Stillman, S. (2007). IVENDOG: Stata module to calculate Durbin. Wu-Hausman endogeneity test after ivreg.

Beck, N., & Katz, J. N. (1995). What to do (and not to do) with time-series cross-section data. *American Political Science Review*, 89(3), 634–47.

Beetsma, R., Giuliodori, M., & Klaassen, F. (2006). Trade spill-overs of fiscal policy in the European Union: a panel analysis. *Economic Policy*, 21(48), 640–87.

Begg, I., Buti, M., Pench, L. R., Weale, M., Enderlein, H., & Schelkle, W. (2004). Reforming fiscal policy co-ordination under EMU: what should become of the Stability and Growth Pact? *Journal of Common Market Studies*, 42(5), 1023–59.

Bernoth, K., Von Hagen, J., & Schuknecht, L. (2004). Sovereign risk premia in the European government bond market. (No. B 26-2003). University of Bonn, ZEI-Center for European Integration Studies.

Berry, W. D. (1990). The confusing case of budgetary incrementalism: too many meanings for a single concept. *The Journal of Politics*, 52(1), 167–96.

Bird, G. (2012). Dealing with global economic imbalances: the political economy of policy coordination. *Global Economic Review*, 41(4), 299–317.

Birdsall, N. (2002). *What Went Wrong in Argentina?* Washington, DC: Center for Global Development, January.

Bishop, G., Damrau, D., & Miller, M. (1989). *1992 and Beyond: Market Discipline CAN Work in the EC Monetary Union*. New York: Salomon Bros.

Blanchard, O. (2012). Review: four hard truths. IMF Direct Blog.

Blyth, M. (2013). *Austerity: The History of a Dangerous Idea*. Oxford: Oxford University Press.

Bodea, C., & Huemer, S. (2010). Dancing together at arm's length? The interaction of central banks with governments in the G7. (No. 120). European Central Bank.

Bohn, H., & Inman, R. P. (1996). Balanced-budget rules and public deficits: evidence from the US states. *Carnegie-Rochester Conference Series on Public Policy*, 45, 13–76.

Bonatti, L., & Cristini, A. (2008). Breaking the stability pact: was it predictable?. *Journal of Policy Modeling*, 30(5), 793–810.

Bovenberg, A. L., Kremers, J. J., & Masson, P. R. (1991). Economic and monetary union in Europe and constraints on national budgetary policies. *Staff Papers*, 38(2), 374–98.

Brainard, L. (2015, April). Coming of age in the Great Recession. Economic mobility: research and ideas on strengthening families, communities, and the economy. Ninth Biennial Federal Reserve System Community Development Research Conference, April (vol. 2).

Breen, M. (2013). *The Politics of IMF Lending*. Basingstoke: Palgrave Macmillan.

Brunnermeier, M. K., James, H., & Landau, J. P. (2016). *The Euro and the Battle of Ideas*. Princeton, NJ: Princeton University Press.

Bryant, R. C., & Portes, R. (1987). Global macroeconomics: policy conflict and cooperation (vol. 84). London: Macmillan, in association with the International Economic Association and the Centre for Economic Policy Research.

Buiter, W. H. (1985). A guide to public sector debt and deficits. *Economic Policy*, 1(1), 13–61.

Buiter, W., Corsetti, G., & Roubini, N. (1993). Excessive deficits: sense and nonsense in the Treaty of Maastricht. *Economic Policy*, 8(16), 57–100.

Bulmer, S., & Paterson, W. E. (2013). Germany as the EU's reluctant hegemon? Of economic strength and political constraints. *Journal of European Public Policy*, 20(10), 1387–1405.

Bundesbank. (2013). Hohe Staatschulden Bergen Inflationsrisiken. http://www.bundesbank.de/Redaktion/DE/Themen/2013/2013_01_11_hohe_staatschulden_bergen_inflationsrisiken.html.

Busemeyer, M. R. (2004). Chasing Maastricht: the impact of the EMU on the fiscal performance of member states. *European Integration Online Papers (EIoP)*, 8(8).

Buti, M. (2009). Strategies for a post-crisis world: enhancing European growth. ECFIN Economic Brief.

Buti, M., & Van den Noord, P. (2003). Discretionary fiscal policy and elections: the experience of the early years of EMU (No. 351). Paris: OECD Publishing.

Buti, M., & Pench, L. R. (2004). Why do large countries flout the Stability Pact? And what can be done about it?. *JCMS: Journal of Common Market Studies*, 42(5), 1025–32.

Buti, M., & Carnot, N. (2012). The EMU debt crisis: early lessons and reforms. *JCMS: Journal of Common Market Studies*, 50(6), 899–911.

Buti, M., Turrini, A., Van den Noord, P., & Biroli, P. (2009). Defying the 'Juncker curse': can reformist governments be re-elected? *Empirica*, 36(1), 65–100.

Cafruny, A. W., & Magnus Ryner, J. (2007). Monetary union and the transatlantic and social dimensions of Europe's crisis. *New Political Economy*, 12(2), 141–65.

Camdessus, M. (1997). Address by Michel Camdessus, Chairman of the Executive Board and Managing Director of the International Monetary Fund to the Board of Governors of the Fund. Hong Kong, China, September 23.

Cameron, D. (1978). The expansion of the public economy: a comparative analysis. *American Political Science Review*, 72(4), 1243–61.

Cameron, D. (2012). *Fiscal Responses to the Economic Contraction of 2008–09*. Paper presented to the annual meeting of the American Political Association, Washington, D.C., September.

Cameron, D. (2013). Economy speech delivered by David Cameron. March 7.

Carstensen, M. B., & Schmidt, V. A. (2015). Power and changing modes of governance in the euro crisis. *Governance*. https://doi.org/10.1111/gove.12318.

Castles, S. (1998). Globalization and migration: some pressing contradictions. *International Social Science Journal*, 50(156), 179–86.

Catao, L. A., & Terrones, M. E. (2005). Fiscal deficits and inflation. *Journal of Monetary Economics*, 52(3), 529–54.

Chang, M. (2006). Reforming the Stability and Growth Pact: size and influence in EMU policymaking. *European Integration*, 28(1), 107–20.

Chari, V. V., & Kehoe, P. J. (2007). On the need for fiscal constraints in a monetary union. *Journal of Monetary Economics*, 54(8), 2399–408.

Chesler, C. (2017). The blood of the crab. *Popular Mechanics*. April 13.

Chodor, T. (2017). The G-20 since the global financial crisis: neither hegemony nor collectivism. *Global Governance: A Review of Multilateralism and International Organizations*, 23(2), 205–23.

Chwieroth, J. M. (2009). *Capital Ideas: The IMF and the Rise of Financial Liberalization*. Princeton, NJ: Princeton University Press.

Clark, W. R. (2009). *Capitalism, Not Globalism: Capital Mobility, Central Bank Independence, and the Political Control of the Economy*. Ann Arbor, MI: University of Michigan Press.

Clift, B. (2008). Economic policy. In A. Cole, P. Le Galès, & J. Levy (eds.), *Developments in French Politics*, 4. Basingstoke: Palgrave.

Clift, B. (2018). *The IMF and the Politics of Austerity in the Wake of the Global Financial Crisis*. Oxford: Oxford University Press.

Clift, B., & Woll, C. (2012). Economic patriotism: reinventing control over open markets. *Journal of European Public Policy*, 19(3), 307–23.

Codogno, L., Favero, C., & Missale, A. (2003). Yield spreads on EMU government bonds. *Economic Policy*, 18(37), 503–32.

Cœuré, B. (2013). Outright monetary transactions, one year on. *American Economic Review*, 76(1), 72–81.

Cohen, B. J. (2012). The future of the euro: let's get real. *Review of International Political Economy*, 19(4), 689–700.

Collender, S. (2010). Bond vigilantes are now deficit cheerleaders. *Capital Gains and Games*, August 3.

Cooper, A. F., & Thakur, R. (2013). *The Group of Twenty (G20)*. London: Routledge.

Corsetti, G. (2012). *Austerity: Too Much of a Good Thing*. A VoxEU.org eCollection of views by leading economists. London: Centre for Economic Policy Research (CEPR).

Corsetti, G., Kuester, K., Meier, A., & Müller, G. J. (2010). Debt consolidation and fiscal stabilization of deep recessions. *American Economic Review*, 100(2), 41–5.

Cottarelli, M. C., Mauro, M. P., Forni, L., & Gottschalk, J. (2010). Default in today's advanced economies: unnecessary, undesirable, and unlikely (No. 2010–2012). International Monetary Fund.

Cukierman, A. (2013). Monetary policy and institutions before, during, and after the global financial crisis. *Journal of Financial Stability*, 9(3), 373–84.

Cukierman, A., & Tommasi, M. (1998). When does it take a Nixon to go to China?. *American Economic Review*, 88(1), 180–97.

Curzio, A. (2011). On the different types of eurobonds. *Economia Politica*, 28(3), 279–94.

Davies, W. (2018). Weaponising paperwork. *London Review of Books*, 40(9), 13–14. Available from: https://www.lrb.co.uk/v40/n09/william-davies/weaponising-paperwork.

Davis, O. A., Dempster, M. A. H., & Wildavsky, A. (1966). A theory of the budgetary process. *American Political Science Review*, 60(3), 529–47.

De Bièvre, D. (2014). A glass quite empty: issue groups' influence in the global trade regime. *Global Policy*, 5(2), 222–8.

Debrun, X., & Kinda, T. (2016). That squeezing feeling: the interest burden and public debt stabilization. *International Finance*, 19(2), 147–78.

Debrun, X., Moulin, L., Turrini, A., Ayuso-i-Casals, J., & Kumar, M. S. (2008). Tied to the mast? National fiscal rules in the European Union. *Economic Policy*, 23(54), 298–362.

De Grauwe, P. (2009). The Euro at ten: achievements and challenges. *Empirica*, 36(1), 5–20.

De Grauwe, P., & Moesen, W. (2009). Gains for all: a proposal for a common euro bond. *Intereconomics*, 44(3), 132–5.

De Grauwe, P., & Ji, Y. (2013). Self-fulfilling crises in the Eurozone: an empirical test. *Journal of International Money and Finance*, 34, 15–36.

De Haan, J., & Sturm, J. E. (2000). On the relationship between economic freedom and economic growth. *European Journal of Political Economy*, 16(2), 215–41.

De Haan, J., Berger, H., & Jansen, D. J. (2003). *The End of the Stability and Growth Pact?* Netherlands Central Bank, Research Department.

Dehousse, R., & Menon, A. (2009). The French presidency. *JCMS: Journal of Common Market Studies*, 47(s1), 99–111.

DeLong, J. B., & Summers, L. H. (2012). Fiscal policy in a depressed economy. *Brookings Papers on Economic Activity*, 2012(1), 233–97.

Delors, J. (1989). Regional implications of economic and monetary integration. Report on Economic and Monetary Union in the European Community. Collection of papers submitted to the Committee for the Study of Economic and Monetary Union, 81.

Delpla, J., & Von Weizsäcker, J. (2011). Eurobonds: the blue bond concept and its implications (No. 2011/02). Bruegel policy contribution.

Devries, P., Pescatori, A., Leigh, D., & Guajardo, J. (2011). A new action-based dataset of fiscal consolidation. *IMF Working Papers: A New Action-Based Dataset of Fiscal Consolidation*, 11(128).

Dewachter, H., & Toffano, P. (2012). Fiscal activism and the cost of debt financing. *International Journal of Finance & Economics*, 17(1), 14–22.

Dolls, M., Fuest, C., & Peichl, A. (2010). Social protection as an automatic stabilizer (No. 18). IZA Policy Paper.

Dornbusch, R. (1996). Euro fantasies. *Foreign Affairs*, 110–24.

Dougherty, K. L. (2003). Public goods theory from eighteenth century political philosophy to twentieth century economics. *Public Choice*, 117(3–4), 239–53.

Draghi, M. (2012). Speech by Mario Draghi, President of the European Central Bank at the Global Investment Conference in London, July 26, 2012.

Drazen, A. (2000a). *Political Economy in Macroeconomics*. Princeton, NJ: Princeton University Press.

Drazen, A. (2000b). The political business cycle after 25 years. *NBER Macroeconomics Annual*, 15, 75–117.

Drezner, D. (2014). *The System Worked: How the World Stopped Another Great Depression*. Oxford: Oxford University Press.

Drukker, D. M. (2003). Testing for serial correlation in linear panel-data models. *Stata Journal*, 3(2), 168–77.

Dullien, S. (2008a). German economists have to take some blame for Merkel's slow reaction. *Eurozone Watch*

Dullien, S. (2008b). Spain: a stimulus package in the wrong country. *Eurozone Watch*.

Dullien, S., & Fritsche, U. (2006). How bad is divergence in the Euro-Zone? Lessons from the United States of America and Germany (No. 5/2006). DEP (Socioeconomics) Discussion Papers, Macroeconomics and Finance Series.

Dunteman, G. H. (1989). *Principal Components Analysis* (No. 69). London: Sage.

Dyson, K. (2014). *States, Debt, and Power: 'Saints' and Sinners' in European History and Integration*. Oxford: Oxford University Press.

Dyson, K., & Featherstone, K. (1999). *The Road to Maastricht: Negotiating Economic and Monetary Union*. Oxford: Oxford University Press.

Ecofin (2008). Main results of the Council, 2894th Council meeting, Economic and Financial Affairs, Luxembourg, 7 October. Available from: http://europa.eu/rapid/press-release_PRES-08-279_en.htm.

Eichengreen, B. (1987). Hegemonic stability theories of the international monetary system (No. 193). CEPR Discussion Papers.

Eichengreen, B. (2010). Out-of-the-box thoughts about the international financial architecture. *Journal of International Commerce, Economics and Policy*, 1(01), 1–20.

Eichengreen, B. (2014). *Hall of Mirrors: The Great Depression, the Great Recession, and the Uses and Misuses of History*. Oxford: Oxford University Press.

Eichengreen, B., & Sachs, J. (1985). Exchange rates and economic recovery in the 1930s. *The Journal of Economic History*, 45(4), 925–46.

Eichengreen, B., & Wyplosz, C. (1998). The Stability Pact: more than a minor nuisance? *Economic Policy*, 13(26), 66–113.

Eichhorst, W., & Hassel, A. (2015). Are there austerity-related policy changes in Germany? (No. 9325). IZA Discussion Papers.

Eijffinger, S. (2004). Reform of the Stability and Growth Pact. Briefing paper for the European Parliament, Tilberg University, the Netherlands, January.

Elster, J. (1985). Rationality, morality, and collective action. *Ethics*, 96(1), 136–55.

Elster, J. (2000). *Ulysses Unbound: Studies in Rationality, Precommitment, and Constraints*. Cambridge: Cambridge University Press.

Emmenegger, P. (2011). Job security regulations in Western democracies: a fuzzy set analysis. *European Journal of Political Research*, 50(3), 336–64.

Enderlein, H. (2004). Break it, don't fix it! *JCMS: Journal of Common Market Studies*, 42(5), 1039–46.

Eurogroup (2008) Declaration on a concerted European Action Plan of the Euro Area Countries. October 12. Available from: http://ec.europa.eu/economy_finance/publications/pages/publication13260_en.pdf.

European Central Bank. (2009). Monthly bulletin July. Frankfurt am Main.

European Central Bank. (2010). Euro area fiscal policies and the crisis. ECB Occasional Paper Series (109).

European Commission. (2004). Public finances in EMU 2004. European Economy No. 3.

European Commission. (2008). Communication from the Commission: from financial crisis to recovery: a European framework for action. 706 final.

European Commission. (2009). Public finances in EMU 2009.

European Commission. (2010a). Public finances in EMU 2010.

European Commission. (2010b). Greece: Commission assessment in relation to the Commission recommendation for a Council decision under Article 104(8) of the Treaty. Available from: http://ec.europa.eu/economy_finance/publications/pages/publication16243_en.pdf [accessed May 14, 2018].

European Commission. (2011a). Public finances in EMU. Available from: http://ec.europa.eu/economy_finance/publications/european_economy/public_finances_emu_en.htm [accessed December 1, 2013].

European Commission. (2011b). Report from the Commission Alert Mechanism.

European Commission. (2012). Fiscal rules database. Available from: https://ec.europa.eu/info/publications/fiscal-rules-database_en [accessed March 22, 2012].

European Commission. (2018). Financial assistance programmes. Available from: https://ec.europa.eu/info/business-economy-euro/economic-and-fiscal-policy-coordination/eu-financial-assistance/which-eu-countries-have-received-assistance/financial-assistance-greece_en [accessed March 14, 2018].

European Monetary Institute (EMI). (1996). Opinion of the European Monetary Institute, CON/96/14. Available from: http://www.ecb.int/ecb/legal/pdf/en_con_96_14.pdf.

Eurostat. (2012). Eurostat supplementary table for the financial crisis, Background note.

Evans, B. (1954). *The Spoor of Spooks: And Other Nonsense*. New York: Knopf.

Fahrholz, C., & Wójcik, C. (2011). A positive framework to analyze sovereign bail-outs within the EMU (No. 15). Working Papers on Global Financial Markets.

Faini, R. (2006). Fiscal policy and interest rates in Europe. *Economic Policy*, 21(47), 444–89.

Farrell, H., & Quiggin, J. (2012). Consensus, dissensus and economic ideas: the rise and fall of Keynesianism during the economic crisis. Center for the Study of Development Strategies, 1–52.

Fatás, A., & Mihov, I. (2003). The case for restricting fiscal policy discretion. *The Quarterly Journal of Economics*, 118(4), 1419–47.

Feldstein, M. (1997). The political economy of the European Economic and Monetary Union: political sources of an economic liability. *Journal of Economic Perspectives*, 11(4), 23–42.

Feldstein, M. (2000). Europe can't handle the Euro. *Wall Street Journal*, February 8.

Fels, J. (2015). The end of fiscal obstruction. PIMCO: Macro Perspectives November.

Ferguson, N., & Schularick, M. (2006). The empire effect: the determinants of country risk in the first age of globalization, 1880–1913. *The Journal of Economic History*, 66(2), 283–312.

Fischer, J. (2005). Swedish budget rules: praise from Brussels, pressure at home. *ECFIN Country Focus*, 2(4), 1–6.

Fleischer, J., & Parrado, S. (2010). Power distribution in ambiguous times: the effects of the financial crisis on executive decision-making in Germany and Spain. Der moderne staat–dms: Zeitschrift für Public Policy, *Recht und Management*, 3(2), 1–16.

Folkerts-Landau, D., & Garber, P. M. (1992). The European Central Bank: a bank or a monetary policy rule (No. w4016). National Bureau of Economic Research.

Fourcade, M., Steiner, P., Streeck, W., & Woll, C.(2013). Moral categories in the financial crisis. *Socio-Economic Review*, 11(3), 601–27.

Franzese Jr, R. J. (2002). Electoral and partisan cycles in economic policies and outcomes. *Annual Review of Political Science*, 5(1), 369–421.

Freitag, M., & Sciarini, P. (2001). The political economy of budget deficits in the European Union: the role of international constraints and domestic structure. *European Union Politics*, 2(2), 163–89.

Frieden, J. A. (2009). Global imbalances, national rebalancing, and the political economy of recovery. Center for Geoeconomic Studies and International Institutions and Global Governance Program Working Paper.

Friedman, T. L. (2000). *The Lexus and the Olive Tree: Understanding Globalization*. New York: Farrar, Straus and Giroux.

Furceri, D., & Mourougane, A. (2009). The effect of financial crises on potential output: new empirical evidence from OECD countries. OECD Economic Department Working Papers, 699, 1.

Geithner, T. F. (2015). *Stress Test: Reflections on Financial Crises*. New York: Broadway Books.

Giavazzi, F., & Pagano, M. (1995). Non-Keynesian effects of fiscal policy changes: international evidence and the Swedish experience (No. w5332). National Bureau of Economic Research.

Giavazzi, F., & Pagano, M. (2009). Issues in the design of a fiscal exit strategy. *Diskussion bei einem informellen ECOFIN-Treffen. Göteborg*, 1(2), 1–52.

Gill, S. (1998). European governance and new constitutionalism: economic and monetary union and alternatives to disciplinary neoliberalism in Europe. *New Political Economy*, 3(1), 5–26.

Girouard, N., & André, C. (2005). Measuring cyclically-adjusted budget balances for OECD countries (No. 434). Paris: OECD Publishing.

Goodharta, C., & Schoenmaker, D. (2009). Fiscal burden sharing in cross-border banking crises. *International Journal of Central Banking*, 5(1), 141–65.

Goldstein, K. (2002). Getting in the door: sampling and completing elite interviews. *PS: Political Science & Politics*, 35(4), 669–72.

González-Páramo, J. M. (2005). The reform of the Stability and Growth Pact: an assessment. Speech by José Manuel González-Páramo, Member of the Executive Board of the ECB Conference on 'New Perspectives on Fiscal Sustainability', Frankfurt (Vol. 13).

Gourevitch, P. (1986). *Politics in Hard Times: Comparative Responses to International Economic Crises*. Ithaca, NY: Cornell University Press.

Gourevitch, P. (2013). Yet more hard times: politics in the new hard times: the great recession in comparative perspective. In M. Kahler and D. A. Lake (eds.), *Politics in the New Hard Times: The Great Recession in Comparative Perspective*. Ithaca, NY: Cornell University Press, 253–74.

Grabosky, P. N. (1995). Using non-governmental resources to foster regulatory compliance. *Governance*, 8(4), 527–50.

Gray, J. (2013). *The Company States Keep: International Economic Organizations and Investor Perceptions*. Cambridge: Cambridge University Press.

Green, S., & Paterson, W. E. (eds.) (2005). *Governance in Contemporary Germany: The Semisovereign State Revisited*. Cambridge: Cambridge University Press.

Gros, D. (2012). On the stability of public debt in a monetary union. *JCMS: Journal of Common Market Studies*, 50(s2), 36–48.

Gros, D., & Belkle, A. (2007). Instability of the Eurozone? On Monetary Policy, House Prices and Labor Market Reforms (No. 2547). Institute for the Study of Labor (IZA).

Guichard, S., Kennedy, M., Wurzel, E., & André, C. (2007). *What Promotes Fiscal Consolidation: OECD Country Experiences* (No. 553). Paris: OECD Publishing.

Gupta, S., Baldacci, E., Clements, B., & Tiongson, E. R. (2005). What sustains fiscal consolidations in emerging market countries?. *International Journal of Finance & Economics*, 10(4), 307–21.

Haggard, S. (2013). The 2008–9 financial crisis in emerging markets. In M. Kahler and D. A. Lake (eds.), *Politics in the New Hard Times: The Great Recession in Comparative Perspective*. Ithaca, NY: Cornell University Press, 52–74.

Hallerberg, M. (2004). *Domestic Budgets in a United Europe: Fiscal Governance from the End of Bretton Woods to EMU*. Ithaca, NY: Cornell University Press.

Hallerberg, M. (2011). Fiscal federalism reforms in the European Union and the Greek crisis. *European Union Politics*, 12(1), 127–42.

Hallerberg, M. (2016). Fiscal governance and fiscal outcomes under EMU before and after the crisis. In J. Caporaso & M. Rhodes (eds.), *The Political and Economic Dynamics of the Eurozone Crisis*. Oxford: Oxford University Press, 145–67.

Hallerberg, M., & Wolff, G. B. (2008). Fiscal institutions, fiscal policy and sovereign risk premia in EMU. *Public Choice*, 136(3–4), 379–96.

Hallerberg, M., Strauch, R., & Von Hagen, J. (2007). The design of fiscal rules and forms of governance in European Union countries. *European Journal of Political Economy*, 23(2), 338–59.

Hallerberg, M., Strauch, R., & Von Hagen, J. (2009). *Fiscal Governance in Europe*. Cambridge: Cambridge University Press.

Hallett, A. H., & Petit, M. L. (1990). Cohabitation or forced marriage? A study of the costs of failing to coordinate fiscal and monetary policies. *Review of World Economics*, 126(4), 662–90.

Hardie, I. (2011). How much can governments borrow? Financialization and emerging markets government borrowing capacity. *Review of International Political Economy*, 18(2), 141–67.

Hardin, R. (1982). *Collective Action*. Baltimore, MD: Johns Hopkins University Press.

Hassel, A. (2014). The paradox of liberalization: understanding dualism and the recovery of the German political economy. *British Journal of Industrial Relations*, 52(1), 57–81.

Hay, C., Riiheläinen, J. M., Smith, N. J., & Watson, M. (2008). Ireland: the outlier inside. In K. Dyson (ed.), *The Euro at Ten: Europeanisation, Power and Convergence*. Oxford: Oxford University Press, 182–203.

Heckelman, J. C., & Berument, H. (1998). Political business cycles and endogenous elections. *Southern Economic Journal*, 64(4), 987–1000.

Heinemann, F., & Winschel, V. (2001). Public deficits and borrowing costs: the missing half of market discipline (No. 01–16). ZEW-Zentrum für Europäische Wirtschaftsforschung/Center for European Economic Research.

Heipertz, M., & Verdun, A. (2010). *Ruling Europe: The Politics of the Stability and Growth Pact*. Cambridge: Cambridge University Press.

Helgadóttir, O. (2016). The Bocconi boys go to Brussels: Italian economic ideas, professional networks and European austerity. *Journal of European Public Policy*, 23(3), 392–409.

Helleiner, E. (1996). *States and the Reemergence of Global Finance: From Bretton Woods to the 1990s*. Ithaca, NY: Cornell University Press.

Helleiner, E. (2011). *The Contemporary Reform of Global Financial Governance: Implications of and Lessons from the Past*. Oxford: Oxford University Press.

Helleiner, E. (2014). The status quo crisis: global financial governance after the 2008 meltdown. Oxford: Oxford University Press.

Heller, P. S. (2005). Understanding fiscal space (No. 05/4). International Monetary Fund.

Heller, W. B. (1997). Bicameralism and budget deficits: the effect of parliamentary structure on government spending. *Legislative Studies Quarterly*, 22(4), 485–516.

Hellwig, T., & Coffey, E. (2011). Public opinion, party messages, and responsibility for the financial crisis in Britain. *Electoral Studies*, 30(3), 417–26.

Henning, C. R. (2017). *Tangled Governance: International Regime Complexity, the Troika, and the Euro Crisis*. Oxford: Oxford University Press.

Hercowitz, Z., & Strawczynski, M. (2005). Government-spending adjustment: the OECD since the nineties. Available from: https://ssrn.com/abstract=2028367 or http://dx.doi.org/10.2139/ssrn.2028367.

Hibbs, D. A. (1977). Political parties and macroeconomic policy. *American Political Science Review*, 71(4), 1467–87.

HM Treasury. (2008). HM Treasury pre-budget report November 2008. Available from: https://www.gov.uk/government/publications/hm-treasury-pre-budget-report-november-2008.

Hodson, D. (2010). The EU economy: the euro area in 2009. *JCMS: Journal of Common Market Studies*, 48(s1), 225–42.

Hodson, D. (2012). The Eurozone in 2011. *JCMS: Journal of Common Market Studies*, 50(s2), 178–94.

Hodson, D. (2013). The Eurozone in 2012: 'whatever it takes to preserve the Euro'? *JCMS: Journal of Common Market Studies*, 51(S1), 183–200.

Hodson, D., & Maher, I. (2001). The open method as a new mode of governance: the case of soft economic policy co-ordination. *JCMS: Journal of Common Market Studies*, 39(4), 719–46.

Högenauer, A. L., & Howarth, D. (2016). Unconventional monetary policies and the European Central Bank's problematic democratic legitimacy. *Zeitschrift für öffentliches Recht*, 71(2), 1–24.

Holtz-Eakin, D., Newey, W., & Rosen, H. S. (1988). Estimating vector autoregressions with panel data. *Econometrica: Journal of the Econometric Society*, 56(6), 1371–95.

Horsman, M., & Marshall, A. (1994). *After the Nation-State: Citizens, Tribalism and the New World Disorder*. New York: HarperCollins.

Howarth, D. (2007). Making and breaking the rules: French policy on EU 'gouvernement économique'. *Journal of European Public Policy*, 14(7), 1061–78.

Howarth, D. (2008). Delegation and Commission leadership in Economic and Monetary Union. In J. Hayward (ed.), *Leaderless Europe*. Oxford: Oxford University Press, 28–46.

Howarth, D., & Rommerskirchen, C. (2013). A panacea for all times? The German stability culture as strategic political resource. *West European Politics*, 36(4), 750–70.

Howarth, D., & Quaglia, L. (2016). *The Political Economy of European Banking Union*. Oxford: Oxford University Press.

Howarth, D., & Rommerskirchen, C. (2017). Inflation aversion in the European Union: exploring the myth of a North–South divide. *Socio-Economic Review*, 15(2), 385–404.

Hübscher, E. (2015). The politics of fiscal consolidation revisited. *Journal of Public Policy*. DOI: 10.1017/S0143814X15000057.

Hübscher, E., & Sattler, T. (2017). Fiscal consolidation under electoral risk. *European Journal of Political Research*, 56(1), 151–68.

Ilzetzki, E., Mendoza, E. G., & Végh, C. A. (2013). How big (small?) are fiscal multipliers? *Journal of Monetary Economics*, 60(2), 239–54.

Imbeau, L., Pétry, F., & Lamari, M. (2001). Left–right party ideology and government policies: a meta-analysis. *European Journal of Political Research*, 40(1), 1–29.

Inman, R. P., & Rubinfeld, D. L. (1992). Fiscal federalism in Europe: lessons from the United States experience. *European Economic Review*, 36(2–3), 654–60.

International Labour Organization. (2009). A review of global fiscal stimulus. EC-IILS Joint Discussion Paper Series (5).

In't Veld, J. (2013). Fiscal consolidations and spillovers in the Euro area periphery and core. European Commission, Directorate-General for Economic and Financial Affairs.

Jabko, N. (2006). *Playing the Market: A Political Strategy for Uniting Europe, 1985–2005*. Ithaca, NY: Cornell University Press.

Jacoby, W., & Hopkin. J. (2017). *Drunk on Conditionality: The Move to Coercive Conditionality in the EU Periphery*. New York: Mimeo.

Jessop, R. D. (2002). *The Future of the Capitalist State*. Cambridge: Polity.

Johnson, J., & Barnes, A. (2015). Financial nationalism and its international enablers: the Hungarian experience. *Review of International Political Economy*, 22(3), 535–69.

Johnston, A. (2016). *From Convergence to Crisis: Labor Markets and the Instability of the Euro*. Ithaca, NY: Cornell University Press.

Jolliffe, I. T. (1986). *Principal Component Analysis*. New York: Springer.

Jones, E. (2009). Shifting the focus: the new political economy of global macroeconomic imbalances. *SAIS Review of International Affairs*, 29(2), 61–73.

Jones, E. (2015). Forgotten financial union. In M. Matthijs and M. Blyth (eds.), *The Future of the Euro*. Oxford: Oxford University Press, 44–69.

Jones, E., Kelemen, R. D., & Meunier, S. (2016). Failing forward? The Euro crisis and the incomplete nature of European integration. *Comparative Political Studies*, 49(7), 1010–34.

Judt, T. (2010). Ill fares the land. *The New York Review of Books*, March 16, 17–19.

Juncker, J.-C., Tusk, D., Dijsselbloem, J., & Draghi, M. (2015). Completing Europe's Economic and Monetary Union. Available from: https://ec.europa.eu/commission/sites/beta-political/files/5-presidents-report_en.pdf.

Kahler, M. (2013). Economic crisis and global governance: the stability of a globalized world. In Miles Kahler and David A. Lake (eds.), *Politics in the New Hard Times: The Great Recession in Comparative Perspective*. Ithaca, NY: Cornell University Press, 27–51.

Kahler, M., & Lake, D. (2013). *Politics in the New Hard Times: The Great Recession in Comparative Perspective*. Ithaca, NY: Cornell University Press.

Kapur, D. (1998). The IMF: a cure or a curse?. *Foreign Policy*, 111 (Summer), 114–29.

Keefer, P. (2010). Database of political institutions: changes and variable definitions. Development Research Group, World Bank.

Kelemen, R. D., & Teo, T. K. (2014). Law, focal points, and fiscal discipline in the United States and the European Union. *American Political Science Review*, 108(2), 355–70.

Keohane, R. (1984). *After Hegemony: Cooperation and Discord in International Political Economy*. Princeton, NJ: Princeton University Press.

Keohane, R. (1992). Compliance with international commitments: politics within a framework of law. In Proceedings of the Annual Meeting (American Society of International Law) (pp. 176–80). The American Society of International Law.

Keohane, R., & Nye, J. (1989). *Power and Interdependence*. 2nd ed. Little, Brown Series in Political Science. Glenview, IL: Scott, Foresman.

Kindleberger, C. P. (1986). *The World in Depression, 1929–1939: Revised and Enlarged Edition* (Vol. 4). Berkeley, CA: University of California Press.

King, M. (1995). Commentary: monetary implications of greater fiscal discipline. In *Budget Deficits and Debt: Issues and Options*, Proceedings of the 1995 Jackson Hole Symposium. Kansas City, MO: Kansas City Federal Reserve, 171–83.

Kirton, J. (2014). The G20 system still works: better than ever. *Caribbean Journal of International Relations and Diplomacy*, 2(3), 43–60.

Klug, G. (2008). Stenographisches Protokoll 761. *Sitzung des Bundesrates der Republik Österreich*, October 21, 2008.

Knedlik, T., & Von Schweinitz, G. (2012). Macroeconomic imbalances as indicators for debt crises in Europe. *JCMS: Journal of Common Market Studies*, 50(5), 726–45.

Konzelmann, S. (2012). *The Economics of Austerity* (No. wp434). ESRC Centre for Business Research.

Kopits, M. G., & Symansky, M. S. A. (1998). *Fiscal policy rules* (No. 162). International Monetary Fund.

Krugman, P. (2010). Appeasing the bond gods. *New York Times*, August 19.

Kuenzel, R., & Ruscher, E. (2013). The future of EMU. *ECFIN Economic Brief*, 22.

Kühn, A. (1963). *The Study of Society: A Unified Approach*. Homewood, IL: The Dorsey Press.

Lake, D. (2010). The state and international relations. In D. Snidal and C. Reus-Smit (eds.), *The Oxford Handbook of International Relations*. New York: Oxford University Press.

Lane, P. R. (2012). The European sovereign debt crisis. *Journal of Economic Perspectives*, 26(3), 49–68.

Lane, T. D. (1993). Market discipline. *IMF Staff Papers*, 40(1), 53.

Larch, M., & Salto, M. (2005). Fiscal rules, inertia and discretionary fiscal policy. *Applied Economics*, 37(10), 1135–46.

Larch, M., & Turrini, A. (2011). Received wisdom and beyond: lessons from fiscal consolidation in the EU. *National Institute Economic Review*, 217(1), R1–R18.

Larch, M., Pench, L. R., & Frayne, C. (2012). SGP 3.0: continuity and innovation in the evolution of the EU fiscal framework. Rules and Institutions for Sound Fiscal Policy after the Crisis, Rome.

Lavigne, R. (2011). The political and institutional determinants of fiscal adjustment: entering and exiting fiscal distress. *European Journal of Political Economy*, 27(1), 17–35.

LeMay-Boucher, P., & Rommerskirchen, C. (2015). An empirical investigation into the Europeanization of fiscal policy. *Comparative European Politics*, 13(4), 450–70.

Levi, M. (1989). *Of Rule and Revenue* (Vol. 13). Berkeley, CA: University of California Press.

Lewis, J. (2005). The Janus face of Brussels: socialization and everyday decision making in the European Union. *International Organization*, 59(4), 937–71.

Lindvall, J. (2012). The political consequences of the Great Depression and the Great Recession: remarkably similar. *Swiss Political Science Review*, 18(4), 514–17.

Lipsmeyer, C. S. (2011). Booms and busts: how parliamentary governments and economic context influence welfare policy. *International Studies Quarterly*, 55(4), 959–80.

Lodge, M., & Wegrich, K. (2012). Executive politics and policy instruments. In M. Lodge and K. Wegrich (eds.), *Executive Politics in Times of Crisis*. London: Palgrave Macmillan, 118–35.

Lojsch, D. H., Rodríguez-Vives, M., & Slavík, M. (2011). *The Size and Composition of Government Debt in the Euro Area* (No. 132). European Central Bank.

Longest, K. C., & Vaisey, S. (2008). Fuzzy: a program for performing qualitative comparative analyses (QCA) in Stata. *Stata Journal*, 8(1), 79.

Lutz, B. F., & Follette, G. (2012). *Fiscal Rules: What Does the American Experience Tell Us?* (No. 2012–38). Board of Governors of the Federal Reserve System (US).

Lux, T. (1995). Herd behaviour, bubbles and crashes. *The Economic Journal*, 105(431), 881–96.

Mabbett, D., & Schelkle, W. (2014). *Searching Under the Lamp-Post: The Evolution of Fiscal Surveillance*, 'Europe in Question' (Discussion Paper 75). London: London School of Economics.

Mabbett, D., & Schelkle, W. (2015). What difference does Euro membership make to stabilization? The political economy of international monetary systems revisited. *Review of International Political Economy*, 22(3), 508–34.

MacKenzie, D., & Millo, Y. (2003). Constructing a market, performing theory: the historical sociology of a financial derivatives exchange. *American Journal of Sociology*, 109(1), 107–45.

Majone, G. (1975). On the notion of political feasibility. *European Journal of Political Research*, 3(3), 259–74.

Maltritz, D. (2012). Determinants of sovereign yield spreads in the Eurozone: a Bayesian approach. *Journal of International Money and Finance*, 31(3), 657–72.

Martin, L. L. (1994). *Coercive Cooperation: Explaining Multilateral Economic Sanctions*. Princeton, NJ: Princeton University Press.

Matthijs, M. (2014). Mediterranean blues: the crisis in Southern Europe. *Journal of Democracy*, 25(1), 101–15.

Matthijs, M., & Blyth, M. (2015). *The Future of the Euro*. New York: Oxford University Press.

Matthijs, M., & McNamara, K. (2015). The euro crisis theory effect: northern saints, southern sinners, and the demise of the eurobond. *Journal of European Integration*, 37(2), 229–45.

Mayer, T. (2011). Quotes from Brussels Economic Forum. Available from: http://ec.europa.eu/economy_finance/bef2011/media/quotes/index.html [accessed June 13, 2017].

McCulley, A. (2001). *The Right Way*. PIMCO: Global Central Bank Focus.

McMenamin, I., Breen, M., & Muñoz-Portillo, J. (2015). Austerity and credibility in the Eurozone. *European Union Politics*, 16(1), 45–66.

McNamara, K. R. (1998). *The Currency of Ideas: Monetary Politics in the European Union*. Ithaca, NY: Cornell University Press.

McNamara, K. R. (2009). Of intellectual monocultures and the study of IPE. *Review of International Political Economy*, 16(1), 72–84.

Menon, A. (2008). Europe: the state of the union. *Survival*, 50(3), 192–3.

Merkel, A. (2009). Rede von Bundeskanzlerin Dr. Angela Merkel in der Debatte zur Situation in Deutschland vor dem Deutschen Bundestag am September 8, 2009 in Berlin.

Merkel, A. (2010). Rede Zum Zehnjährigen. *Financial Times Deutschland*.

Merler, S., & Pisani-Ferry, J. (2012). *Who's Afraid of Sovereign Bonds?* (No. 2012/02). Bruegel Policy Contribution.

Meyer, C. (2004). The hard side of soft policy co-ordination in EMU: the impact of peer pressure on publicized opinion in the cases of Germany and Ireland. *Journal of European Public Policy*, 11(5), 814–31.

Mierau, J. O., Jong-A-Pin, R., & De Haan, J. (2007). Do political variables affect fiscal policy adjustment decisions? New empirical evidence. *Public Choice*, 133(3–4), 297–319.

Miller, M. J. (ed.) (2003). *Credit Reporting Systems and the International Economy*. Cambridge, MA: MIT Press.

Mink, M., & De Haan, J. (2006). Are there political budget cycles in the euro area?. *European Union Politics*, 7(2), 191–211.

Molander, P. (2000). Reforming budgetary institutions: Swedish experiences. In R. R. Strauch and J. von Hagen (eds.), *Institutions, Politics and Fiscal Policy*. Boston, MA: Springer, 191–214.

Molnar, M. (2013). Fiscal consolidation. *OECD Journal: Economic Studies*, 2012(1), 123–49.

Morris, L. (1997). A cluster of contradictions: the politics of migration in the European Union. *Sociology*, 31(2), 241–59.

Morris, R., Ongena, H., & Schuknecht, L. (2006). The reform and implementation of the stability and growth pact. The International Relations Committee Task Force on Enlargement.

Moschella, M. (2014). Monitoring macroeconomic imbalances: is EU surveillance more effective than IMF surveillance? *JCMS: Journal of Common Market Studies*, 52(6), 1273–89.

Moschella, M. (2017). When some are more equal than others: National Parliaments and intergovernmental bailout negotiations in the Eurozone. *Government and Opposition*, 52(2), 239–65.

Moser-Boehm, P. (2006, March). The relationship between the central bank and the government. Central banks and the challenge of development, A special meeting of governors held at the BIS, Basel (pp. 14–15).

Mosley, L. (2000). Room to move: international financial markets and national welfare states. *International Organization*, 54(4), 737–73.

Mosley, L. (2003). *Global Capital and National Governments*. Cambridge: Cambridge University Press.

Mosley, L. (2004). Government–financial market relations after EMU: new currency, new constraints?. *European Union Politics*, 5(2), 181–209.

Mukherjee, B. (2003). Political parties and the size of government in multiparty legislatures: examining cross-country and panel data evidence. *Comparative Political Studies*, 36(6), 699–728.

Mulas-Granados, Carlos (2003). The political and economic determinants of budgetary consolidation in Europe. *European Political Economy Review*, 1(1), 15–39.

Nickel, C., Rother, P., & Zimmermann, L. (2010). Major public debt reductions: lessons from the past, lessons for the future (No. 1241). ECB Working Paper.

Nikiforakis, N. (2008). Punishment and counter-punishment in public good games: can we really govern ourselves?. *Journal of Public Economics*, 92(1–2), 91–112.

Nordhaus, W. D. (1975). The political business cycle. *The Review of Economic Studies*, 42(2), 169–90.

Nordhaus, W. D. (1991). To slow or not to slow: the economics of the greenhouse effect. *The Economic Journal*, 101(407), 920–37.

North, D. (1990). *Institutions, Institutional Change, and Economic Performance: The Political Economy of Institutions and Decisions*. Cambridge: Cambridge University Press.

OECD. (2008). Handbook on constructing composite indicators: methodology and user guide. Available from: http://www.oecd.org/sdd/42495745.pdf.

OECD. (2011). Fiscal consolidation: targets, plans and measures. *OECD Journal on Budgeting*, 11(2). http://dx.doi.org/10.1787/budget-11-5kg869h4w5f6.

Oliver, P. (1980). Rewards and punishments as selective incentives for collective action: theoretical investigations. *American Journal of Sociology*, 85(6), 1356–75.

Olson, M. (1965). *The Logic of Collective Action*. Cambridge, MA: Harvard University Press.

Olson, M., & Zeckhauser, R. (1966). An economic theory of alliances. *The Review of Economics and Statistics*, 48(3), 266–79.

Oneal, J. R., & Bryan, A. L. (1995). The rally 'round the flag effect in US foreign policy crises, 1950–1985. *Political Behavior*, 17(4), 379–401.

Osborne, George. (2012). Commons debate. Available from: http://www.publications.parliament.uk/pa/cm201213/cmhansrd/cm121205/debtext/121205-0002.htm [accessed May 4, 2015].

Ostrom, E. (1986). An agenda for the study of institutions. *Public Choice*, 48(1), 3–25.

Ostrom, E. (1990). *Governing the Commons: The Evolution of Institutions for Collective Action*. Cambridge: Cambridge University Press.

Ostrom, E. (1998). A behavioral approach to the rational choice theory of collective action: Presidential address, American Political Science Association, 1997. *American Political Science Review*, 92(1), 1–22.

Ostry, J. D., Ghosh, A. R., Kim, J. I., & Qureshi, M. S. (2010). *Fiscal space*. International Monetary Fund, Research Department.

Otero-Iglesias, M. (2012). The (in) tangible Euro challenge to the dollar: insights from the financial elites in Brazil and China. *Cambridge Review of International Affairs*, 25(1), 123–42.

Oye, K. (1986). *Cooperation Under Anarchy*. Princeton, NJ: Princeton University Press.

Padoa-Schioppa, T. (2002). Reflections on recent financial incidents. Speech given at the Third Joint Central Bank Research Conference on Risk Measurement and Systemic Risk, Basel (Vol. 8).

Pampel, F. C., & Williamson, J. B. (1988). Welfare spending in advanced industrial democracies, 1950–1980. *American Journal of Sociology*, 93(6), 1424–56.

Parrado, S. (2012). The executive at work during times of crisis. In M. Lodge and K. Wegrich (eds.), *Executive Politics in Times of Crisis*. London: Palgrave Macmillan, 197–221.

Parenteau, R. W. (2005). The late 1990s US bubble: financialization in the extreme. In *Financialization and the World Economy*, G. Epstein, 11–48.

Passarelli, F., & Tabellini, G. (2013). *Emotions and Political Unrest* (No. 4165). CESifo Working Paper: Fiscal Policy, Macroeconomics and Growth.

Pauly, L. W. (2009). The old and the new politics of international financial stability. *JCMS: Journal of Common Market Studies*, 47(5), 955–75.

Perotti, R. (1999). Fiscal policy in good times and bad. *The Quarterly Journal of Economics*, 114(4), 1399–436.

Peters, B. G. (2011). *Institutional Theory in Political Science: The New Institutionalism*. New York: Bloomsbury Publishing.

Peterson, J. (2017). Juncker's political European Commission and an EU in crisis. *JCMS: Journal of Common Market Studies*, 55(2), 349–67.

Phillips, L. (2012). Politics, policy and financial market volatility in advanced economies. Mimeo. Available from: https://piigsty.files.wordpress.com/2013/06/phillips.pdf [accessed January 23, 2015].

Pierson, P. (1996). The path to European integration: a historical institutionalist analysis. *Comparative Political Studies*, 29(2), 123–63.

Pisani-Ferry, J. (2014). *The Euro Crisis and Its Aftermath*. New York: Oxford University Press.

Plümper, T., Troeger, V. E., & Manow, P. (2005). Panel data analysis in comparative politics: linking method to theory. *European Journal of Political Research*, 44(2), 327–54.

Pollin, R. (2012). US government deficits and debt amid the great recession: what the evidence shows. *Cambridge Journal of Economics*, 36(1), 161–87.

Pontusson, J., & Raess, D. (2012). How (and why) is this time different? The politics of economic crisis in Western Europe and the United States. *Annual Review of Political Science*, 15, 13–33.

Portes, R. (1993). EMS and EMU after the fall. *The World Economy*, 16(1), 1–15.

Poteete, A. R., & Ostrom, E. (2004). Heterogeneity, group size and collective action: the role of institutions in forest management. *Development and Change*, 35(3), 435–61.

Poterba, J. M. (1995). Balanced budget rules and fiscal policy: evidence from the states. *National Tax Journal*, 48(3), 329–36.

Poterba, J. M. (1996). *Do Budget Rules Work?* (No. w5550). National Bureau of Economic Research.

Prager, R. (2012). Days of tight bid: ask spreads gone, Blackrock tells investors. *Financial Post.*

Puetter, U. (2004). Governing informally: the role of the Eurogroup in EMU and the Stability and Growth Pact. *Journal of European Public Policy*, 11(5), 854–70.

Puetter, U. (2012). Europe's deliberative intergovernmentalism: the role of the Council and European Council in EU economic governance. *Journal of European Public Policy*, 19(2), 161–78.

Quaglia, L. (2011). The 'old' and 'new' political economy of hedge fund regulation in the European Union. *West European Politics*, 34(4), 665–82.

Ragin, C. (1987). *The Comparative Method: Moving Beyond Qualitative and Quantitative Methods*. Berkeley, CA: University of California Press.

Ragin, C. (2000). *Fuzzy-Set Social Science*. Chicago, IL: University of Chicago Press.

Ramo, J. C. (2004). *The Beijing Consensus* (p. 3). London: Foreign Policy Centre.

Ramsey, J. B. (1969). Tests for specification errors in classical linear least-squares regression analysis. *Journal of the Royal Statistical Society. Series B (Methodological)*, 31(2), 350–71.

Rao, T. R., & Kalpagam, U. (1977). Mixed public goods, consumption externality, and economic growth. *Zeitschrift für Nationalökonomie*, 37(3–4), 385–94.

Rehn, O. (2012). Vice President Olli Rehn speaks on restoring growth in Europe through confidence, reforms and investment, May 5.

Reinhart, C. M., & Rogoff, K. S. (2010). Growth in a time of debt. *American Economic Review*, 100(2), 573–78.

Rippert, U. (2009). Europe turns to protectionism as industry plummets. World Socialist Website. Available at: https://www.wsws.org/en/articles/2009/02/euro-f14.html [accessed May 13, 2018].

Rodrik, D. (1997). *Has Globalization Gone Too Far?* New York: Columbia University Press.

Rommerskirchen, C. (2015). Debt and punishment: market discipline in the Eurozone. *New Political Economy*, 20(5), 752–82.

Rommerskirchen, C., & Snaith, H. (2017). Bringing balance to the force? A comparative analysis of institutionalisation processes in the G20's mutual assessment process and the EU's macroeconomic imbalances procedure. *New Political Economy*, 23(4), 391–406.

Rugman, A. M. (2001). *The End of Globalization: Why Global Strategy Is a Myth and How to Profit From the Realities of Regional Markets*. New York: Amacom.

Sadeh, T. (2006). *Sustaining European Monetary Union: Confronting the Cost of Diversity*. Boulder, CO: L. Rienner Publishers.

Safire, W. (1995). On language: exit strategy. *New York Times*, December 24.

Sandbu, M. (2017). *Europe's Orphan: The Future of the Euro and the Politics of Debt*. Princeton, NJ: Princeton University Press.

Saramo, Peter (2012). Email exchange with Peter Saramo, Director EU Secretariat, Parliament of Finland.

Sarkozy, N. (2009). 19th Ambassadors' Conference: speech by Nicolas Sarkozy, President of the Republic, Paris.

Sarkozy, N. (2011). 9th Ambassadors' Conference: speech by Nicolas Sarkozy, President of the Republic, Paris.

Sbragia, A. (2000). Governance, the state, and the market: what is going on? *Governance*, 13(2), 243–50.

Schadler, S., & Luengnaruemitchai, P. (2007). Do economists' and financial markets' perspectives on the new members of the EU differ? No. 7–65. International Monetary Fund.

Schaechter, A., Budina, N., Weber, A., & Kinda, T. (2012). Fiscal rules in response to the crisis: toward the 'next-generation' rules: a new dataset. IMF Working Paper. 12(187).

Schaefer, A., & Streeck, W. (eds.) (2013). *Politics in the Age of Austerity*. Cambridge: Polity.

Scharpf, F. W. (2011). Monetary union, fiscal crisis and the pre-emption of democracy. *Zeitschrift für Staats-und Europawissenschaften (ZSE)/Journal for Comparative Government and European Policy*, 9(2), 163–98.

Schäuble, W. (2010). Warum Das Maßnahmenpaket Richtig Ist, Brief Von Bundesfinanzminister Dr. Wolfgang Schäuble an Die Mitglieder Der Cdu/Csu-Bundestagsfraktion Und Der Fdp-Bundestagsfraktion.

Schäuble, W. (2011a). Die Märkte Wollen Taten Sehen. *RPOnline*, December 19.

Schäuble, W. (2011b). A comprehensive strategy for the stabilization of the Economic and Monetary Union. Speech by the German Federal Minister of Finance Dr Wolfgang Schäuble Brussels Economic Forum 2011. Available from: http://ec.europa.eu/economy_finance/bef2011/media/files/speech-brussels-economic-forum-schauble.pdf.

Schelkle, W. (2005). The political economy of fiscal policy co-ordination in EMU: from disciplinarian device to insurance arrangement. *JCMS: Journal of Common Market Studies*, 43(2), 371–91.

Schelkle, W. (2009). The contentious creation of the regulatory state in fiscal surveillance. *West European Politics*, 32(4), 829–46.

Schelkle, W. (2011). A tale of two crises: the euro area in 2008/09 and in 2010. *European Political Science*, 10(3), 375–83.

Schelkle, W. (2012). Policymaking in hard times: French and German responses to economic crisis in the Euro area. In Jonas Pontusson and Nancy Bermeo (eds.), *Coping With Crisis: Government Reactions to the Great Recession*. New York: Russell Sage Foundation, 130–62.

Schelkle, W. (2017). *The Political Economy of Monetary Solidarity: Understanding the Euro Experiment*. Oxford: Oxford University Press.

Schick, A. (2009). Budgeting for fiscal space. *OECD Journal on Budgeting*, 9(2), 1–18.

Schmidt, V. A. (2016). Reinterpreting the rules 'by stealth' in times of crisis: a discursive institutionalist analysis of the European Central Bank and the European Commission. *West European Politics*, 39(5), 1032–52.

Schmidt, V. A., & Thatcher, M. (eds.) (2013). *Resilient Liberalism in Europe's Political Economy*. Cambridge: Cambridge University Press.

Schneider, C. Q., & Wagemann, C. (2010). Standards of good practice in qualitative comparative analysis (QCA) and fuzzy-sets. *Comparative Sociology*, 9(3), 397–418.

Schuknecht, L. (2004). EU fiscal rules: issues and lessons from political economy (No. 421). ECB Working Paper.

Schuknecht, L., Von Hagen, J., & Wolswijk, G. (2009). Government risk premiums in the bond market: EMU and Canada. *European Journal of Political Economy*, 25(3), 371–84.

Schumpeter, J. A. (1995 [1918]). The crisis of the tax state. In Joseph A. Schumpeter, *The Economics and Sociology of Capitalism*, edited by R. Swedberg. Princeton, NJ: Princeton University Press, 99–140.

Schwab, S. C. (2011). After Doha: why the negotiations are doomed and what we should do about it. *Foreign Affairs*, May/June, 104–17.

Schwarzer, D. (2012). Crisis management and integration at gun point. Available from: http://euro.boellblog.org/2012/12/13/crisis-management-and-integration-at-gun-point.

Seabrooke, L., & Tsingou, E. (2018). Europe's fast-and slow-burning crises. *Journal of European Public Policy*, DOI: 10.1080/13501763.2018.1446456.

Singer, J. D. (1961). The level-of-analysis problem in international relations. *World Politics*, 14(1), 77–92.

Sinn, H. W. (2014). *The Euro Trap: On Bursting Bubbles, Budgets, and Beliefs*. Oxford: Oxford University Press.

Snidal, D. (1994). The politics of scope: endogenous actors, heterogeneity and institutions. *Journal of Theoretical Politics*, 6(4), 449–72.

Spilimbergo, M. A., Schindler, M. M., & Symansky, M. S. A. (2009). *Fiscal Multipliers* (No. 2009–2011). International Monetary Fund.

Stark, J. (2010). Taking stock: where do we stand in the crisis? Speech delivered at BMW Stiftung Herbert Quandt, Washington D.C., April 15.

Steinbrück, P. (2008a). Germany's way out of the crisis. *Wall Street Journal*.

Steinbrück, P. (2008b). *Plenary Session 16*. Deutsche Bundestag, Berlin.

Steinbrück, P. (2010). *Unterm Strich*. Hamburg: Hoffmann und Campe.

Stiglitz, J. E. (2004). *The Roaring Nineties: A New History of the World's Most Prosperous Decade*. New York: W.W. Norton & Company.

Strange, S. (1998). *Mad Money*. Manchester: Manchester University Press.

Streeck, W. (2014). How will capitalism end?. *New Left Review*, 87, 35–64.

Tanzi, V. (2004). The Stability and Growth Pact: its role and future. *Cato Journal*, 24, 57.

Te Velde, D. W. (2011). Economic policies in G-20 and African countries during the global financial crisis: who's the apprentice, who's the master? *African Development Review*, 23(4), 380–406.

Thomson, R., Torenvlied, R., & Arregui, J. (2007). The paradox of compliance: infringements and delays in transposing European Union directives. *British Journal of Political Science*, 37(4), 685–709.

Thygesen, N. (1993). Towards monetary union in Europe: reforms of the EMS in the perspective of monetary union. *JCMS: Journal of Common Market Studies*, 31(4), 447–72.

Thygesen, N. (2010). Rebuilding Euro governance. Project Syndicat, September 23.

Tornell, A., & Lane, P. R. (1999). The voracity effect. *American Economic Review*, 89(1), 22–46.

Tsebelis, G. (2002). *Veto Players: How Political Institutions Work*. Princeton, NJ: Princeton University Press.

Vail, M. I. (2014). Varieties of liberalism: Keynesian responses to the great recession in France and Germany. *Governance*, 27(1), 63–85.

van Riet, A. (2017). Monetary policy stretched to the limit: how could governments support the European Central Bank?, ADEMU Working Paper Series, No. 75, December 28.

Van Rompuy, H., Barroso, J. M., Juncker, J. C., & Draghi, M. (2012). Towards a genuine economic and monetary union. Consilium.Europa.eu, December 5.

Van Rompuy Task Force Report. (2010). *Strengthening Economic Governance in the EU: Report of the Task Force to the European Council.* Brussels: Publications Office of the European Union.

Varoufakis, Y. (2017). Greece's fiscal waterboarding continues. *Al Jazeera.*

Varughese, G., & Ostrom, E. (2001). The contested role of heterogeneity in collective action: some evidence from community forestry in Nepal. *World Development*, 29(5), 747–65.

Vaubel, R. (1983). The moral hazard of IMF lending. *World Economy*, 6(3), 291–304.

Verkuilen, J. (2005). Assigning membership in a fuzzy set analysis. *Sociological Methods & Research*, 33(4), 462–96.

Victor, D. G. (2011). *Global Warming Gridlock: Creating More Effective Strategies for Protecting the Planet.* Cambridge: Cambridge University Press.

Visco, I. (2011). Quotes from Brussels Economic Forum. Available from: http://ec.europa.eu/economy_finance/bef2011/media/quotes/index.html [accessed May 12, 2018].

Vives, X. (2001). Competition in the changing world of banking. *Oxford Review of Economic Policy*, 17(4), 535–47.

Volkerink, B., & De Haan, J. (2001). Fragmented government effects on fiscal policy: new evidence. *Public Choice*, 109(3–4), 221–42.

von Hagen, J. (2006). Fiscal institutions. In B. Weingast and D. Wittman (eds.), *The Oxford Handbook of Political Economy*. Oxford: Oxford University Press, 464–79.

von Hagen, J., & Harden, I. J. (1995). Budget processes and commitment to fiscal discipline. *European Economic Review*, 39(3–4), 771–9.

von Hagen, J., Pisani-Ferry, J., & Von Weizsäcker, J. (2009). A European exit strategy (No. 328). Inter-American Development Bank, Research Department.

von Hagen, J., Bordignon, M., Grewal, B. S., Peterson, P., Seitz, H., & Dahlberg, M. (2000). Subnational government bailouts in OECD countries: four case studies (No. 3100). Inter-American Development Bank, Research Department.

Wallich, H. C. (1984). Institutional cooperation in the world economy. In J. A. Frenkel and M. L. Mussa (eds.), *The World Economic System: Performance and Prospects*. Dover, MA: Auburn House Publishing, 85–99.

Watt, A. (2009). A quantum of solace? An assessment of fiscal stimulus packages by EU Member States in response to the economic crisis. ETUI, Brussels, ISSN 1994-4446.

Webb, M. (1995). *The Political Economy of Policy Coordination: International Adjustment Since 1945*. Ithaca, NY: Cornell University Press.

Weber, Axel (2016). Investors now facing 'unprecedented situation' and they need to get used to it. *CNBC.*

Wehner, J. (2010). Cabinet structure and fiscal policy outcomes. *European Journal of Political Research*, 49(5), 631–53.

Weingast, B. R., Shepsle, K. A., & Johnsen, C. (1981). The political economy of benefits and costs: a neoclassical approach to distributive politics. *Journal of Political Economy*, 89(4), 642–64.

Weiss, L. (1997). Globalization and the myth of the powerless state. *New Left Review*, 225, 3.

Wellhausen, R. L. (2015). Investor–state disputes: when can governments break contracts? *Journal of Conflict Resolution*, 59(2), 239–61.

White, W. R. (1998). Promoting international financial stability: the role of the BIS. *Regulatory and Supervisory Challenges in a New Era of Global Finance*. Forum on Debt and Development (Fondad).

Wildavsky, A. (1964). *Politics of the Budgetary Process*. New York: Little, Brown.

Willett, T. D., & Chiu, E. M. (2012). Power relationships and the political economy of global imbalances. *Global Economic Review*, 41(4), 341–360.

Winkler, B. (1999). Is Maastricht a good contract? *JCMS: Journal of Common Market Studies*, 37(1), 39–58.

Wintour, P. (2009). Labour stakes its reputation on second gamble. *Guardian*, January 19.

Woll, C. (2014). *The Power of Inaction: Bank Bailouts in Comparison*. Ithaca, NY: Cornell University Press.

Wolswijk, G., & de Haan, J. (2005). *Government Debt Management in the Euro Area: Recent Theoretical Developments and Changes in Practices* (No. 25). European Central Bank.

Woodruff, D. M. (2016). Governing by panic: the politics of the Eurozone crisis. *Politics & Society*, 44(1), 81–116.

Wooldridge, J. M. (2002). *Introductory Econometrics: A Modern Approach*. 2nd edition. Oxford: Nelson Education.

World Bank (2010). *Global Economic Prospects: Crisis, Finance and Growth*. Washington, DC: World Bank.

Wyplosz, C. (2006). European Monetary Union: the dark sides of a major success. *Economic Policy*, 21(46), 208–61.

Wyplosz, C. (2011). The ECB, the EFSF (and the ESM): roles, relationship and challenges. European Parliament, Monetary Dialogue.

Wyplosz, C. (2013). Europe's quest for fiscal discipline (No. 498). Directorate General Economic and Financial Affairs (DG ECFIN), European Commission.

Yamagishi, T. (1986). The provision of a sanctioning system as a public good. *Journal of Personality and Social Psychology*, 51(1), 110.

Zohlnhöfer, R. (2007). The politics of budget consolidation in Britain and Germany: the impact of blame avoidance opportunities. *West European Politics*, 30(5), 1120–38.

Zohlnhöfer, R. (2011). Between a rock and a hard place: the grand coalition's response to the economic crisis. *German Politics*, 20(2), 227–42.

Index

Index